SOME OLD SCOTS JUDGES

Photo, Swan Watson

LORD KAMES

From the Painting by David Martin in Scottish National Portrait Gallery, Edinburgh

SOME OLD SCOTS JUDGES

ANECDOTES AND IMPRESSIONS

BY

W. FORBES GRAY

LONDON
CONSTABLE AND COMPANY LTD.
1914

PREFACE

WHILE this volume treats of a group of Scots judges who flourished in the latter half of the eighteenth century, and the earlier decades of the nineteenth, it is primarily addressed, not to the man of law, but to the general reader. These pages are in nowise an attempt to explicate or estimate judicial character from a legal standpoint. Naturally in a series of biographical portraits such as are here presented, the position of Kames, Monboddo, and the rest as lawyers, cannot altogether be ignored; but what little has been said merely recapitulates in the most general terms the opinion of competent authorities.

My main object lies in quite another direction, *i.e.* to present an adequate picture, by means of anecdotes and contemporary testimony, of the personalities of certain old Scots judges who are remembered more by their debt to adventitious circumstance than by their judicial eminence. The twelve senators here portrayed widely differed in intellectual and moral worth, but they had two things in common—they were all Scotsmen, and they were all men of marked individuality. To describe them merely as eminent lawyers would be to do them scant justice. They were lawyers, and a great deal more. They are interesting to the student of literature, of science, of art, and, above all, of human nature. Moreover, the manifold activities in spheres remote from the law of the earlier members of the group, their amazing eccentricities, and their still more amazing foibles are so completely at variance with the modern conception of those holding high judicial position, that one marvels how such men ever found their way to the Bench. Certainly the judges here depicted cannot but arouse interest, though they may not always excite admiration.

In the spirit of Pope's dictum that "the proper study of mankind is man," I have essayed the task of elucidating the characters of these extraordinary men, most of whom sat on the judgment seat in the days when Scott was young. I have attempted, with what success the reader must judge, to show what manner of men those old Scots jurisconsults were—to present a conspectus of their philosophy of life. Accordingly, much space is devoted to setting forth their ideas and ideals, to recording their habits, their daily walk and conversation, their studies, their recreations, their manner of comporting themselves in the various relationships of life. In short, every effort has been made to shed as much light as possible upon their morals and their manners, their wit and their wisdom.

As will be apparent to every student of the period covered by these sketches, I have not gone to any recondite sources for my materials. My debt to such works as Cockburn's *Memorials of his Time*, Ramsay's *Scotland and Scotsmen*, Kay's *Edinburgh Portraits*, and the writings of the late Rev. Henry Grey Graham (one of the most brilliant representatives of the school of literary historians) is quite obvious. But while relying largely on these works, and others acknowledged in the footnotes, I have endeavoured to give my own impressions of the judges who form the subject-matter of this book. In sketching their personal characteristics, I have sought not only to bring them into relation with the social, literary, and political life of their own time, but to make clear the ethical gulf which separates their day from ours.

In the matter of the sedition trials of 1793–94, and particularly Braxfield's judicial conduct in connection therewith, I have mainly followed Cockburn. As is indicated in the chapters dealing with this discreditable episode in the annals of Scottish jurisprudence, Cockburn's Whiggery no doubt influenced his judgment to some extent, and occasionally led him to be more severe in his castigation than the circumstances warranted; but it seems to me that no one can read the records of those trials with a desire to be fair, without arriving at the conclusion that Cockburn's view in the main was substantially correct. It needs no legal acumen to perceive that the conduct of Braxfield, Eskgrove, and some of the other judges was, for the most part, wholly indefensible; their behaviour was, in fact, nothing short of a negation of the elementary ideas of justice.

Perhaps I ought to add that my selection of individuals is purely arbitrary. There may have been, doubtless were, other judges of that far-off time who deserved commemoration in these pages; but in choosing those here treated, I was merely asserting a personal preference. I think it will be generally acknowledged, however, that the Scots judges who find a place in this volume were all men of commanding, in some cases of astounding, personality, and that their life and work well repay study.

W. F. G.

April 1914.

CONTENTS

LIST OF ILLUSTRATIONS

I

LORD KAMES

(1696–1782)

DEAN RAMSAY, the genial author of *Reminiscences of Scottish Life and Character,* writing some fifty years ago, used these words : " There is no class of men which stands out more prominent in the Reminiscences of the last hundred years than that of our Scottish Judges. They form, in many instances, a type or representative of the leading *peculiarities* of Scottish life and manners. They are mixed up with all our affairs, social and political. There are to be found in the annals of the Bench rich examples of pure Scottish humour, the strongest peculiarity of Scottish phraseology, acuteness of intellect, cutting wit, eccentricity of manners, and abundant powers of conviviality. Their successors no longer furnish the same anecdotes of oddity or of intemperance."

No one who has even a superficial acquaintance with the sayings and doings of this group of Scottish judges will be disposed to cavil at Dean Ramsay's statement. They were, indeed, an extraordinary class of men—probably the most extraordinary that ever was entrusted with the administration of justice in these islands. Surely the most bitter fate that can overtake a judge is that he should be remembered not for intellectual worth, judicial rectitude, and intimate acquaintance with, and able administration of, the law, but rather as the type and exemplar of certain frailties and oddities which ill comport with senatorial dignity. Yet this is precisely what has happened in the case of most of the Scottish jurisconsults who flourished in the good old days when George the Third sat on the throne and Henry Dundas worked his own sweet will in shaping the political destinies of His Majesty's northern kingdom. They were cynically indifferent to the proprieties of the Bench to an extent which now may well seem incredible. Uncouth in appearance, profane in speech, frequently harsh and contemptuous in the discharge of their judicial functions, addicted to the wildest eccentricities, and exhibiting at all times a decided penchant for deep potation and the coarse and boisterous joviality of the tavern, Kames and his colleagues unquestionably present a phase of human character of singular interest.

Of course, it must not be supposed that the ugly traits to be found, for example, in the characters of Braxfield and Hermand were common to all the jurists who form the subject of this book. With the advent of a higher standard of morals, and the consequent improvement of manners, the grosser elements disappeared ; but the more reputable characteristics of the school—which were seen to perfection in

Hailes—lingered on until the days of Henry Cockburn. It ought also to be made clear that grave injustice would be done were Kames, Monboddo, and the others held up to posterity as types of the degeneracy of the Scottish judiciary of the period. It would be foolish to judge the conduct of these men by the standard of judicial comportment prevailing to-day. As a simple statement of fact, "even-handed justice" was never more ably dispensed than it was by Kames, Monboddo, and Hailes. Despite their foibles, their ribaldry, and their whimsicalities, the judges of those days, or at least most of them, were sound lawyers whose acquaintance with Scottish jurisprudence might even now be envied. Moreover, if none possessed genius, or ever showed signs of becoming formidable competitors in the race for immortality, several were men of undoubted culture, and three made their mark in literature. One of the trio was Henry Home, Lord Kames, whose dexterous intelligence, versatile learning, and literary craftsmanship earned him a great reputation, though its lustre has long since departed.

Judge, author, metaphysician, agricultural pioneer, and convivialist, Henry Home was born in 1696. Paternally, he was descended from an ancient family, being the great-grandson of Sir John Home of Renton, Lord Justice-Clerk in the reign of Charles II., whose ancestor was a cadet of the family of the Earl of Home. His father was George Home of Kames, Berwickshire, where the future judge was born, and from which he derived his judicial title. Home's parent was a landed proprietor in little more than in name. His fields were untilled, his farm-houses were dilapidated, and he himself was thriftless. On the maternal side, Home could also boast distinguished lineage. His mother was a daughter of Mr. Walkinshaw of Barrowfield, and grand-daughter of Robert Baillie, that celebrated Covenanting divine who refused to preach in favour of Laud's service-book, and whose *Letters and Journals* throw much light upon dark and troublous times.

Considering his family and station, Home received a wretched education. An improvident and careless father could hardly be expected to pay much attention to the moral and intellectual equipment of his son. But if Home did not receive a liberal education, he could at least take consolation in the fact that he was no worse off than many sons of good families, for, sad to relate, the Scottish gentry of that day were forsaking the educational ideals of their forefathers. They were content if their sons acquired sufficient knowledge to qualify them for a desk in a mercantile house; as for their daughters, they were not supposed to require any.

Home, therefore, had to rest satisfied with what learning he could pick up from a tutor, Wingate by name, who to severity added dullness and incompetency. Wingate's harshness Home never forgot, and by and by Nemesis claimed its victim. Years after, Wingate, who had amassed enough wealth to buy a little land, repaired to his quondam pupil, now a Senator of the College of Justice, to ascertain whether the title-deeds were in order. After scrutinising the parchments, Kames, looking very serious, asked his old tutor if the bargain was concluded. "Not only so," replied Wingate, "but the price is paid." "Good heavens! how unlucky this is," exclaimed the judge, who proceeded to point out flaw after flaw in the titles until the sweat poured from the brows of the hapless pedagogue. Perceiving that his revenge was complete, Kames summarily closed the interview with the following admonition: "Mr. Wingate, you may remember how you made me smart in days of yore for very small offences. Now, I think our accounts are cleared. Take up your parchments, and go home with an easy mind; your titles are excellent."

With a scanty education and still scantier means, but with the determination to win his way to fame and fortune on the strength of his own talents, Home, aged fifteen, quitted the paternal roof and journeyed to Edinburgh, where he entered the office of a Writer to the Signet, a dignity which he himself fondly hoped some day to attain. But an interview with Sir Hew Dalrymple, President of the Court of Session, to whom he had been sent one evening on business, convinced him that the donning of the wig and gown of an advocate was the true goal of legal aspiration. Tytler (afterwards Lord Woodhouselee), in his authentic but much too favourable biography of Kames, gives a somewhat rhapsodical account of this interview. When young Home was shown into the parlour of Dalrymple's suburban villa at the end of Bristo Street, he found a daughter of the house performing on the harpsichord while the venerable judge sat by her with a book in his hand. Music was suspended, and after a conversation, in the course of which Dalrymple was impressed by Home's legal knowledge, the young lady made tea, which was followed by the playing and singing of Scots airs. This scene of domestic felicity the Writer to the Signet's apprentice regarded as "the fruits of eminence" in the law, and he returned to his humble lodgings fired with the ambition to participate in the coming years in all the "elegant enjoyments that affluence justly earned can command." [1]

Home now bent all his energies to repairing the defects in his education. In addition to his legal studies, he applied himself diligently to the classics, natural philosophy, logic, mathematics, and especially to metaphysics, for which his zeal was more apparent than his aptitude; but of this more anon. In 1723 he entered into erudite correspondence with Andrew Baxter, whose *Inquiry into the Nature of the Human Soul* was rescued from oblivion by Warburton's encomium in the *Divine Legation of Moses.*

Baxter was then residing at Dunse Castle, a few miles from Kames, and between him and the ambitious lawyer an intimacy sprang up. But metaphysics is rather a slender foundation on which to rear an abiding friendship, and ere long the young philosophers were behaving most unphilosophically. Worsted in a metaphysical argument, Home lost his temper, and terminated the intercourse with a proposal that Baxter and

[1] Tytler's *Life of Kames*, i. 9-10.

he should burn the correspondence and their "philosophical heats" with it.

One would have thought that after this experience Home would have given metaphysics a wide berth. No sooner, however, had he finished his bout with Baxter than he re-entered the lists with a much more redoubtable champion —Dr. Samuel Clarke, whose famous *Discourse concerning the Being and Attributes of God* turned the tables upon the Deists of his day. Compared with Clarke, Home was a mere fledgeling in things metaphysical, but the disparity did not prevent him from writing an unconscionably long and grandiose epistle to the English divine, in which, with more temerity than knowledge, he criticised several of the arguments in the *Discourse*. Clarke received these random reflections of "a young philosopher and a stranger" with the utmost docility, and even favoured his correspondent with an elaborate and carefully worded reply.

Home was called to the Scottish Bar in 1724. His practice for some time was meagre in the extreme, partly because he was without influential connections, and partly because there were already at the Bar three men of conspicuous forensic talent—Duncan Forbes of Culloden, Robert Dundas of Arniston, and Sir James Fergusson of Kilkerran, all of whom subsequently found their way to the Bench. In those lean years when briefs were few, money scarce, and ambition boundless, Home showed his good sense by persistently grinding at his law-books, and broadening the basis of his general culture. For four years he was the humblest of advocates, but with the publication in 1728 of his *Remarkable Decisions of the Court of Session from 1716 to 1728*—which proved a godsend to many an overworked barrister—he began to bask in the sunshine of legal favour, and before long he was striding the highway of promotion.

With a nimble intelligence, argumentative ability, persuasive speech, and a knowledge of the most subtle and complicated doctrines of Scots law, Home combined a style of pleading singularly original and impressive. Colloquial rather than oratorical, his appeal was to the intellect, never to the emotions. His object at all times, says Tytler, was more "to rear his own argument upon a solid basis, than to cavil with or impugn the reasoning of his antagonist."[1] Equally characteristic was his ill-concealed contempt for precedent. The stamp of immemorial usage signified nothing to him. He valued rules and maxims only in so far as they conformed to, and were grounded in, rational principle.

Despite his multifarious studies, his metaphysical correspondence, and his struggles to make a living at the Bar, Home found time to become a man of fashion, in which capacity he cut quite a respectable figure. He loved literature and philosophy, but he was human enough to love Society still more. And Society loved him. "The vivacity of his wit and of his animal spirits," says one authority, ". . . rendered his company not only agreeable, but greatly solicited by the *literati*, and courted by ladies of the highest rank and accomplishments."[2] But,

[1] Tytler's *Life of Kames*, i. 45. [2] Smellie's *Literary Lives*, p. 145.

great as was his capacity for social enjoyment, it does not appear that it ever took the form of low company and buffoonery, as it did in the case of many of his professional brethren. Not that he was immaculate by any means. On occasion he could be coarse in his speech and brutal in his behaviour. The man who could use the epithet (quite unprintable) which Home is credited with having used when parting with his colleagues at the close of a long judicial career is not likely to earn a testimonial either for good breeding or refinement. True, his biographer is silent regarding this incident, which is perhaps natural in the case of a panegyrist; but the story comes from well-authenticated sources. Moreover, it accords only too well with other lamentable episodes in Home's career.

Home, then, was a beau, but a beau who discriminated. He liked fops with brains and some pretensions to literary culture. Surely there is food for reflection here, for if brainy fops flourished in Home's day they are now as extinct as the dodo. Who, then, were these fine gentlemen whose handsome presence, polished manners, and mental fitness satisfied the ideal of the meticulous young advocate? Three may be singled out as typical of the rest—William Hamilton of Bangour, whose poem, "The Braes of Yarrow," has given him a secure place in Scottish literature; Colonel Forrester, author of a tract entitled *The Polite Philosopher* (of him Dr. Johnson wrote: "He was himself The Great Polite he drew"); and Lord Binning, an obscure writer of Scots songs.

Between "The Great Polite" and Home a correspondence passed which sheds some light upon the topics which then absorbed the thoughts of young men of fashion. The letters are written in a stilted style, and are a strange mixture of the sublime and the ridiculous. In one epistle, after an allusion to an elaborate poem to be prefixed to the *Opera Homiana*, Forrester proceeds to discuss so mundane a subject as female coquetry, to which, by the way, he assigns somewhat high antiquity. Eve, he affirms, plainly established her coquetry when she evinced surprise at seeing herself reflected in the watery mirror in the Garden of Eden.

With Hamilton of Bangour, Home seems to have been specially intimate. The bond of friendship was poetry, in which both dabbled. Home very soon discovered, however, that he had not been born to achieve distinction in that line, and after sending a few pieces to the *Edinburgh Miscellany*, he ignominiously closed his career as versifier. He retained, however, a keen relish for the fustian of his friend, particularly when it had reference to himself, for Home was so excessively vain that, as a friend said, one might flatter him at all times with "a safe conscience." Tytler says it may be doubted if Home was ever more highly gratified by any incident in his legal career than by the lines Hamilton addressed to "H. H. in the Assembly." They are as follows:

While crown'd with radiant charms divine,
Unnumber'd beauties round thee shine,
When Erskine leads her happy man,
And Johnston shakes the flutt'ring fan;

When beauteous Pringle shines confest,
And gently heaves her swelling breast,
Her raptur'd partner still at gaze
Pursuing thro' each winding maze;
Say, Harry, canst thou keep secure
Thy heart, from conquering Beauty's power?

Hamilton himself had answered the question in the negative, and was playing the part of the importunate lover. In one of his letters to Home, after discoursing on Horace, he declares his whole heart about Jeannie Stewart, an amiable young lady, who was annoyed by his attentions, and consulted Home as to the most effectual way of giving Hamilton the *coup de grâce*. "You are his friend," said the unhappy lady. "Tell him he exposes both himself and me to the ridicule of our acquaintance." "No, madam," replied Home, "you shall accomplish his cure yourself, and by the simplest method. Dance with him at to-night's assembly, and show him every mark of kindness, as if you believed his passion sincere and had resolved to favour his suit. Take my word for it, you'll hear no more of him." The lady did so, and the fickle poet was completely cured.[1]

Home was a curious compound of sobriety and silliness. Few things came amiss to him. He pored over theology and metaphysics with the same ardour as he treaded "the light fantastic toe" at Miss Nicky Murray's assemblies, or became hilarious with the wits who foregathered at Balfour's coffee-house. It need therefore cause no surprise to learn that at a time when he was

[1] Tytler's *Life of Kames*, i. 69.

revelling in an atmosphere of dilettantism, bombast, and love-making, he should also be trying to inveigle Bishop Butler into a correspondence regarding certain conclusions in his newly published *Analogy of Religion, Natural and Revealed*. Home was a sciolist, and like all sciolists he lost himself in the mazes of his own profundity. The second Lord President Dundas on one occasion neatly summed up the situation by remarking, after Kames had delivered a metaphysical opinion: "Lord Kames, I do not understand a word of what you have been saying all this while; *it is too deep for me*."[1] Be that as it may, Home had read Butler's book with avidity, and, disagreeing with certain portions, he must needs, as in the case of Dr. Samuel Clarke, try to set the author right. Home craved a personal interview, but this the Bishop declined on the ground "that the cause of truth might . . . suffer from the unskilfulness of its advocate,"[2] a reply behind the touching modesty of which there may have lurked a modicum of guile. Butler and Home never met to compose their theological differences; but they remained friends, Home having the sagacity to perceive, and the grace to acknowledge, the moral and intellectual worth of an opponent whose shoe-latchets he was not worthy to unloose.

Bishop Berkeley also came in for a share of his attention. Ramsay of Ochtertyre chronicles a story to the effect that Home, when on a visit to London, went, without previous introduction, to

[1] Ramsay's *Scotland and Scotsmen*, i. 186 (*n.*).
[2] Tytler's *Life of Kames*, i. 87.

the lodgings of the distinguished prelate and philosopher, who received him with more courtesy than he deserved. Home at once plunged into a metaphysical argument. Berkeley, doubtless not relishing the idea of crossing swords with a tyro, tried to divert the conversation into lower channels, but finding this impossible, he wisely maintained silence.[1]

But while devoting much time to metaphysics and frivolity, Home never forgot that his main business was the law. As has been indicated, his progress at first was discouraging enough; but before the Jacobite Rebellion he was enjoying a large practice, and, in the course of the next ten or twelve years, acquired no small fortune. When a young advocate, his best client was an East Lothian lady who was both litigious and censorious. On one occasion, while Home was visiting her, she fell foul of a neighbour to the embarrassment of her guest. Home, wishing to calm her turbulent spirit, told her he had brought Bishop Butler's *Sermons*, one of which he asked permission to read. The lady assented. Whereupon Home proceeded to read a sermon which happened to treat of the government of the tongue, but had not gone far before he began to fear that it would lose him a good client, so exactly did it apply to his hostess. But his misgivings were groundless, for the lady pronounced the sermon excellent, and added that it "would fit our neighbour Scotston to a T."[2]

In 1752 Home was raised to the Bench, taking his seat with the title of Lord Kames. Eleven

[1] Ramsay's *Scotland and Scotsmen*, i. 196 (*n.*). [2] *Ibid.* i. 184-5 (*n.*).

years later he became one of the Lords of Justiciary, a post which he personally solicited at the hands of an influential nobleman. Kames exercised judicial functions for more than thirty years. Tytler says that "as a judge, his opinions and decrees were dictated by an acute understanding, an ardent feeling of justice, and a perfect acquaintance with the jurisprudence of his country."[1] Kames may have been an acute and erudite lawyer—of that Tytler was well qualified to judge—but whether he was the paragon of judicial rectitude his biographer would have us believe, any novice may determine on the evidence adduced.

Now it so happens that certain stories, notorious and uncontradicted, have come down to us, the cumulative effect of which is to convey an unfavourable impression of Kames, not only as a judge but as a man. No doubt the times allowed more latitude to judges than they do now, but when all that may reasonably be said in mitigation has been said, the ugly fact remains that Kames in his judicial capacity was very frequently vindictive, and, in criminal cases, needlessly severe.[2] "In trials of life and death," says Ramsay, "he sometimes lowered the majesty of justice by the levity or harshness of his expressions. . . . To gravity and appearances he paid perhaps too little attention, and therefore did not check those petty ebullitions of spleen or impatience as he ought to have done."[3]

He also indulged in a type of humour in-

[1] Tytler's *Life of Kames*, i. 152. [2] *Ibid.* ii. 2.
[3] Ramsay's *Scotland and Scotsmen*, i. 189.

describably coarse. Readers of *Redgauntlet* will remember Scott's allusion to this undesirable trait, while those who have read that amusing poem of Boswell's, "The Court of Session Garland," hardly need to be reminded of the couplet in which Kames's fondness for a certain word, more expressive than elegant, is caustically referred to. His usual mode of salutation was: "Well, ye brute, how are ye to-day?" Once, in company with Burns's friend, John Rankine, whose daughter, Annie, claimed to be the heroine of "The Rigs o' Barley," his lordship, having indulged his rudeness more than his wont, turned to his companion and exclaimed: "Brute, are you dumb? Have ye no queer sly story to tell?" "I hae nae story," said Rankine, "but last night I had an odd dream that I was dead, and that for keeping other than good company on earth I was sent downstairs. When I knocked at the low door, wha should open it but the deil; he was in a rough humour, and said: 'Wha may ye be, and what's your name?' 'My name,' quoth I, 'is John Rankine, and my dwelling-place was Adamhill.' 'Gae 'wa' wi' ye,' quoth Satan, 'ye canna be here; ye're ane o' Lord Kames's brutes.'"[1] This timely rebuke is said to have not gone unheeded.

An amazing example of Kames's judicial manner is furnished by Cockburn,[2] who had the story from his relative, Lord Hermand, one of the counsel at the trial in which the incident happened. In 1780 at Ayr, Kames tried Matthew

[1] Chambers's *Life of Burns*, new ed, i. 120 (*n.*).
[2] Cockburn's *Memorials of His Time*, 1856, p. 117 (*n.*).

Hay (with whom he used to play chess) on a charge of murder. On learning that a verdict of guilty had been returned, his lordship exclaimed, "That's checkmate to you, Matthew!" Lockhart, in the first edition of his *Life of Scott*, foisted this anecdote on Braxfield, which was very unfortunate, since the "Hanging Judge," as will be shown later, had quite enough misdeeds of his own to answer for.

Kames seems to have reserved all his eccentricities and Rabelaisian wit for the Bench. The profane and brutal judge was in private life the most exemplary of men. He had once drank very hard, but "having fallen out of conceit with claret, which had long been his favourite liquor," [1] and given up the tavern, he had become the pride of the family circle—amiable, refined, chivalrous. He delighted in the society of young people, and took "extraordinary pains to form the taste and improve the knowledge of young ladies distinguished for beauty or talents," [2] telling them what books to read and instructing them in the canons of criticism. His counsels are said to have greatly influenced his fair hearers, though the world did not approve of a judge, who had passed the allotted span, "philandering with them with all the sprightliness of an ensign of the Guards." [3]

Much of his domestic happiness was due, as he himself admitted, to the admirable lady who, in 1741, became his wife. Agatha, younger daughter of James Drummond of Blair Drum-

[1] Ramsay's *Scotland and Scotsmen*, i. 203.
[2] *Ibid.* i. 205. [3] *Ibid.* i. 206.

mond, brought Kames beauty, wealth, and an affectionate nature. She had only one failing—an inordinate love of old china. Soon after her marriage, she made such inroads on her patrimony in pursuit of her hobby that her husband had to intervene. But how to cure his wife of this propensity without hurting her feelings was the problem. Kames excogitated long and anxiously, but with excellent results. He framed a will bequeathing to his spouse the whole china that should be found in his possession at his death. This deed he put into his wife's hands, and she was effectually cured.

If Kames found much time for social enjoyment, it was not because he ate the bread of idleness. He was at all times a hard worker. Being methodical in his habits, and dexterous in body and mind, he managed to get through an amount of work in one day which other men would not have done in several. In summer he was usually abroad between five and six o'clock in the morning; in winter generally two hours before daybreak. The time before breakfast was devoted to preparing for the business of the Court. There the forenoon was spent. Soon after mid-day he quitted the Bench, and there was an hour or two to spare before dinner for a walk with a friend, or for study. The labours of the day over, he would join the ladies in the drawing-room, and take part in a game of whist, which he played well. Frequently he attended the theatre, or the concert-hall, or the assembly, for advancing years never lessened his interest in the diversions of the *beau monde*. The evening generally closed with the entertaining of his friends to supper "in a style," says Ramsay, "so perfectly his own that it deserves commemoration as a relic of the old manners of Edinburgh."[1]

But much as Kames loved the pleasures of Edinburgh society, he was always ready to surrender them for the quiet joys and sober occupations of country life. Farming and planting were then becoming fashionable among lairds, who were to be seen hard at work in the fields and woods at almost any hour of the day. Lord Auchinleck, the father of Dr. Johnson's biographer, used to rise at five o'clock every morning for the purpose of pruning his young wood, while Kames, when he chanced to arrive at his country home after dark, would take a lantern in his hand, and by the aid of its feeble rays try to discover what progress his plantation had made during his absence.[2]

Kames was a poor metaphysician, but an excellent farmer. He was not only passionately fond of agriculture, but he was skilled in it. If not the first, he was certainly one of the first in Scotland to practise farming on scientific lines, and his strenuous efforts to introduce improved modes of husbandry are worthy of all praise. He was extremely well circumstanced for giving effect to his agricultural ideals. Comparatively early in life he inherited the paternal estate in Berwickshire, which had been wofully neglected through the indolence and impecuniosity of his

[1] Ramsay's *Scotland and Scotsmen*, i. 203.
[2] Graham's *Social Life of Scotland*, 1901, p. 59.

father. This gave Kames his opportunity, and after much hard work and vigilant care what had been little better than a dreary waste became a productive piece of land.

With Kames it was an incontrovertible doctrine that the inferiority of Scottish farmers to their southern neighbours was due not so much to a poorer soil and a more trying climate as to lethargy, crass ignorance, and a slavish adherence to obsolete methods and implements. Accordingly, when residing at Kames, his Berwickshire seat, he would spend several hours every day supervising the operations of the farm servants, and occasionally labouring with his own hands. A friend, calling one day, found his lordship so absorbed in the task of clearing stones from an enclosure that he had no time for conversation. "Well, my lord," said the visitor when the dinner-hour arrived, "you have truly wrought for your meal; and pray let me ask you, how much you think you will gain by that hard work at the end of the year?" Instantly came the reply: "Why, really, my good sir, I never did calculate the value of my labour; but one thing I will venture to assert, that no man who is capable of asking that question will ever deserve the name of *farmer*." [1]

Caustic though the reply was, it was an honest opinion. And with enthusiasm and practical skill Kames combined enterprise. He devised implements for the economising of agricultural labour. He also interested himself in the growth and storage of winter fodder, the improving of

[1] Tytler's *Life of Kames*, i. 111.

the breed of sheep, the enclosure and culture of wastes and moors, the rearing of timber, and the draining and cultivation of mosslands. On the estate of Blair Drummond, to which his wife succeeded in 1766, he initiated a variety of improvements which were then thought marvellous.

His most notable performance was the irrigation of the Moss of Kincardine, a swamp of about four miles in length, and from one to two miles in breadth. The largest portion lay within the Blair Drummond policies, and was covered with moss from eight to nine feet in thickness. Kames conceived the idea of floating this moss into the river Forth in order that the soil of rich clay and vegetable mould, which was known to exist underneath, might be brought under cultivation. The project was regarded as chimerical; but Kames lived to see about one-third of this extensive marsh made agriculturally profitable, while not long after his death, no fewer than 620 persons were settled upon the land, all of whom were engaged in raising valuable crops.

Nothing could daunt Kames's enthusiasm for agriculture, and it was quite characteristic that when bordering on four-score years he should take pen in hand and proceed to enlighten his countrymen as to how farming might be improved, if conducted on rational principles. Judged by the standards of the twentieth century, *The Gentleman Farmer*, which was published in 1776, contains many queer maxims, but it was by far the most useful manual of its kind that had appeared up to that time, and was the means of giving a fresh impetus to almost every branch of husbandry. Among other services to farming, Kames advocated the establishment of a Board of Agriculture for Scotland, an idea which was subsequently realised to some extent in the Highland and Agricultural Society.

In other ways also Kames proved himself a true builder of the national prosperity. He wrote a pamphlet advocating the culture of flax of native growth. He strongly supported the movement for the construction of a canal between the Forth and Clyde rivers. He was an active member of the Board of Trustees for the Encouragement of the Fisheries, Arts, and Manufactures of Scotland, and a Commissioner for the management of the forfeited estates annexed to the Crown, the rents of which were applied to bettering the condition of the natives of the Highlands and Islands. He also conducted a voluminous correspondence with eminent doctors, natural philosophers, mathematicians, botanists, and social reformers.

And what Kames did for the furtherance of national industry and social well-being, he did, only in a lesser degree, for literature, the fine arts, and incipient science. Boswell, boasting to Dr. Johnson on one occasion of the progress of literature in Scotland, exclaimed, "But, sir, we have Lord Kames." Quick came the retort, "You *have* Lord Kames. Keep him, ha, ha, ha! We don't envy you him."[1] The gibe was a trifle acrid. In a less whimsical moment, the Doctor would have been the first to admit that

[1] Boswell's *Life of Johnson*, Hill's ed., ii. 53.

Kames, by encouraging Hugh Blair to publish his *Sermons*, had at least performed one literary service. But if Johnson was unnecessarily severe, the claim of Kames's friend, Smellie, was preposterous. To couple the name of Kames with that of Pliny the Elder[1] is as absurd as it would be to rank the poems of Pope alongside those of Mark Akenside.

A just estimate of Kames will recognise the important part he played in the literary revival which occurred in Scotland in the middle of the eighteenth century, and which made Edinburgh, rather than London, the true home of letters until the death of Scott. "Though too old to unlearn his native dialect, he wished the rising generation to speak (and write) English with grace and propriety, reprobating only affectation and vulgarism."[2] He was indefatigable in his efforts to purge the writings of his countrymen of Scotticisms, maintaining, with Hume and Robertson, that the fact that an author was a Scotsman was no valid reason why he should write bad English. And certainly, when Beattie had to confess that Scotsmen were obliged "to study English for books like a dead language,"[3] and thought it necessary to publish a collection of Scotticisms as a warning to his countrymen, the ardour of the literary reformers was not misplaced.

But the mischief was that Kames and other Scots authors, in striving to rid their pages of the provincial idiom, attained to a standard of

[1] Smellie's *Literary and Characteristical Lives*, 139.
[2] Ramsay's *Scotland and Scotsmen*, i. 212.
[3] Forbes's *Life of Beattie*, ii. 203.

English, the only recommendation of which was its correctness. That complete mastery of the tongue, which would have enabled them to write it not only correctly, but with grace and ease, they never attained. Indeed, it is doubtful if literary culture of this nature ever gave them a thought. Correct English is what they aimed at, and correct English in large measure they attained; but nothing more. Their style might be pure as far as Scotticisms were concerned; but it was crabbed and stilted, for they knew not the genius of the language of Shakespeare, and Milton, and the Book of Common Prayer.

The strength and the weakness of the Scots literary revival, and of Kames's connection with it, are accurately expressed in a notice of Kames's *Sketches of the History of Man* which appeared in the *Edinburgh Magazine and Review*. Says the reviewer: "There are few writers to whom Scotland is more indebted than to the author of the present performance. At a period when literature was neglected, and the public ear unrefined, he applied himself to enlighten his fellow-citizens, and to accommodate his compositions to an English standard. His example was contagious. . . . The peculiarities of the Scottish idiom wore away; loose and inaccurate modes of diction were reprobated. Men, studious to excel, became skilled in the delicacies of the language which they could not speak; and there remains not, perhaps, an obstruction to retard a most general diffusion of *a correct and an elegant taste* in this quarter of the island." Correctness and elegance were the true goal instead of rhythm, charm, and naturalness.

In other directions, besides driving out the Scotticism, Kames promoted the cultivation and improvement of polite literature. He was one of the most active members of the Select Society. Founded by Allan Ramsay, the painter, in 1754, the Society met on Friday evenings in the Advocates' Library for literary and philosophical discussion, and for the improvement of its members in public speaking. It certainly did not belie its name. Fifteen of its members were, or became, peers, and eighteen were either holding judicial posts or were judges in the making. "The Select Society," wrote Hume to its founder, "has grown to be a national concern. Young and old, noble and ignoble, witty and dull, laity and clergy, all the world are ambitious of a place amongst us." [1]

Kames was also President of the Philosophical Society of Edinburgh, founded in 1731 for the advancement of medical knowledge. Before this learned body he read three papers—on the "Laws of Motion," on the "Advantages of Shallow Ploughing," and on "Evaporation." Then it was his patronage more than anything else which originated the course of lectures on Rhetoric which Adam Smith delivered in 1748–50, and Hugh Blair in 1783. We cannot greatly admire those lectures, but they represented the high-water mark of literary discernment at that time, and materially furthered the study of letters in Scotland. But more important was the con-

[1] *Letters of David Hume* (ed. by Hill).

spicuous part Kames took in founding in 1762 the Chair of Rhetoric in Edinburgh University—indeed, he is usually spoken of as its founder—a Chair which has had many illustrious occupants. It may be doubted if there is another academic centre in the country which has done more, not only to elucidate the treasures of English literature but to augment them.

While Kames, like Scott in later times, made literature his staff and not his crutch, he laboured strenuously in producing books which, in point of quantity, would have done credit to a professional man of letters. Of his legal writings we can say nothing, save that they were numerous and were at one time quoted with the same respect as an English lawyer quotes Coke or Blackstone.

Kames's other writings range over a wide field, and vary much in style and value. During their author's life-time they had a great vogue, but their interest now is purely historical. No publisher who values his business reputation would ever dream of reprinting Kames's works; but those who are curious may still find them reposing under a thick layer of dust on the top-most shelf of a second-hand bookseller's shop. Nor is this neglect wholly unmerited, for Kames was crude and superficial as a thinker, and unattractive as a writer. Nevertheless, if one has time and, still more, the patience to search whole acres of dithyrambic prose, he shall have his reward. Occasionally Kames did stumble upon an idea which showed him to be in advance of his time, though his grasp was usually so precarious that it amounted to little more than an adumbration. When Sir Gilbert Elliot sought his guidance regarding some obscure point of political economy, he got the advice: "Go and write a book upon it if you want to understand it."[1] Kames himself acted too much on this principle.

His first notable work, *Essays on the Principles of Morality and Natural Religion* (1751), had a curious effect. Intended to counteract the principles of Hume's *Treatise on Human Nature*, and "to prepare the way for the proof of the existence of a Deity," it yet brought its author under a suspicion of scepticism and impiety, for which he narrowly escaped the censure of the Kirk. Confutant and confuted (or at least supposed to be) were both banned as writers of infidel books. The work is a medley of nebulous thought and inconclusive reasoning; and it is easy to sympathise with the view of Baron Maccara who, when asked by Lady Frances Moray of Abercairney what he thought of the *Essays*, nonchalantly replied: "Why, madam, I wish its author may understand it. Sure I am it is some points above my reach."[2] Kames fights valiantly against the empiricism of Locke and the utilitarian conception of morality espoused by Hume. But he flounders hopelessly when he comes to establish his own position, maintaining, with strange illogicality, that man is not a free agent, but, because he acts as if he were one, he is morally responsible.

[1] Tytler's *Life of Kames*, i. 61.
[2] Ramsay's *Scotland and Scotsmen*, ii. 342.

In the belief that thinking was in danger of becoming a lost art, Kames published in 1761 his *Introduction to the Art of Thinking*. The work is quite a literary curiosity. It was specially written for children, but judging by the maxims it contains, the children of Kames's day must have been precocious with a vengeance. John Stuart Mill, who began Greek at three,[1] and at fourteen had read extensively in that language and in Latin, might have proved equal to Kames's manual, but it is difficult to imagine the normal child, or even the normal adult, construing his lordship's wisdom. Tytler, with delicious *naïveté*, remarks that some of the maxims are suited to a more advanced period of education. Here are a few of the aphoristic gems which Kames would feign have taught the luckless child of his day :

He who incessantly vaunts of his probity and honour, and swears to gain belief, has not even the art of counterfeiting.

It is harder than is commonly thought to dissemble with those we despise.

Self-conceit is none of the smallest blessings from heaven.

You may sooner expect a favour from him who has already done you one, than from him to whom you have done it.

To women that have been conversant with the world, a gardener is a gardener, and a mason a mason : to those who have been bred in a retired way, a gardener is a man, and a mason is a man.

In the first passion, women have commonly an affection for the lover ; afterwards they love for the pleasure of loving.

---

[1] Mill's *Autobiography*, new ed., p. 3.

To show precipices on all sides is the best way to bring weak persons into your path.

The concentrated wisdom of some of these maxims is undeniable: they would have adorned a page of Marcus Aurelius or of Bacon. There is nothing extravagant in Benjamin Franklin's remark: "I think I never saw more solid useful matter contained in so small a compass."[1] Nevertheless, the book, both in form and substance, was utterly unsuited to children. That so wise a man should not have seen this makes one almost believe that there is an occult alliance between wisdom and stupidity.

The *Elements of Criticism* (1762) is Kames's most pretentious work, as it is the one by which he is best remembered. Before it was published Rollin's *Belles Lettres* held the field, but no sooner did Kames's book appear than the scholarly Frenchman's "instantly vanished," and "gave place to greater genius and greater utility." Tytler claimed that the *Elements of Criticism* inaugurated the science of philosophical criticism,[2] a view which was partially endorsed by Dugald Stewart, who regarded the work as the first serious attempt to set forth the metaphysical principles of the fine arts—a work possessing "in spite of its numerous defects both in point of taste and of philosophy, infinite merits."[3] Johnson and Goldsmith showed the other side of the shield. "A pretty essay," said the Doctor, but much of it "chimerical."[4]

[1] Tytler's *Life of Kames*, i. 262. [2] *Ibid.* i. 273.

[3] "First Preliminary Dissertation," *Ency. Brit.*, 8th ed., i. 222.

[4] Boswell's *Life of Johnson*, Hill's ed., i. 394.

"Goldy," on the other hand, dismissed it with the scarifying remark that it was easier to write than to read.[1]

Though running into three volumes, the *Elements of Criticism* is the most readable of Kames's writings. The author sets aside the traditional canons of literary criticism, and seeks to discover the rules in the constitution of the human mind, and the nature of the passions and affections. That there is an air of artificiality about the critical principles expounded may be admitted. The work, however, reveals much learning, ingenious reasoning, and a little sound criticism. But assuredly the latter quality was not displayed in referring to the *Mourning Bride* as "the most complete of English dramas," or to Gothic art as being suited only to the "rude, uncultivated" places where it was invented.

The work, despite its admixture of sense and silliness with the balance decidedly inclining towards the latter, brought Kames many admirers, for intellectual people were then busy overhauling their ideas regarding taste and beauty, mainly as the result of the recent publication of Burke's essay *On the Sublime and Beautiful.* But there were others who laughed it to scorn. Shortly after the *Elements of Criticism* appeared, Kames, meeting his colleague, Monboddo, asked him if he had read his book. "No, my lord," was the withering reply, "you write a great deal faster than I am able to read."[2] Bishop Warburton commented on it with more vehemence

[1] Boswell's *Life of Johnson*, Hill's ed, ii. 90.
[2] Ramsay's *Scotland and Scotsmen*, i. 356 (*n.*)

than judgment. Voltaire, in his retreat at Ferney, skimmed the pages of "Makames' (*sic*) *Elements*," and, no doubt, thought that an excellent opportunity for reprisal had arrived, Kames, whom he described as a "Justice of the Peace in Scotland," having ventured to say some unkind things about his *Henriade*. At all events, the *Elements* was made a target for a fine display of Voltairean ridicule. What most tickled the "brilliant Frenchman's" fancy was that "from remote Scotland should come rules for taste on all matters from an epic to a garden."

In 1774, at the mature age of seventy-eight, Kames gave to the world his *Sketches of the History of Man*. The book is a singular instance of the frailty of the human mind, affording, as it does, convincing proof that even the ablest of jurisconsults may develop a genius for irrelevancy. Kames, it is true, occasionally stumbles upon his theme, but such is his discursiveness that we must be content to catch glimpses of the history of Man through a haze of moralisings on politics, economics, poor-laws, moral philosophy, women, and many other subjects. Even the Ossianic poems are dragged in. But perhaps we ought not to be wholly ungrateful for this *pot-pourri* of reflections on things in general. If Kames leaves the history of Man very much where he found it, it is only fair to say that he does here and there foreshadow truths which have since come to play a great part in the world. For example, he draws attention to the analogy between animals and plants. Facts, again, drove him to the conclusion that distinct races of man had peopled the earth from the beginning, but then a literal interpretation of the Book of Genesis told a different story, so the logic of facts had to be given the cold shoulder.

It was in the domain of political economy, however, that Kames's prescience was shown, perhaps, to the best advantage. The *Wealth of Nations* was not published until two years after the appearance of the *Sketches of the History of Man*, but the latter work contains the germ of the new doctrines of commerce promulgated by Adam Smith. The enlightened views of Kames may be gathered from the following: "A commerce in which the imports exceed in value the exports will soon drain a nation of its money, and put an end to industry." Again: "It appears to be the intention of Providence that all nations should benefit by commerce, as by sunshine." These are now the commonplaces of economic science, but that they should have been proclaimed two years before Adam Smith launched his epoch-making work is truly wonderful. Of course, it may be that Kames, so far from being original, was merely heralding the views of Smith, who was then hard at work on his *Wealth of Nations*. Smith had a high opinion of Kames's judgment. He once said of his friend: "We must every one of us acknowledge Kames for our master."[1] It is conceivable, therefore, that he discussed knotty points with the judge and that the latter, having got the drift of Smith's work, made use of some of his ideas in his *Sketches*. But of this we cannot be certain.

[1] Tytler's *Life of Kames*, i. 160.

Kames's book came in for a good deal of adverse criticism. Johnson censured it for "misrepresenting Clarendon's account of the appearance of Sir George Villiers's ghost, as if Clarendon were weakly credulous; when the truth is, that Clarendon only says that the story was upon a better foundation of credit, than usually such discourses are founded upon."[1] Johnson also fell foul of Kames's statement "that virtue is natural to man, and that if we would but consult our own hearts we should be virtuous." "Now," adds the Doctor, "after consulting our own hearts all we can, and with all the helps we have, we find how few of us are virtuous. This is saying a thing which all mankind know not to be true."[2]

Something has already been said of the friends of Kames's earlier years. Those of his manhood and old age included almost every eminent person in the Scotland of his day. His acquaintance with David Hume began about 1735 and lasted, despite differences in religion and philosophy, until the latter's death in 1776. As has been shown, Hume's *Treatise on Human Nature* caused the judge much searching of heart, and drove him eventually to combat the views therein expressed in the interests of orthodoxy. His antipathy to the *Treatise*, however, did not prevent Kames complying with Hume's request for an introduction to Bishop Butler. Hume, on the other hand, had more than respect for Kames. Soon after the appearance of his *Treatise*, he wrote the judge to the effect that he

[1] Boswell's *Life of Johnson*, Hill's ed., iii. 351. [2] *Ibid.* iii. 352.

aspired to his approbation, and "next to that, to your free censure and criticism." Hume also read Kames's *Essays upon Several Subjects concerning British Antiquities* (1747) with "great satisfaction," adding that "the reasons are solid, the conjectures ingenious, and the whole instructive." Generous praise surely on the part of Hume for a critic who thought his *Treatise* subversive of morality, let alone religion.

The truth is, Kames presented a curious psychological problem. Always a stickler for orthodoxy, he yet was unorthodox himself, and chose his most intimate friends from the ranks of those who almost counted heterodoxy a virtue. And yet speculative differences never seem to have brought about estrangement. Kames reviled Hume's writings, and Hume returned good for evil.

Adam Smith's *Theory of Moral Sentiments* pleased Kames no more than did Hume's *Treatise.* To the system there expounded he strongly objected, and not very tactfully sent Smith a transcript of his criticisms, with the intimation that he proposed to insert them in a third edition of his *Essays on Morality.* Smith replied in a letter which put his character for magnanimity decidedly high. Both men were strongly opinionative, but both seem to have recognised that a man may be better than his books. At all events their intimate relationship remained unimpaired.

Probably of all his friends, Blair, Robertson, Boswell, and Thomas Reid, the father of the Scottish school of Philosophy, were those with whom he had most in common. It is regrettable that Kames did not meet Johnson when the latter paid his visit to the Hebrides in 1773, for then it might have been found that the lexicographer and the Scottish judge were not so far apart after all. Kames, however, met an equally commanding personality in Benjamin Franklin, who, together with his son, was the guest of the judge at his Berwickshire seat for a few days in 1759. The versatile American and Kames drew together at once, and a lifelong friendship was begun. "Whenever I reflect," wrote Franklin grandiloquently, "on the great pleasure and advantage I received from the free communication of sentiments in the conversations we had at Kames, and in the little agreeable rides to the Tweed-side, I shall for ever regret our premature parting."[1] But, though unduly effusive, this epistle seems to have been perfectly sincere. During his visit Kames offered his guest a portrait of Penn, but this the latter declined as being "too valuable a curiosity" for him to think of accepting, but he desired "the favour of leave to take a copy of it," to which, no doubt, his lordship graciously consented.

As indeed may be conjectured from his manifold activities, Kames was a man of wonderful vitality. "At eighty-three he is as gay and as nimble as he was at twenty-five; his sight, hearing, and memory perfect; . . . he is a most entertaining companion,"[2] wrote his old literary friend, Mrs. Montagu, who had attracted his

[1] Tytler's *Life of Kames*, i. 264.
[2] Doran's *Lady of the Last Century*, p. 247.

lordship by her "Parnassian coquetry" long years before. At eighty-five, Tytler tells us, he was free from any chronic ailment or even from bodily infirmity, which certainly argues a robust constitution, since it must not be forgotten that Kames's "manner of living was sociable, and at no time repugnant to moderate indulgences."[1] Now "moderate indulgences" is an eighteenth-century euphemism signifying that the limits to excess were lightly drawn. We may therefore conclude that Kames's constitution was often put to a severe test. Happily, regular exercise, plenty of fresh air, and frequent journeys would in a measure counteract debilitating influences.

But even Methuselah must run his course. The first premonitions occurred in his eighty-sixth year, when he was seized with an internal complaint. But the dauntless spirit of the man buoyed him up. Despite the fact that he was suffering much pain, he continued to discharge his judicial functions, and also to conduct a lengthy philosophical correspondence with his friend, Thomas Reid. On starting for the autumn circuit in 1782, he said to his daughter-in-law: "It is very possible that this journey may shorten my life a little space; but what then? Have I not lived long enough?" He dreaded outliving his faculties, and when friends asked about his health, he would reply with some irritation: "Don't talk of my disease. I have no disease but old age."

Kames left Blair Drummond, where he had spent the vacation, in the beginning of November,

[1] Tytler's *Life of Kames*, ii. 227.

and the Court of Session meeting soon after, he took his seat on the first day of the term as usual. The spirit was undoubtedly willing, but the flesh was weak. For some time he took his full share of the work of the Court. Gradually, however, he became conscious that his strength was ebbing away, and that the place which had known him for almost sixty years must know him no more. On the last day of his attendance he took a separate and affectionate farewell of each of his brethren on the Bench.

Two days before his death he told his friend, Dr. Cullen, with grim humour, that he earnestly wished to be gone, because he was exceedingly curious to learn the nature and manners of the next world. "Doctor," he added, "as I never could be idle in this world, I shall willingly perform any task that may be imposed upon me" in the next.[1] Some one coming into the sick-chamber, and finding Kames, notwithstanding his weakness, engaged in dictating to an amanuensis, expressed surprise. "How, man," said the dying judge and philosopher, "would you hae me stay wi' my tongue in my cheek till death comes to fetch me?"[2] On December 27, 1782, Kames passed "into that still country, where the hail-storms and fire-showers do not reach, and the heaviest-laden wayfarer at length lays down his load."[3]

Kames was tall and thin. Though he had not a striking presence, he was far from being

[1] Smellie's *Literary Lives*, p. 147.
[2] Kay's *Edinburgh Portraits*, Pop. ed., i. 26.
[3] Carlyle's "Essay on Burns."

ungainly, except "when intent on some abstract speculation or novel theory." Then he would "throw his body into an awkward attitude, his head being sometimes depressed as low as his knees, whilst his body formed somewhat of a semicircle."[1] In his declining years he had a decided stoop, but when in the vigour of manhood, his appearance, according to Tytler, who knew him, was "uncommonly becoming. His countenance, though not handsome, was animated and intelligent. . . . In ordinary discourse, his accent and pronunciation were like those of the better educated of his countrymen. . . . The tone was not displeasing from its vulgarity ; and though the idiom, and frequently the phrases, were peculiar to the Scottish dialect, his language was universally intelligible."[2]

This word-portrait of Tytler's is worth quoting, if for no other reason than because of its quaintness. To say that Kames's speech was vulgar and yet not displeasing is to estimate somewhat poorly the judgment of his contemporaries. Moreover, it is evident that, however successful Kames was in purging his writings of Scotticisms, he retained them in his speech, though it is comforting to know that they did not preponderate to such an extent as to make his conversation unintelligible to the southron.

From all accounts Kames appears to have been a man whose talk was worth listening to. Ramsay, of Ochtertyre, no mean judge, goes so far as to say that "a collection of Lord Kames's

[1] Ramsay's *Scotland and Scotsmen*, i 209.
[2] Tytler's *Life of Kames*, ii. 239-40.

table-talk, like that of Selden or of Johnson, as given by Boswell, would be a precious and interesting relic of him."[1] That it would be shrewd, and witty, and allusive, and entertaining can well be imagined, but that it would be reflective, high-souled, epigrammatic is at least open to doubt. Ramsay says that all delighted in Kames's conversation because they were edified thereby, but as he accuses him of prurience of speech, and classifies him "as one of the very few lively persons whom liquor rendered more joyous and sprightly,"[2] it is difficult to see where the edification came in.

Kames was a typical product of his age, and of his class. Greatness was not his, nor genius, but he was not by any means a mediocrity. A man of strong though not wholly attractive individuality, he had considerable natural endowments combined with wide and varied interests and boundless activity, which enabled him to make some mark in law, in literature, in philosophy, and in agriculture. He was not a scholar in the true sense, for though he studied hard, he often studied to little purpose. His knowledge was neither deep nor trustworthy; and if he had imagination it never soared high. But he had a genuine love of intellectual pursuits. It pleased him, however, to flit from one subject to another without thoroughly mastering any. His perception was sometimes surprisingly acute. Truths to which the world has hearkened since, he saw, but as through a glass darkly. The creative intelligence he had not, but he some-

[1] Ramsay's *Scotland and Scotsmen*, i. 212. [2] *Ibid.* i. 213.

times turned to excellent account what other men had originated.

Perhaps the best that can be said for Kames, and it is no small admission, is that he gave a decided impetus to everything that tended to the improvement of Scotland in law, literature, commerce, manufactures, and agriculture. He was thus a true builder of national prosperity at a time when men of that sort were none too many.

The traits of his character have already, to some extent, been expiscated. Versatile in his talents, he was no less versatile in his foibles. If he accounted knowledge above riches, he set fame above knowledge. He was unswervingly loyal to the spirit of his own maxim: "Self-conceit is none of the smallest blessings from heaven." He was vain beyond all believing, and when you have said that you have robbed a man of his place in the first rank, and possibly in the second. Then he sinned against the lesser proprieties of behaviour, and a few of the greater. He was a curious mixture of virtues and vices. He united culture with vulgarity, geniality with moroseness, catholicity with the spirit of all uncharitableness, orthodoxy with scepticism, shrewdness with eccentricity. His humour was grim, mordant, sometimes obscene; but he was no misanthrope. He felt the joy of life. He loved good men, good books, and good talk. And if his social instincts implied a degree of conviviality which cannot be condoned by twentieth-century opinion, it is only just to remember that the temper and standard of his age was not ours.

It was not decreed that the chaplet of renown should rest on Kames's brow. At least half a dozen of his contemporaries far surpassed him in originality and learning, but in character, attainments, and idiosyncracies he may be taken as a representative of the normal type of cultured Scotsman of the eighteenth century.

II

LORD MONBODDO

(1714–1799)

I.—The Man

James Burnet, Lord Monboddo, one of the most extraordinary men who ever sat on the judgment seat—" a character rarely to be met with in common life ; being fitter for a comedy or novel than anything else " [1]—was born in 1714 of a family more ancient than opulent. His paternal ancestors could be traced back to the days of King Robert the Bruce, and were the owners of the Deeside property of Leys. His father, James Burnet, was the proprietor of a small estate in Kincardineshire, known as Monboddo, in the unpretentious and somewhat dilapidated mansion-house of which the future judge first saw the light. Burnet's lineage on the maternal side was also distinguished, his mother being the only daughter of Sir Arthur Forbes, Bart., of Craigievar.

Of the parents there are few personal details. The father was a strong Jacobite and, along with many other landed gentlemen, got into trouble

[1] Ramsay's *Scotland and Scotsmen*, i. 355.

in connection with the Rebellion of 1715. He was present at the battle of Sheriffmuir, and one incident, recorded by Ramsay, of Ochtertyre,[1] shows him in rather an amiable light. An English officer, who had been stunned by a fall from his horse, perceiving, on his recovery, a gentleman on horseback near him, said: "Sir, I am your prisoner." "No," answered the other (who saw the King's troops approaching), "I am your prisoner." "If that be the case," said the officer, "dismount, and I will protect you." Burnet of Monboddo accordingly walked, while the officer rode his horse, and brought him safely to Stirling Castle.

Burnet received his first schooling from a Robert Milne, designated in the family archives "Tutor to Monboddo's bairns." Monboddo, however, does not seem to have rated the tutor's gifts very highly, for in 1722 we find him writing a doleful letter to his spouse from Edinburgh, expressing doubts as to the efficacy of home tuition, and gravely assuring her that "Jamie will be lost" if she does not send him to a proper school. The advice was taken, and "Jamie" was despatched forthwith to the parish school of Laurencekirk, where he was taught by Thomas Ruddiman who, in later years, shone as a prince among Latin grammarians and as Keeper of the Advocates' Library, an office in which he was succeeded by no less a person than David Hume. Ruddiman was an apt teacher, a scholar, and, if all reports be true, a gentleman. But, notwithstanding these excellent qualifications, Monboddo

[1] Ramsay's *Scotland and Scotsmen*, i. 351 (*n.*).

LORD MONBODDO
From the Portrait by Kay

had still gloomy forebodings that " Jamie " was in danger of being " lost." The result was that the boy was early recalled from the parish school, and home tuition was given another trial—this time under Dr. Francis Skene.

Under his new tutor Burnet made satisfactory progress, and imbibed that love of Greek literature and philosophy which was to become the ruling passion of his life. Skene remained at Monboddo until his appointment to the Chair of Philosophy in King's College, Aberdeen. Thither his pupil followed him. He is even said to have lived under his tutor's roof; but, however that may be, it is certain that, inspired by Skene and Principal Blackwell, the latter one of the most ardent champions of Greek study in Scotland, Burnet became an enthusiastic disciple of Aristotle and Plato, and a contemner of Bacon, Locke, Newton, Hume, and other mere moderns.

Having graduated Master of Arts at Aberdeen University, he removed to Edinburgh, where he began to equip himself for the Scottish Bar. He afterwards went to Holland to learn the maxims of the great Dutch jurists (which then had great weight in the Parliament House), to see the world, and to converse with strangers of figure and fashion. Monboddo, in after years, prided himself not a little upon the fact that he had spent three years studying Civil Law at Groningen, and never lost an opportunity of advocating a similar education for all promising Scottish lawyers.

Returning to Scotland, he happened to arrive in Edinburgh on the day when the notorious

Captain Porteous expiated his crime on a dyer's pole in the Grassmarket. When about to retire to rest, Burnet's curiosity was aroused by a tumultuous crowd hurrying along the thoroughfare beneath his window. Instead of going to bed, he made his way to the street, where his scantily clad condition and the nightcap which he wore added a touch of humour to a situation tragic in the extreme. Speedily becoming entangled with the crowd, he soon found himself in the Grassmarket, where he was an involuntary witness of the scene which Scott has painted in indelible colours in his *Heart of Midlothian.* Burnet was so shocked by what he saw that he passed a sleepless night, and next morning seriously meditated leaving Edinburgh as a place unfit for a civilised being to live in. Better counsels prevailed, however, for on learning how Porteous had come by his miserable end, he heroically resolved to hazard his life among the turbulent populace of the Scottish capital.

Burnet became an advocate in 1737 and, with a true sense of the fitness of things, went to reside in Advocates' Close. Here he practised the simple life, partly because briefs were few, and partly because his capacity for convivial enjoyment was limited. One good story has come down to us of those days when Burnet's plight seems to have been that suggested by the cheerless line in Johnson's *London* :

> Slow rises worth by poverty dépress'd.

He was junior counsel for the Laird of Stracathro and the tacksman of the Edzell fishings in an action which they had brought against Mr. Scott of Brotherton with reference to the construction of certain "cruive fishings" near the mouth of the North Esk. The cruives had to be inspected, and Burnet, in doing this, fell into a deep pool. Efforts were made to rescue him, but Scott, the defender, thought this a work of supererogation. "Let him alone," he cried, "the young man wants to go to the bottom of the cause." Burnet, however, was saved, and did get to the bottom of the cause, though in a different way from what the defender in the case expected.

As a young man, Burnet sedulously attended social entertainments of all kinds, and in fashionable society he speedily rose to honour. There was no more familiar figure at the assemblies in Bell's Wynd, where he generally appeared in a suit of white velvet. Adorned in this garb, which he thought might well have become the person of the Chancellor of France, he would dance a minuet in truly Dutch style, to the delight of the ladies, and to the no small satisfaction of himself. He was unfailing, too, in his devotion to theatricals, though, as will be shown later, his ideas of the drama were decidedly peculiar. When West Digges and the captivating Mrs. Ward appeared in the Edinburgh playhouse, Burnet was nightly in attendance, and found scope for his energies in handing the ladies to their seats. He was also fond of hunting and other manly exercises.

The outbreak of the Jacobite rebellion in 1745 brought about a temporary cessation of business in the Court of Session, and Burnet, loathing civil strife, hurried off to London to cement a number of literary and philosophical friendships. In the Metropolis, which, in later life, he visited annually, he mixed in the best society, his company being much sought after by wits, men of letters, and fashionable ladies. Indeed, he knew almost everybody worth knowing, not excepting the King. Among his most intimate London acquaintances were Thomson, the poet of the *Seasons*, in whose house at Richmond he passed many a pleasant hour; David Mallet, that notorious literary adventurer who changed his name "from Scotch Malloch to English Mallet," and tried to filch from Thomson the honour of having written "Rule, Britannia"; and Dr. John Armstrong—frugal, taciturn, splenetic—who divided his time between a lucrative medical practice and the Muses, cultivating the latter with profit to himself, if not with advantage to the human race.

Burnet was also intimate with a group of law lords, including the great Thurlow, who is remembered by Fox's jest, "No man was so wise as Thurlow looked," and the greater Mansfield, one of the finest intellects that ever added lustre to the King's Bench. Then there was Mrs. Montagu, "a faded beauty, a wit, a critic, an author of some fame" who "might have been admired by the first order of minds, had she not been greedy of more praise than she was entitled to."[1] It was at Mrs. Montagu's that Burnet met Hannah More, whom he exasperated by

[1] Alex. Carlyle's *Autobiography*, 3rd ed., p. 461.

defending slavery because the Ancients did so, and by maintaining that Home's *Douglas* was the greatest of tragedies. Nor must we forget Mrs. Garrick, of whom he saw a good deal in the days of her widowhood. The lady still retained her beauty and charm of manner, so much so that the eccentric judge—now a widower of some years' standing—fell deeply in love with her. Twice the widower offered marriage to the widow, and twice it was politely declined.

Last, but not least, Burnet basked in the sunshine of royal favour. George III. became quite interested in the Scottish judge, and frequently welcomed him at the Court of St. James. One day Burnet was walking on the terrace at Windsor Castle, when the King, recognising him, desired him to be called. "My Lord," said His Majesty with much affability, "how did you travel from Scotland?" "On horseback, please your Majesty." "That was too much at your time of life, and in the late bad weather, when even my dragoon officers took chaises; but, tell me, does your lordship call a wheel-carriage a *box*?" "Sire," replied Monboddo, "I am afraid I gave it a worse name; for I called it a *close box*."[1]

Burnet won his legal spurs in the Douglas Cause, which began in 1762. This, by far the most famous of Scottish lawsuits of the eighteenth century, centred in a very small point, regarding which, however, the evidence was extremely conflicting, namely, "whether Archibald Stewart was or was not the son of Sir John Stewart of

[1] Ramsay's *Scotland and Scotsmen*, i. 358 (*n.*).

Grandtully and Lady Jane Douglas, sister of the Duke of Douglas." The case created immense interest and excitement, as upon it hung the succession to the extensive estates of the last Duke of Douglas, for which there were several claimants.

"Briefed" on behalf of the Duke of Queensberry, Burnet acquitted himself so well as to make his elevation to the Bench inevitable. His industry and success in collecting evidence amazed his friends and disconcerted his opponents. Thrice did he visit France for this purpose, where his mastery of the language, a legacy of the Groningen days, was of great service. The Paris lawyers employed in the case were not very hopeful of success, and actually drafted a letter to the Duke of Queensberry counselling withdrawal, but Burnet would not hear of his client being so easily vanquished, and the letter was destroyed. Subsequent events fully justified the line he took. The pleadings lasted no fewer than thirty-one days, Burnet sustaining his part brilliantly all the while. It is true that the Court of Session, by the casting vote of the Lord President, decided against him; but when the case was taken to the House of Lords, where sat Camden and Mansfield, the Douglas side won an easy victory. So ably did Burnet plead his case that the Supreme Court of Appeal, without a vote, reversed the decision of the Scottish judges, who had decided that Archibald Stewart was not the son of Sir John Stewart.

The death in 1767 of Andrew Fletcher, Lord Milton, created a vacancy among the ordinary

Lords of Session, and Burnet became his successor, assuming the title of Lord Monboddo. As the Douglas Cause was not yet finally decided, efforts were made to delay the appointment, and not unnaturally, for Burnet's elevation at that moment meant that he would be placed in the invidious position of being called upon to pronounce judgment in a case in which he had played a leading part as an advocate. Burnet, it must be confessed, acted in this matter neither with discrimination nor delicacy, for he allowed the Duke of Queensberry, who was not slow to appreciate the advantage of transforming the man who had pled his cause into being its judge, to go to the King, and secure his appointment. Surely no judge was ever placed in a more embarrassing position than was Monboddo, for on the first occasion on which he appeared in his judicial capacity, the Douglas Cause came up for disposal.

But however inauspicious was the beginning of Monboddo's judicial career, it was fully atoned for. He is credited with having been not only a master of legal principle, but a wise, independent, impartial, and learned judge. Monboddo would probably have subscribed to the dictum of the American orator, " One man with God is a majority." Certainly, he often differed from his brethren, and found himself in a minority of one ; but it says much for his soundness as a lawyer that his judgments were seldom, if ever, reversed by the House of Lords. Paradoxical Monboddo was in his books and in his talk, but he seems to have kept this dubious accomplishment under rigorous restraint while on the Bench.

Not less creditable is the fact that he was instrumental to some extent in getting rid of the "law's delay." One notable improvement instituted by him in a court in which circumlocution had become almost a fetish, was the substitution of what is known, in legal terminology, as "hearings" for "pleadings." Monboddo might have become a judge in the Court of Justiciary, but he declined all overtures, because the duties would have interfered with the pursuit of his Greek studies in the vacation.

The personality of Monboddo is puzzling beyond all belief. He was typically Scottish in his shrewdness, wit, thrift, and "dourness," but there was also a quixotic element in his nature which unmistakably differentiated him from the normal type of Scotsman. He was not exactly winsome, yet it would be a perversion of truth to say that he had no heart. A staunch if candid friend, an excellent host, a lover of cultivated society, an honest advocate of respectability in high places, and a latitudinarian churchman, Monboddo sat under his own vine and fig tree, none daring to make him afraid.

It cannot be said that he was prepossessing, looking, says Chambers, "rather like an old stuffed monkey dressed in a judge's clothes, than anything else. His face, however, 'sicklied o'er' with the pale cast of thought, bore traces of high intellect."[1] His manners were brusque; his habits plain, methodical, and frequently odd.

[1] Chambers's *Traditions of Edinburgh*, new ed., p. 148.

He was abstemious, which is saying much, orgies being then in fashion. He was a thorough-going champion of sunlight and fresh air, which his contemporaries rigidly economised; and he unfeignedly believed that cleanliness was next to godliness, a doctrine more honoured in the breach than in the observance by his neighbours.

It was his custom, summer and winter, to take a cold bath on rising, usually at a very early hour. When staying at his Kincardineshire seat, he enjoyed this luxury in a structure erected for the purpose at some distance from the mansion, and near a running stream which supplied the water. He took a light dinner about noon, but considerably neutralised his excellent system of hygiene by making his supper the heaviest meal of the day. Before retiring to rest he indulged in an air-bath, and then did homage to the Ancients (for whom he considered no sacrifice too great), by applying to his body a lotion composed of rose-water, olive oil, saline, aromatic spirit, and Venetian soap. Besmeared with this formidable concoction, he slept the sleep of the just.

It has been well said that Monboddo earned more fame by his eccentricities than by his acuteness and learning. Unquestionably, he both said and did very odd things—things so odd as to give rise to serious apprehension regarding his sanity. He called forth more ridicule than any other public character of his time. The vagaries of Adam Smith (and they were singular enough) were insignificant compared with the oddities of Monboddo. The queer sayings and doings of this judge were not excrescences, the offspring of affectation; they were part of the man himself. Monboddo could no more do obeisance to tradition and conventionality than he could admit that Shakespeare was a great dramatist, or David Hume an influential philosopher. And this obliquity of conduct and speech, simply because it was innate, has always weighed most in the popular judgment of Monboddo. Whimsical people are often tantalising, but no one can say they are ever dull.

To chronicle all the stories about this crotchety man would be impossible, and even if it could be done no good purpose would be served, but one or two may be retailed as characteristic. What would be said nowadays of a judge who dispensed justice not from the Bench, but from the well of the court? This Monboddo invariably did. Several reasons have been given for his singular conduct. It is said that when he made his first appearance as a judge, he felt the awkwardness of his situation in connection with the Douglas Cause, and, with doubtful expediency, sought relief from a wounded conscience by delivering his "opinion" from the well of the court. Cockburn says[1] that some slight had made Monboddo resolve never to sit on the same bench with Lord President Dundas. He, however, adds that by sitting at the clerk's table, Monboddo was enabled to get easily in and out of the court, a more likely reason, for "whenever there was a pause he was sure to slip off, gown and all, to have a talk in the Outer House."

[1] *Memorials of his Time*, 1856, p. 111.

But Chambers[1] gives another version. The story goes that his lordship once embroiled himself in an action respecting a horse which he had committed when sick to a farrier, with instructions to give the animal a certain medicine. The farrier, thinking to improve the occasion, administered, along with the medicine, a liberal dose of treacle, no doubt surmising that a horse was as fond of its medicine being made palatable as a child. Unfortunately, the horse died next morning, and the farrier found himself the unhappy victim of a prosecution at the hands of Monboddo, who pleaded his own cause at the Bar. He lost the case, however, and became, Chambers alleges, "so enraged in consequence at his brethren, that he never afterwards sat with them upon the bench, but underneath, amongst the clerks."

In Butler's *Hudibras* there is a line which says:

> Great on the bench, great in the saddle.

These words might be fitly applied to Monboddo. He despised a carriage for two reasons. First, because he thought it was degrading to be dragged at the tails of horses instead of being mounted on their backs; and, secondly, because carriages were not in universal use among the Ancients. One wonders what would have been Monboddo's attitude had he lived in this era of motor cars and aeroplanes. The truth is that, apart from his partiality for classical habits, he was very fond of horses. No one delighted more than he

[1] *Traditions of Edinburgh*, new ed., p. 147.

in the pleasures of the chase. Mounted on Alburac, his favourite nag, he would scour the country in all weathers. And he was proud of the performance. He told Ramsay of Ochtertyre[1] once that, in a journey from Dalhousie Castle to Monboddo, he had met but one traveller who, to avoid the blast, rode with his face to the tail.

His annual journeys to London were invariably made on horseback. These equestrian performances continued until he was upwards of eighty years of age. On his last journey he took ill, and it was with great difficulty that a friend, who had overtaken him on the road, persuaded him to enter a carriage, which sorely touched his dignity as well as cast a slur upon the Ancients. But he was ill at ease, and, on the following day, he again mounted Alburac, and arrived in Edinburgh without further mishap.

In May 1785, Monboddo was in the court of the King's Bench when a rumour that the building was falling caused a general stampede. The Scottish judge, however, took the matter very coolly, as the following extract from a contemporary newspaper sufficiently testifies: "In the curious rout of the lawyers' corps, it is singular that the only person who kept his seat was a venerable stranger. Old Lord Monboddo, one of the Scots judges, was in the court of the King's Bench, and being short-sighted and rather dull in his hearing, he sat still during the tumult, and did not move from his place. Afterwards, being questioned why he did not bestir himself to avoid the ruin, he coolly answered 'that he

[1] *Scotland and Scotsmen*, i. 354 (*n.*).

thought it was *an annual ceremony* with which, as an alien to our laws, he had nothing to do!' "

When the colonel in *Guy Mannering* informs Mr. Pleydell that the usual hour of supper will be anticipated, the latter gaily expresses his delight, and remarks, " I am of counsel with my old friend Burnet. I love the *cœna*, the supper of the Ancients." The allusion is to Monboddo's custom of entertaining his friends to what he called " learned suppers," in imitation of the Ancients. These took place fortnightly at his residence in St. John Street. Here of an evening would gather as choice a company of intellectual aristocrats as could be found anywhere, for the colloquial fare was as substantial as the repast. The supper was usually at an early hour, and had all the variety and abundance of the chief meal of the day, Monboddo, in his unquenchable enthusiasm for the Ancients, being intent on reviving as much of the glory of the Attic banquets as was possible in an unattractive house in murky Edinburgh. The table was strewn with roses, for did not Horace love to have it so at his beautiful home among the Sabine hills? Similarly, the master of the feast would garland his flasks of excellent Bordeaux, as Anacreon was wont to do at the court of Polycrates of Samos. And as the sumptuous feast proceeded, Monboddo, who loved to unbend after the labours of the day to a select and admiring company, would discourse upon many things ancient and modern with wit, vivacity, and learning, or would expound some of his eccentric theories regarding the savage state or the diminution of the human race with an ingenuity and eloquence which might have been expended in a better cause.

While Monboddo's conversational powers were exhibited to most advantage at the suppers of the Ancients, his brilliant dialectical skill was in evidence at the meetings of the Select Society. There he met foemen worthy of his steel who by argument, and, occasionally, by sarcasm, sought to demolish his most cherished ideas. But he usually proved more than a match for his antagonists. On one occasion he had an animated encounter with Wedderburn who, in after years, found his way to the Woolsack. The future Lord Chancellor had ventured to say something derogatory to the Ancients which, immediately, brought Monboddo to his feet. "Mr. Preses," he said, "the Ancients roasted *above* the fire; the Moderns roast *before* the fire; but methinks this young gentleman would fain roast without any fire at all!"

An ingenious though unsound philosopher, a scholar whose knowledge was extensive rather than profound, a trafficker in paradox, and a man of letters whose judgment ran counter to that of most of his contemporaries, Monboddo had his full share of the trials of the man who is misunderstood. And like most misunderstood men, he made not a few enemies, partly by his intellectual singularity, and partly by a certain acerbity towards those who happened to differ from him. He quarrelled with Hume, whose "wretched philosophy" he could not abide; he despised his colleague, Kames, and, with perhaps a touch of jealousy, made light of his metaphysics; and he had no love for Dr. Johnson because, among other reasons, he had not "genius enough to comprehend the beauties of Milton," and held very unorthodox views concerning the Ancients.

Foote said of Monboddo that he was "an Elzevir edition of Johnson"[1]—a pretty compliment, though some, perplexed as to whether Foote really meant what the phrase usually implies, have asserted that he was only thinking of a pocket edition. Be that as it may, Monboddo and Johnson could forget their feuds, and meet as gentlemen. Boswell, however, was not at all sure on this point, and believing for once that discretion is the better part of valour, he cautiously "sounded" Monboddo as to whether a visit from Johnson, who was then trudging to the Hebrides, would be acceptable.

It was the vacation, and the judge was as usual living in the guise of a farmer on the ancestral estate. Thither Boswell despatched a letter announcing that Johnson had, with touching magnanimity, expressed a wish to "go two miles out of his way to see Lord Monboddo." Boswell's wish was gratified. Lexicographer and judge met, and if they did not fall upon each other's neck nor always return the soft answer which turns away wrath, they, on the whole, spent a pleasant time, and parted better friends than they were when they met.

Boswell gives a fairly full and graphic description of the interview:[2] "Lord Monboddo

[1] Boswell's *Johnson*, Hill's ed, ii. 189 (*n*). [2] *Ibid.* v. 77-81.

received us at his gate most courteously; pointed to the Douglas arms upon his house, and told us that his great-grandmother was of that family. 'In such houses (said he) our ancestors lived, who were better men than we.' 'No, no, my lord (said Dr. Johnson). We are as strong as they, and a great deal wiser.' This was an assault upon one of Lord Monboddo's capital dogmas, and I was afraid there would have been a violent altercation in the very close, before we got into the house. But his lordship is distinguished not only for 'ancient metaphysics' but for ancient *politesse* . . . and he made no reply."

"His lordship," Boswell continues, "was drest in a rustic suit, and wore a little round hat; he told us, we now saw him as Farmer Burnet, and we should have his family dinner, a farmer's dinner. He said: 'I should not have forgiven Mr. Boswell, had he not brought you here, Dr. Johnson.'" The ice once broken, the two men talked genially concerning many topics in which they had a common interest, and soon became conscious that they were not so far apart after all. Both, of course, spoke highly of Homer. "Johnson: 'He had all the learning of his age. The shield of Achilles shows a nation in war, a nation in peace; harvest sport, nay stealing.' Monboddo: 'Ay, and what we (looking to Boswell) would call a Parliament House scene; a cause pleaded.' Johnson: 'That is part of the life of a nation at peace. And there are in Homer such characters of heroes, that the united powers of mankind ever since have not produced any but what are to be found there.' Monboddo : ' Yet no character is described.' "

Then the conversation turned to history. " Monboddo : ' The history of manners is the most valuable. I never set a high value on any other history.' Johnson : ' Nor I ; and therefore I esteem biography, as giving us what comes near to ourselves, what we can turn to use.' Boswell : ' But in the course of general history, we find manners. In wars we see the dispositions of people, their degrees of humanity, and other particulars.' Johnson : ' Yes ; but then you must take all the facts to get this ; and it is but a little you get.' Monboddo : ' And it is that little which makes history valuable.' "

Monboddo and Johnson then sharpened their wits on such subjects as the decay of learning, the attainments of bishops, and the momentous problem as to whether a savage or a London shopkeeper had the best existence, the judge characteristically casting his vote for the savage. Johnson subsequently examined his host's son, Arthur, in Latin, an ordeal which the youth seems to have stood fairly well. It remains to be added that Johnson ate a hearty dinner, and that the judge suspected him of gourmandism.

It would have been surprising had Monboddo escaped the unpopularity which ever awaits the man whose tongue is not only sharp but indiscreet. He rushed in where angels fear to tread. His likes and dislikes he expressed with the utmost freedom, regardless of consequences. Candour is a virtue, but if not linked to prudence it may do endless havoc. Monboddo and Kames, between whom there was no love lost, once found themselves at Gordon Castle as guests of Jane, Duchess of Gordon. For this great lady Monboddo had much respect. "Sir," he once remarked to a friend, "her Grace has a brilliancy and radiance about her like the rays round the head of an apostle!"—clumsy but genuine appreciation which ill accorded, however, with the incident[1] about to be mentioned. Discussing his favourite topic—the Ancients—Monboddo remarked to the Duchess that few Moderns could write with elegance. It was suggested that Kames (who was present) was at least one exception to the rule. But Monboddo, with amazing tactlessness, declined to admit the exception. Kames, who thought himself as good as any Ancient, was, of course, highly offended. Happily, the noble hostess, not relishing the prospect of a literary duel in her drawing-room, adroitly relieved a desperate situation by proposing that the protagonists should dance a reel with her.

Monboddo's domestic life was clouded by bereavement. In 1760 he married Miss Farquharson, a relative of Marshal Keith, but the lady died in giving birth to her third child. Then his only son was taken at an early age, and, in 1790, his second daughter, who was the light of his eyes and the pride of his heart, fell a victim to consumption. Her remarkable beauty was the talk of Edinburgh; and she is supposed to have been the person who was elegantly praised in one of the papers of the *Mirror* as rejecting

[1] Ramsay's *Scotland and Scotsmen*, i. 355 (*n.*).

the most flattering offers of marriage in order that she might tend her father in his old age. Burns, who met her on the occasion of his first visit to Edinburgh, surrendered at once to her charms. "Well," said his friend Geddes to him when he arrived back in his native Ayrshire, "and did you admire the young lady?" "I admired God Almighty more than ever. Miss Burnet is the most heavenly of all His works," was the unhesitating reply. Writing later to William Chalmers,[1] the bard explained that "Fair B—— is heavenly Miss B., daughter of Lord Monboddo, at whose house I have had the honour to be more than once. There has not been anything nearly like her, in all the combinations of beauty, grace, and goodness, the great Creator has formed, since Milton's Eve on the first day of her existence."

It would have been strange, indeed, if Burns had not followed up such superlative laudation by singing the praises of Monboddo's fair daughter in verse. Accordingly, there is the well-known allusion to her in the "Address to Edinburgh":[2]

> Fair Burnet strikes th' adoring eye,
> Heav'n's beauties on my fancy shine;
> I see the Sire of Love on high,
> And own His work indeed divine!

Miss Burnet's death, however, impelled the poet to try something more ambitious, and after several months' "hammering," he produced the fine elegy[3] of seven stanzas beginning:

---

[1] Chambers's *Life of Burns*, new ed., ii. 30. [2] *Ibid.* ii. 25.
[3] *Ibid.* iii. 231.

Life ne'er exulted in so rich a prize
As Burnet, lovely from her native skies;
Nor envious Death so triumph'd in a blow
As that which laid th' accomplish'd Burnet low.

Even Clarinda was forced to acknowledge the bewitching beauty of Monboddo's daughter. To "dear Sylvander," she wrote:[1] "Miss Burnet sat just behind me. What an angelic girl! I stared at her, having never seen her so near. I remembered you talking of her, etc. What felicity to witness her 'softly speak and sweetly smile!' How could you celebrate any other Clarinda! Oh, I would have adored you, as Pope of exquisite taste and refinement, had you loved, sighed, and written upon her for ever!" Whatever foibles Clarinda may have had, certainly jealousy was not one of them.

The death of his beloved daughter was a blow from which Monboddo never recovered. It is said that, after she died, his son-in-law covered her portrait to spare the old man's feelings. "Quite right—quite right," said Monboddo, casually looking up from his book. "Never," says Ramsay, "did Lord Monboddo appear in a more advantageous light. . . . He bore his loss like a hero and a Christian, returning to his studies and duties seemingly with increased ardour."[2] Monboddo survived his daughter for nine years. Shortly before his own death, which occurred at his house in Edinburgh on May 26, 1799, he said to Dr. Gregory, his medical adviser and friend: "I know it is not in the power of

[1] Chambers's *Life of Burns*, new ed., ii. 304.
[2] *Scotland and Scotsmen*, i. 360.

Art to cure me: all I wish is euthanasia—a happy death." And euthanasia he got, for he died in harness.

Monboddo was fortunate in many things—fortunate in possessing a fine intellect, a sound heart, and a good conscience. But his estimable qualities and his undoubted learning were buried beneath as ludicrous a mass of crotchets and idiosyncrasies as ever were credited to a man outside of bedlam. Ridicule was his only portion during his lifetime, and it has not forsaken his memory—so hard is the way of the man who habitually trades in paradox. Of Monboddo's writings something will be said in the next chapter; but here, having regard solely to his personality, there is little to cavil at in the inflated lines which Dr. H. W. Tytler, author of *Pædstrophia,* wrote in memory of his friend:

> If wisdom, learning, worth, demand a tear,
> Weep o'er the dust of great Monboddo here;
> A Judge upright, to mercy still inclined;
> A generous friend, a father fond and kind;
> His country's pride, for skill in Grecian lore,
> And all Antiquity's invalued store.

III

LORD MONBODDO

II.—His Writings

Monboddo tells us, in one of his letters, that he "had resolved like Varro the Roman never to publish anything upon the subject of philosophy, because the learned would not read me and the unlearned would not understand me." The resolution was not kept, and the consequences have followed that Monboddo foretold. The learned do not read his pages unless to be amused, and the unlearned, we may be certain, are not even aware of their existence. Nor need we quarrel with what the gods have decreed. When the virtue has gone out of a book, it must surely die, and the virtue had wholly escaped from Monboddo's works before their author had been many years in his grave.

Professor Knight says that "as a man of learning, Monboddo has had no rival amongst the philosophers of Scotland except Sir William Hamilton."[1] Be it so; but it is a fame to which no crown of glory attaches. Monboddo's learning may have benefited himself (though even that may be doubted); it certainly has not benefited

[1] *Monboddo and his Contemporaries*, p 27.

mankind. Incoherent, discursive, archaic, lifeless, Monboddo discovered no fresh truth, enunciated no new law, proclaimed afresh no doctrine that had become partially obscured. His legacy to the human race consisted of certain fantastical ideas, which caused his contemporaries to laugh and succeeding generations to blaspheme. His writings are read, or rather scanned, not for their sense but for their nonsense — surely the hardest of all perverse destinies with which earth can perplex an author's fame.

But, apart altogether from their subject-matter, Monboddo's books are portentously long, badly arranged, and prolix *ad nauseam.* He admired the rolling periods of Demosthenes, Thucydides, Cicero, Milton, and Clarendon, rather than what he called the "shorthand" of Voltaire. He had a genius for tautological expression, and he rambled from one subject to another in a manner lamentably at variance with the logical precision one expects in a lawyer — and so acute a lawyer as Monboddo is reputed to have been.

His lordship once planned a work on the history of man which he fondly believed would be "the greatest work of History, Philosophy, and Learning, that has been published in this country"—a resolution which did credit to his vanity rather than to his sagacity. But, alas! the *magnum opus* never was written; and Monboddo was driven to compress his wisdom into the twelve portly volumes that comprise the essay on the *Origin and Progress of Language* (6 vols., 1773–1792) and the treatise on *Antient Metaphysics* (6 vols., 1779–99). Gibbon took nearly nineteen years to write the *Decline and Fall of the Roman Empire*, but it took Monboddo twenty-six to tell all he knew about primeval man and his lingual faculty, and to vindicate the learning and wisdom of the Ancients.

The first volume of the *Origin and Progress of Language*, which contains nearly all that is germane to the subject, and is by far the most interesting, was, to a considerable extent, the work of Professor John Hunter of St. Andrews University, who was then his secretary. As for the remaining five volumes, all that can be said for them is that they bring together so enormous a mass of curious and recondite lore as almost to persuade us of the truth of the saying of Monboddo's old age, " I have forgot a great deal more than most other men knew." But most of this learning is so hopelessly irrelevant and so absurd that one marvels how a man who was so shrewd in judging others should have viewed his own verbosity with so lenient an eye.

The *Origin and Progress of Language* is primarily an eloquent plea for a more enthusiastic study of the ancient masters of wisdom, particularly Aristotle and Plato. Monboddo deserves credit for championing the cause of Greek scholarship when the literature and thought of the ancient world had little or no significance for his countrymen. In Scotland in the eighteenth century, classical learning had reached a low ebb — so low that the Greek possessed by the most enlightened of Monboddo's contemporaries would have disgraced a public-schoolboy of to-day. Monboddo was a Grecian of a most uncompromising type. As Rousseau counselled a return to Nature, so Monboddo counselled a return to Antiquity. Nothing, he was wont to say, "could save us and all Europe from absolute destruction and annihilation, but the study of ancient men and ancient manners." The literature and philosophy of Greece was the fountainhead of all wisdom, knowledge, and virtue. Only as modern culture was informed by its spirit and regulated by its canons could it hope to play a worthy part in the world.

And this absorbing devotion to Greek was accompanied by a most irrational contempt for Latin, and practically for all modern, literature. Roman literature, in his estimation, derived what potency it had entirely from Greek sources. Modern philosophic thought, on the other hand, could boast of no name of conspicuous eminence, unless it was that of his "worthy and learned friend, Mr. Harris," whose *Hermes* was a work that would be "read and admired so long as there is any taste for philosophy and fine writing in Britain." To insist upon the great value of Greek culture was right and proper, but to do so at the expense of all modern culture which did not directly draw its sustenance from Aristotelian and Platonic sources was both foolish and reprehensible. Had Monboddo contented himself with championing the claims of ancient learning as the best foundation on which to rear a liberal education, he would have rendered excellent service: but this was alien to his purpose. He idealised the masters of Greek thought. "No one ignorant of Greek," he contended, "could write a page of good English"; but if Monboddo's own prose is to be taken as an example, he who aspires to write good English had better give Greek a wide berth.

This meticulous regard for the Ancients and undisguised contempt for the Moderns led Monboddo to pen a series of literary and philosophical judgments both silly and mendacious. He laments that Shakespeare "knew so little of the nature of poetry," and that he had been set up as a standard "for the English taste of poetry." All the merit Monboddo could allow the dramatist was that he was an excellent mimographer. "Perhaps," he adds pontifically, "I should not have allowed him that praise, if any of the ancient mimic pieces had come down to us." How fortunate that Shakespeare had not filched from him this last shred of honour! Home's tragedy of *Douglas* seems to have been Monboddo's idea of dramatic excellence. It is, we learn, "most happily executed, and exceeds anything of the kind I know, either ancient or modern, without excepting even the famous discovery in the *Oedipus Tyrannus* mentioned by Aristotle as a model of the kind."

Milton's classicism, as may be readily inferred, appealed to Monboddo. He is more generous in his estimate of the Puritan poet than of any other modern writer. Milton is the only English poet that can be compared with Homer, and he commiserates Dr. Johnson for not having genius enough to apprehend that it was so. *Paradise Lost*, however, is not quite satisfactory. The poet "wants that without which neither poem nor picture can have any great degree of excellence, I mean the choice of a proper subject. I hold *Comus* to be the better poem of the two."

Monboddo's estimates of the leading representatives of modern philosophy were equally extraordinary. Bacon was certainly astray, while the philosophy of Hume is dismissed as "wretched." Locke also comes in for a good deal of rough handling. The famous *Essay* is little more than "a hasty collection of crude, undigested thoughts, by a man who thought and reasoned by himself upon subjects of the greatest difficulty and deepest speculation, without assistance of learning." This is Monboddo on Locke: it would have been interesting to have had Locke on Monboddo. Berkeley fares no better, his theory being "as poor a piece of sophistry as ever I saw composed by a man who seems to be in earnest." But Monboddo reserved his most derogatory criticism for a man compared intellectually with whom, he was the merest pigmy —Isaac Newton. Knowing next to nothing of physical science, and therefore unable to grasp the fundamental positions of the Newtonian system, he had the temerity to cross swords with the author of the *Principia*, and, with amazing presumption, to claim that he had improved upon Newton's ideas.

The real interest of the *Origin and Progress of Language*, however, does not lie in Monboddo's extravagant praise of the Ancients, nor yet in his belittlement of the Moderns, but in what he wrote about the origin of man. He has been proclaimed a forerunner of Darwin. But such a claim can only be admitted with important qualifications. Monboddo undoubtedly foreshadowed the evolutionary principle which, nearly a century later, was to transform the whole realm of thought; but the idea was grasped in a vague and incoherent way, was entirely unsupported by evidence, and was hedged round with so many ludicrous notions that the discovery amounted to little more than a guess. If Monboddo was an evolutionist, then he must have been in the same awkward predicament as Monsieur Jourdain, an amusing character in one of Molière's plays, who learned that he had been talking prose for more than forty years without knowing it.

Monboddo held that "language is not natural to man," first, because of "the origin and nature of the ideas expressed by it"; and, secondly, because of "the nature of articulation." In arguing this view, he asserted that man had certain points of affinity with the orang-outang monkey. The passage containing this theory is as follows: "Not only solitary savages, but a whole nation, if I may call them so, have been found without the use of speech. This is the case of the Ouran Outangs that are found in the kingdom of Angola in Africa, and in several parts of Asia. They are exactly of the human form; walking erect, not upon all-four, like the savages that have been found in Europe; they use sticks for weapons; they live in society; they make huts of branches of trees, and they carry off negro girls, whom they make slaves of. . . . These facts are related of them by Mons. Buffon in his *Natural History*. . . . But though from the particulars above mentioned it appears certain that they are of our species, and though they have made some progress in the arts of life, they have not come the length of language."

Now to maintain on the strength of this statement that Monboddo was an evolutionist is as absurd as it would be to ignore the rules of the syllogism. Huxley once said that the man of science has learned to believe in justification, not by faith but by verification. With Monboddo there is much faith, but no verification. His statement that the Angola monkeys are undeveloped specimens of the human species has not even the charm of novelty. In a letter to his friend, Sir John Pringle, he admits that he was indebted for the suggestion to M. Jussieu of Paris. Moreover, Monboddo, so far from being convinced of the truth of what he propounded, had a haunting suspicion that he had expressed himself too strongly with regard to "the exact conformity of the anatomy of the orang-outang with that of a man," and he promised Sir John Pringle that he would modify what he had written on this point.

Notwithstanding all this, however, the notion that Monboddo forestalled Darwin dies hard. Many years ago, when the praises of the author of the *Origin of Species* were on every tongue, Lord Neaves, a distinguished Senator of the College of Justice, thus gave rhymic utterance to the popular delusion :

'Tis strange how men and things revive
Though laid beneath the sod, O !

I sometimes think I see alive
Our good old friend Monboddo !
His views, when forth at first they came,
Appeared a little odd, O !
But now we've notions much the same ;
We're back to old Monboddo.

Alas ! the good lord little knew,
As this strange ground he trod, O !
That others would his path pursue,
And never name Monboddo !
Such folks should have their tails restored,
And thereon feel the rod, O !
For having thus the fame ignored
That's due to old Monboddo.

Though Darwin now proclaims the law,
And spreads it far abroad, O !
The man that first the secret saw
Was honest old Monboddo.
The architect precedence takes
Of him that bears the hod, O !
So up and at them, Land o' Cakes,
We'll vindicate Monboddo.

The truth is, Monboddo was one of the most credulous of men. The *Origin and Progress of Language* is full of incidents which might be pardonable in the pages of Sir John de Mandeville, but hardly do credit to a man of judicial capacity living in the eighteenth century. Monboddo believed not only that men with long hairy tails existed, but men who had the feet of goats, also horns and other bovine attributes. So convinced was he of the truth of his theory of human tails that whenever a child happened to be born in his house, he contrived to see it in its first state, having a notion that the tails were removed immediately after birth. "Most men," said Dr. Johnson, "endeavour to hide their tails; but Lord Monboddo is as vain of his as a squirrel."[1] No wonder, then, that Edinburgh society was highly amused by the speculations of the pedantic old judge, and that Kames should have insisted upon Monboddo walking in front of him in order that he might see his tail.

If, however, Monboddo's anthropological speculations cannot be rated very high, he is at least entitled to the credit of having, in an age when science was still in swaddling clothes, employed a sound scientific method. Instead of wasting time in futile theorising, he laboriously studied the manners and customs of savage races, interviewed travellers, and sought to obtain authentic information whereby light might be thrown upon the problems of civilization. Unquestionably Monboddo possessed some of the divine afflatus of the truth-seeker, notwithstanding the fact that he was often under the dominion of the wildest ideas.

Monboddo's other work, *Antient Metaphysics*, must also be consigned to the museum of literary curiosities, though it sets forth fewer ludicrous notions. The work took many years to write and, like the *Origin and Progress of Language*, extends to six quarto volumes. *Antient Metaphysics* does not increase our respect for Monboddo as a philosopher, hardly even as a man of common sense. It is more rhapsodical than relevant. To wander through those tomes is to wander through whole acres of arid speculation, hasty

[1] Ramsay's *Scotland and Scotsmen*, i. 357.

and false generalization, and wearisome reiteration. The work is a panegyric on Greek philosophy, coupled with much adverse criticism of modern systems. Newton's philosophy is examined at great length and found wanting, while the scepticism of Locke and Hume are ruthlessly attacked.

It is said that Monboddo wrote this work in the full assurance that it would be despised by his contemporaries, though firmly convinced that in later times it would command the attention of cultured Europe. Vain delusion! If his rummagings in the dust-heap of ancient lore were not approved by the enlightened classes of his own day, they have certainly not found favour since. But if his writings have long ago been consigned to the limbo of forgetfulness, it is consoling to reflect that the man was better than his books. While people laughed at Monboddo's eccentric ways and made merry over his preposterous ideas, they did homage to his intrinsic personal worth.

IV

LORD GARDENSTONE

(1721–1793)

If you had lived towards the close of the eighteenth century, and had chanced to bend your steps towards the southern slopes of Edinburgh on a fine summer morning, you might have seen toiling up the hill a jaded steed on whose back sat a decrepit old gentleman, preceded by his favourite dog Smash, and followed by a kilted barefooted lad. Had you been curious, you would have learned that the gentleman was the benevolent but extremely eccentric judge, Lord Gardenstone, and that the lad was a personal attendant, whose duty it would be to take charge of Rosinante when his master arrived at the Parliament House. His lordship appears to have been rather an indifferent equestrian. At all events, it was his horsemanship which appealed to John Kay, the caricaturist, and no one can think of Gardenstone without associating him with the droll etching in the *Original Edinburgh Portraits*.

Gardenstone does not live in history as a great judge. For some years after his elevation to the Bench he did make some figure, being "much admired for the elegance, clearness, and force of his opinions,"[1] but, as he grew older, he became indolent, and shirked his judicial duties "to the great indignation of his brethren, whose admonitions and remonstrances he did not regard."[2] Tytler appraises him[3] as "an acute and able lawyer of great natural eloquence," and with this judgment we may rest content. Doubtless he would have occupied a higher place in the annals of Scottish jurisprudence had not the habits of a "loose liver"[4] and an ample fortune diminished his powers of application.

"A mixed character" is Ramsay's sententious but rather vague judgment of Gardenstone.[5] A close study of his personality seems to warrant the view that he was fundamentally a good man with strong natural endowments, but that exuberant spirits, a talent for conviviality, and a capricious temperament drove him into devious courses which undermined his health, impoverished his mind, wrecked his fortune, and counteracted his influence as a generous and enlightened philanthropist. A man of strong passions, and with a rollicking wit, he was no anchorite passing his days in the idle mortification of the flesh. He loved the pleasures, and revelled in the coarse buffoonery, of the tavern.

But he prided himself most on his whimsicality. "A man who has no whims," he once told Kames, "is, in my opinion, a stupid man. I am sure mine are . . . altogether innocent, and, in some particulars, useful."[6] And Gardenstone was

[1] Ramsay's *Scotland and Scotsmen*, i. 372. [2] *Ibid.* i. 379.
[3] *Life of Kames*, ii., App., p. 99 (*n.*) [4] *Scotland and Scotsmen*, i. 371.
[5] *Ibid.* i. 373. [6] *Life of Kames*, ii., App., p. 100.

LORD GARDENSTONE
From the Portrait by Kay

whimsical with a vengeance. Nothing surely could be more singular than his partiality for pigs. Upon one of these animals he bestowed so much care and affection that, like Mary's little lamb, it repaid his kindness by following him wherever he went. It even shared his bed. This arrangement, however, ultimately became inconvenient, and the animal ceased to be his lordship's bedfellow. But it was not expelled from the bedroom, for Gardenstone made a couch for it out of his own clothes. There is a story to the effect that a visitor, happening to call one dark winter morning before his lordship had risen, stumbled over something in his bedroom which gave a loud grunt, whereupon Gardenstone blandly remarked: "It is just a bit sow, poor beast, and I laid my breeches on it to keep it warm all night."

But if the imperious hand of caprice lay rather heavily upon Gardenstone, it is pleasant to remember that he found time and opportunity to cultivate more normal and likeable traits of character. He was not continually doting upon "grunters." He had some highly laudable ambitions, which his great wealth enabled him to realise to a considerable extent. He tried to increase the sum of human happiness; and to say this is to admit that his nature was far from being irredeemably corrupt. His means were at the disposal of many beneficent causes. But he was no dispenser of indiscriminate charity; he put brains into his philanthropy.

It is also to his credit that he was a zealous political reformer when no stone was being left unturned to preserve the *status quo*, and when even to hint that the people were not living under the best of all possible governments, was enough to bring a man of Gardenstone's position to the brink of social ostracism. While he did not court such a calamity, he had too much force of character to allow it to have any terrors for him. That the government of his day was inefficient, tyrannical, and hopelessly venal was to him self-evident, and like a good subject of the King he strove to eradicate these evils.

Francis Garden, Lord Gardenstone, was the second son of Alexander Garden of Troup, Banffshire, and of his wife, Jean, eldest daughter of Sir Francis Grant, who became a Senator of the College of Justice with the title of Lord Cullen. His uncle was Lord Prestongrange, whom he much resembled in outward features,[1] if not in character and attainments. He was born in Edinburgh in 1721. Of his childhood almost nothing is known. He was educated at the High School, and at Edinburgh University, where his career was no better than it ought to have been.

At the early age of twenty-three he was admitted an advocate, and ere long he became a "popular and well-respected barrister"[2] with a lucrative practice. His person was ungainly, his features harsh, his voice tremulous, but he pled with a grace and brilliancy which proved most effective. On the other hand, his law papers, if "somewhat too gorgeous and splendid

[1] Ramsay's *Scotland and Scotsmen*, i. 373. [2] *Ibid.* i. 371.

in their language,"[1] were informed by vigorous common sense. Altogether "his early appearances at the Bar," says Ramsay,[2] "made his friends entertain sanguine expectations of his future eminence when years should have cooled his passions."

Much importance attaches to the proviso, for at this time the young lawyer had developed a turn for dissipation and gaming, and was fast becoming "the prince of jolly livers." What that meant may be inferred from the fact that the man who then aspired to honours as a convivialist had to reckon with many formidable rivals. But this feat Garden seems to have accomplished. His days were spent in pursuing the sober avocation of the law; his nights in hard drinking. It is said that after a prolonged carouse, and without having studied his papers, he would appear in court and plead eloquently from what he had picked up from the opposing counsel, which at least says much for his mental agility.

These orgies did ultimately play havoc with his constitution, as indeed they were bound to do; but maturer years brought with them no upbraidings over a misspent youth. One would have thought that having wasted his substance in riotous living, the part of the prodigal would have been very acceptable. But it was not so. When he had become a valetudinarian, and could no longer worship at the shrine of Bacchus, his only regret was that he could not live over again those halcyon days—a frame of mind not usually

[1] Ramsay's *Scotland and Scotsmen*, i 370 [2] *Ibid.* i. 370

associated with decayed topers. Kames having flouted him on one occasion with the failings of his youth, he turned to his colleague, whose parsimony was notorious, and said: "Gang to the Deil, my lord; my fauts are growin' the langer the less; and your ain the langer the waur."

The Jacobite rising of 1745 put Garden's patriotism to the test; but he did not emerge from the ordeal with flying colours. No doubt he meant well, as most of us do; but, unfortunately, his love of strong drink got the better of his love of king and country, and he cut rather a sorry figure. Enlisting as a volunteer, he was despatched by the Royalist commander, Sir John Cope, with a companion in arms, to watch the movements of the Highland army in the vicinity of Prestonpans. Passing through Musselburgh, Garden and his companion chanced to see a tavern where they had often regaled themselves with oysters and sherry, and which they could not resist entering in order to renew old memories. The time passed merrily enough, and the revellers thought no more of Sir John Cope and his instructions, till a straggling Highland recruit entered the tavern and took them prisoners. It was suggested that they should be hanged, but their helpless condition doubtless convinced the Highlanders that they were more likely to do valiant service for King Bacchus than for King George. At all events they were soon after liberated.[1]

In the early days of his career, Garden's

[1] Kay's *Edinburgh Portraits*, Pop. ed., i. 34.

practice, as has been said, was lucrative, but it was not until the advent of the Douglas Cause that his star was plainly seen to be in the ascendant. With Monboddo, his future colleague on the Bench, he went to France, and took part in the earlier stages of the case, pleading before the Parliament of Paris, where he was opposed by the brilliant Wedderburn. All accounts agree that he acquitted himself with distinction, his eloquence, his legal ability and learning, and his mastery of the French tongue, gaining him golden opinions.

When the case was transferred to the Court of Session, Garden's services were again employed, but, amidst its many vicissitudes, he was raised to the Bench in 1764 as Lord Gardenstone, and, like Monboddo, had the novel but very undesirable experience of pronouncing judgment in a litigation in which he had formerly acted as counsel. It is only fair to add, however, that the Douglas Cause had by this time undergone so many changes that Gardenstone was less in danger of being suspected of bias than Monboddo.

Twelve years later, in 1776, he was appointed a Lord of Justiciary, a post from which he retired in 1787 with a pension of £200 a year. This step was rendered the more easy by his succession, in 1785, to the family estates in Banffshire and Aberdeenshire (which yielded £3000 a year), and a fortune of £40,000. The windfall did not come a moment too soon, for he was in dire financial straits consequent upon a huge expenditure in connection with his village at Laurencekirk, of which more presently. Indeed his impecuniosity was so great that he was compelled to sell his Edinburgh residence, and to live in a style very unsuited to his position. But his brother's fortune placed him at once in affluent circumstances, and for a number of years he lived in great style. Unhappily, he was both extravagant and unbusinesslike, and shortly before the end he was again, according to Ramsay,[1] in embarrassed circumstances, a considerable portion of his landed property being sold after his death, to pay off his debts.

Gardenstone signalised his entry into the possession of the family estates by taking a prolonged holiday, partly for the benefit of a sadly impaired constitution, the legacy of a dissipated youth, and partly to gratify a somewhat belated taste for foreign travel. In the autumn of 1786, he set out on a pleasure trip which was to last until the summer of 1788. He first visited France, and saw Paris on the eve of the Revolution. But, unlike the noted English traveller, Arthur Young, who visited the city about the same time, he does not seem to have been even remotely conscious of the approach of the momentous event, which was soon to startle the civilised world. A portion of the first winter was spent at Marseilles; and in the spring of 1787 he made his way by slow stages to Geneva.

A visit to Voltaire's home at Ferney left him unimpressed. Though the great French writer had been dead barely nine years, the village which he had helped to rear had fallen

[1] *Scotland and Scotsmen*, i. 380.

into so dilapidated a state that Gardenstone could not help congratulating himself upon the prosperous state of his own village at Laurencekirk. The remainder of the "grand tour" was spent in leisurely wanderings through Italy, Germany, and the Netherlands, where he was a diligent collector of curios.

Gardenstone returned home with a sense of superiority, for had he not been privileged to see more of the world within eighteen months than most of his countrymen had seen in a lifetime? It was, therefore, most fitting that he should turn this singular experience to account, and relate for the benefit of less favoured Scotsmen all that had befallen him in distant lands. This he did in three duodecimo volumes, two of which were published in his lifetime, and the third after his death. The work, which constitutes Gardenstone's single literary performance, is entitled *Travelling Memorandums made in a Tour upon the Continent of Europe in the Years 1786, 1787, and 1788.*

The contents are about as jejune and colourless as the title. A more vapid production there could hardly be. Perhaps the word "Memorandums" was intended to cover a multitude of literary sins. Anyhow, one need have no hesitation in endorsing the view that the work as a whole "can give little pleasure to a thinking mind, searching for digested and useful information." Some of the author's remarks on men and manners are shrewd, but little or no attempt is made to clarify ideas or to visualise impressions. Indeed, had the author set himself deliberately to be as little informative as possible, he could not have accomplished his purpose better.

The *Travelling Memorandums* has been spoken of as Gardenstone's sole claim to authorship, but there are those who believe that he was also the author of a work entitled *Miscellanies in Prose and Verse*. The evidence is certainly conflicting. Ramsay says [1] that a number of the pieces were supposed to be written by his lordship, but adds that it is difficult to distinguish them from those written by his friends, notably Callander Thomson, one of the "Friends of the People," and a boon companion of his lordship. But the question of authorship need not detain us, since the work is one which no man of letters worthy of the name would wish to own. The verses, as a rule, do not rise above the level of doggerel, and some of them are decidedly indecent. That a work, which displays the indelicacy of Swift without Swift's genius, should have reached a second edition within two years, is certainly no compliment to the literary taste or moral character of Gardenstone's contemporaries.

Though it may truthfully be said of his lordship's literary writings what some one said of Dr. Johnson's Latin poems, "All are bad but some are worse than others," his literary understanding is not to be despised. It was much sounder than that of Monboddo who, as has already been pointed out, thought Home's tragedy of *Douglas* superior to any of Shakespeare's plays. Gardenstone knew better than

[1] *Scotland and Scotsmen*, i. 375.

to talk such arrant nonsense. It says much for his literary discernment that he should not only have fully appreciated the greatness of Shakespeare, but should have displayed an intimate knowledge of the Elizabethan drama when interest in this stage of our literary history was rather meagre. "Few men," says Ramsay,[1] "ever studied Shakespeare more than his lordship, insomuch that a great deal of this inimitable poet's phrases and idioms entered into his discourse and writings."

Tytler is within the mark when he says[2] that Gardenstone's letter to Kames on the merits of the old English drama exhibits "much ingenious and just criticism." The occasion of the letter was his desire to obtain the opinion of the author of *Elements of Criticism* regarding some alterations which he had made on Massinger's comedy, *The City Madam.* His effort to improve Massinger is of no consequence, but the letter which accompanied the suggested emendations contains some penetrating criticism. For Massinger, he had rightly conceived a high regard. "There is in his works, I think, a rich store of materials, a precious mine of dramatic entertainment, though encumbered with a mass of superfluous rubbish" —a testimony which will hardly be gainsaid by the most fastidious critic of to-day. He is, too, in full accord with modern criticism when he denounces the unwarrantable liberties which Garrick and other actors of his time took with the Shakespearian text. Gardenstone also held that the Restoration was equally the era of bad

[1] *Scotland and Scotsmen*, i. 374. [2] *Life of Kames*, ii, App., p. 99.

morals and of bad taste. The remark sounds trite enough in our ears, but it took some courage to utter it in the noontide of the eighteenth century.

His lordship warmly patronised letters, and sat among the metaphysicians, which was then the "correct thing" for a man in his position to do. He befriended James Beattie, author of the *Minstrel*, the bond of sympathy no doubt being strengthened by the fact that the poet was a native of his favourite Laurencekirk. Then he rescued from a debtor's prison, Dr. John Brown, founder of "the Brunonian system of medicine," and author of some medical works in which he propounded the dubious doctrine that all diseases that could not be removed by debilitating medicines, such as opium, could be cured by stimulants, notably wine and brandy. Burns, it ought to be added, sent Gardenstone a copy of his *Poems*,[1] but whether or not the latter hailed the Ayrshire bard as a rising genius is not recorded.

Scott's ambition was to be the progenitor of a noble family: Gardenstone who, by the way, was never married, wished to perpetuate his name by founding a village, the inhabitants of which would be prosperous, contented, and happy. There was nothing visionary about the project, though it did not meet with the success he anticipated. On the contrary, he demonstrated how much a landlord who combines enlightened views with enterprise and munificence, may accomplish within a comparatively limited area.

[1] Chambers's *Life of Burns*, new ed., ii. 177.

In 1762, he purchased the estate of Johnston adjoining Laurencekirk in Kincardineshire, and, three years later, began to build a new village. At that time Laurencekirk contained only fifty-four inhabitants, but by the year 1779, the community had increased to such an extent as to warrant Gardenstone obtaining a royal charter erecting the village into a burgh of barony. No father could have shown more solicitude for the welfare of his child than did his lordship for the little community which had sprung up around his Kincardineshire home. Money, time, and brain-power were bestowed upon it with a lavish hand. In a letter addressed to the inhabitants of his model village when they had reached 500 souls, he wrote: "I have tried in some measure a variety of the pleasures which mankind pursue; but never relished anything so much as the pleasure arising from the progress of my village."

One has only to note the nature and extent of his schemes to be convinced that these were not empty words. He caused a line of street, six furlongs in length, to be formed on his estate; he offered land on extremely moderate terms to induce people to settle in his village; he founded a library and museum for the use of the villagers; he built a commodious inn and an episcopal chapel; and last, but by no means least, he furnished the capital for starting various industries.

Gardenstone may safely be claimed as the pioneer of the public library movement, at least in Scotland. The institution which he founded somewhere about the year 1765 was called by him "The Public Library of Laurencekirk." It was a modest establishment, and not, of course, to be compared with those with which Mr. Carnegie's munificence has made us familiar; but the idea was similar. Books were scarce then, but the founder managed to get together a goodly collection, and the mental improvement of the villagers no doubt grew apace. In the unpretentious building containing the library, there was also placed the nucleus of a museum in the shape of stuffed birds, shells, and minerals.

"His lordship," says Dean Ramsay,[1] "was much taken up with his hotel or inn, for which he provided a large volume for receiving the written contributions of travellers who frequented it. It was the landlady's business to present this volume to the guests and ask them to write in it during the evenings, whatever occurred to their memory or their imagination. In the mornings it was the favourite amusement of Lord Gardenstone to look it over." One of the visitors to avail themselves of this privilege was Miss Burnet, the beautiful daughter of Lord Monboddo. This lady invariably accompanied her father on horseback to and from the ancestral seat of Monboddo, and as the road lay through Laurencekirk, she frequently halted at Gardenstone's inn. On one occasion, Miss Burnet, who had some poetic talent, inserted in the visitors' book a short address to his lordship, modelled on the prologue to the second Duke of Buckingham's comedy, *The Rehearsal* (1671). It ran thus:

[1] *Reminiscences of Scottish Life and Character.*

We well might call this bloated book of yours
A poesy of weeds, and not of flowers;
Yet such have been presented to our noses,
And some there are, I fear, who've thought them roses.

Gardenstone was much offended, and, below the objectionable verse, wrote: "This plagiary writer censures without sense; for tho' there are some things improper, yet every person will reap much entertainment from the variety of quotations." But Miss Burnet was not to be so easily vanquished, and returned to the charge with the following *jeu d'esprit*:

My Lord, do not growl
'Cause the verses are stole,
Altho' you smart under their lash;
Should you purge your chaste Olio
Of each borrowed folio,
I fear you'd leave little but trash.

Yet your Lordship should know,
That a dangerous blow
From no such a fair arm could come,
For the stroke of a wand
From a Lady's soft hand
Is a compliment paid your album.

Then don't take it ill
That a feminine quill
Has ventured to tickle your Toby;
But allow her to urge
That, if you will purge,
You first should consult Dr. Boby.[1]

In his Letter to the people of Laurencekirk, already referred to, Gardenstone, with a strange lack of humour, exhorted the villagers to cultivate

[1] Chambers's *Life of Burns*, new ed., ii. 24 (*n.*).

habits of industry, frugality, and sobriety. He also seems to have had an eye to their religious welfare, though he himself "did not pretend much zeal for revealed religion." But however that may be, he built an episcopal chapel, the majority of those settling in his village belonging, curiously enough, to England. To his own lands he attached the burden of the upkeep of both incumbent and building. To the former he gave three acres of ground, and stipulated that he should receive annually the sum of £40 sterling, and forty bolls of meal. He also, according to Dean Ramsay,[1] placed in the vestry "a most respectable library."

But Gardenstone's practical sagacity and philanthropy were perhaps shown to best advantage by what he did to stimulate industry. He succeeded in converting "a paltry kirk town into a neat and flourishing village."[2] He encouraged all sorts of manufacturers to settle in Laurencekirk, and gave substantial monetary support to several of their undertakings. In particular, he was interested in the making of a type of snuff-box for which Laurencekirk was long famous. These snuff-boxes, a peculiarity of which was their being fitted with invisible hinges, appear to have been very fine pieces of workmanship. Gardenstone himself was an inveterate snuffer, though, singularly enough, he kept the article not in a box, but in a leather waistpocket. So addicted was he to snuff that he used to say that if he had a dozen noses he would feed them

[1] *Reminiscences of Scottish Life and Character.*

[2] Ramsay's *Scotland and Scotsmen*, i. 370.

all. Every fold of his waistcoat was filled with the article, and there is a legend that from these receptacles the villagers, when conversing with him, frequently helped themselves (without his knowledge) to a pinch.[1]

With all his enthusiasm, generosity, and public spirit, Gardenstone had to learn the hard lesson that the best-laid schemes "gang aft a-gley." His village could not be launched on the full tide of prosperity without a large drain on his purse and on his patience. But disappointment and failure did not quench his indomitable spirit. To the last, the welfare of the little community of Laurencekirk was uppermost in his thoughts. The bibulous, rakish lawyer of earlier years had, in his old age, become an ardent social reformer and an enlightened philanthropist—truly a remarkable transformation!

Of all faddists those who belong to the valetudinarian order are among the worst. Their days are passed either in prating about their ailments, or in trying to give practical effect to their gospel of health. Gardenstone, who midway through life had become pretty much of an invalid, did both. His constitution, as was naturally to be expected in the case of a man who had spent his youth in an endless round of dissipation, was certainly not robust, but as he lived beyond the allotted span, it may be assumed that he magnified his ailments. Anyhow, he found the problem of how to keep well one of absorbing interest.

So circumstanced, it is not difficult to realise

[1] Kay's *Edinburgh Portraits*, Pop. ed., i. 36.

how the discovery of a mineral spring on the banks of the Water of Leith would gladden the heart of the portly old gentleman. As the well, named St. Bernard's, was in the vicinity of Edinburgh, he regularly partook of its waters, was the first to herald its praises; and as a token of gratitude he erected over it an elegant Doric temple after the model of the one at Tivoli. Under the dome was placed a fine statue of Hygeia by Coade of London, and into the foundation stone was sunk a metal plate bearing the following inscription: "Erected for the benefit of the Public at the sole expense of Francis Garden, Esq., of Troup, one of the Senators of the College of Justice, A.D. 1789. Alex. Naismith, Archt. John Wilson, Builder."

In the fortunes of St. Bernard's Well, which is now a notable feature of the landscape which greets the eye from the dizzy heights of the Dean Bridge of Edinburgh, Gardenstone took an interest only less profound than that evinced in his village of Laurencekirk. To be keeper of the well, he appointed one, George Murdoch, of whose "honesty and decent manners," his lordship had had long experience. For this official's guidance, he drew up an elaborate list of instructions, which were obviously framed with a view to the public deriving the greatest possible benefit from the well.

For a sum of five shillings a person might partake during the season (May to October) of the waters every morning from six to nine o'clock; but those unable or unwilling to pay were entitled to free access between the hours of ten and one.

Occasional visitors were to be charged one penny, while those who desired to draw water to be used at a distance were to pay at the rate of a half-penny per Scots pint. All poor people on presenting a certificate from a doctor or apothecary in Edinburgh were to have the advantages of the well free. Evidently anticipating a crush, one rule declared that there was to be no loitering after having drunk; another prohibited bathing at or in sight of the well during the morning; and a third bound the keeper to see that "no water was carried away in open vessels but in corked ones"—an injunction not so superfluous then as it would be now.

This interesting document winds up with a request by the proprietor for hints "for the better regulation and public use of the waters," together with a promise that "some account of the virtues of this mineral well, and of certain remarkable cures performed by the use of it," would soon be published by "a medical gentleman of character and experience." Then Gardenstone adds, presumably as an afterthought, that "the effects of this water, when used in making either tea or punch, are remarkably agreeable." The virtues of St. Bernard's Well, after the lapse of more than one hundred and twenty years, are still proclaimed, but judging by the numbers who now go to get their morning glass, the prospect of congestion in the sense anticipated by Gardenstone's rule regarding loitering, is, to say the least, somewhat remote.

There is no incident in Gardenstone's career more creditable than his bold stand against the political and civic tyranny of his time. In days when Scotland owned no man master save Henry Dundas, when the land from end to end was seething with corruption, when "violent Tory judges sentenced remorselessly to transportation honest enthusiasts for political reform, like Muir, Palmer, Margarot, and Gerrald,"[1] it required infinite courage for a man like Gardenstone to come forward, and try to inaugurate a new and better state of things. What chiefly stirred the judge's indignation was the lamentable state of the Scots burghs. Writing in the *Scots Magazine* in 1789, he gives vent to his feelings, and points the way to just and necessary reform. "I must frankly confess," he says, "it seems to me surprising that many of our men of considerable landed property, and some spirited and good characters, even among our magistrates themselves, are yet either inimical or indifferent to this great question (the government of the Scots burghs). . . . It is perfectly evident, that the honour and true interest of our landed men in all ranks, are connected with the independence and prosperity of our burghs. In proportion as the neighbouring burghs are flourishing, industrious, and rich, their properties grow in value, and their patronage in importance."

This was strange doctrine to a generation which had become reconciled to jobbery, perquisites, and secret conclaves; but Gardenstone pursued his course unflinchingly. He called upon the *perfervidum ingenium Scotorum* to exert itself in this matter with wisdom and constancy.

[1] Graham's *Social Life of Scotland*, 1901, p. 537.

Let all honest, moderate, and constitutional means be taken to abolish the monstrous system of self-elected magistrates and councillors; to restore "the original just right of election by the burgesses"; to end the notorious maladministration and embezzlement of burgh revenues; and to make magistrates, like other people, amenable to the law of the land.

But Scotland was not yet prepared for so drastic an instalment of reform, and things went on very much as before for another generation. That, however, is no reason why those of us who live in more propitious times should not gratefully remember that Gardenstone risked much in championing a most necessary reform fully half a century before it was conceded. Furthermore, it ought not to be forgotten that he eloquently pleaded the cause of liberty—not the liberty to be lawless, but that true liberty which allows a man the utmost freedom consistent with social well-being. He was a lover of democracy, long before democracy had come to its own.

Gardenstone was neither scholar, littérateur, poet, nor philosopher, but he had riches, wit, and, at all events in his younger days, an insatiable desire for hilarious excitement. He was a hedonist, and as such, found his way easily into the best convivial circles of Edinburgh. "There was a sprightliness and urbanity in his discourse, a candour and generosity in his sentiments, that pleased people of the most discordant taste."[1] His social attainments must have been con-

[1] Ramsay's *Scotland and Scotsmen*, i. 370.

siderable, for "he could render himself exceedingly acceptable to the grave and the aged, whilst the young and the frolicsome delighted in his society."[1]

In his later years, by compulsion rather than by choice, he lived plainly, though his devotion to the wine-cup remained to the end. Shortly before his death he is said to have divided his time between the pleasures of the table and his bed, resorting to the latter when his jovial friends were gone.[2] His dress, if not eccentric, was usually shabby, a circumstance which partially gave rise to an incident highly characteristic.

The story goes that he was returning from London, and had purchased a ticket for the outside of the coach, having observed that some young bucks had secured seats in the inside. On arriving at an inn where breakfast was to be served, his lordship was shown into an inferior room, while his better-dressed fellow-travellers were conducted to the best. Desiring to test the calibre of the young gentlemen, he sent a request that they would permit him to have the honour of breakfasting with them. Back came the answer that Gardenstone expected, namely, that they could keep no company with *outside* passengers. Whereupon his lordship ordered a bottle of claret, and asked the landlord to share it with him. At the same time he requested that a post-chaise and four horses be got ready for him immediately. This done, he instructed the coachman to try and reach the next stage simultaneously with the coach containing his former

[1] Ramsay's *Scotland and Scotsmen*, i. 370. [2] *Ibid.* i. 379.

fellow-travellers, a feat which was duly accomplished. The result, as may be imagined, was rather disconcerting to the snobbish young men, who, now repenting of their conduct, sent a polite note regretting the incident of the morning, and requesting his lordship to honour them with his company to dinner. But his lordship only returned the verbal answer that he could keep no company with people whose pride would not permit them to use their fellow-travellers with civility.[1]

Gardenstone's old age, though marred by ill-health and the alienation of the friends of his riper years consequent upon his advocacy of political reform, was on the whole serene and peaceful. At his beautiful home in Morningside overlooking the Pentland Hills, the days passed pleasantly in the society of a few political associates, and in advancing the welfare and prosperity of his village. He died on July 22, 1793, and, two days later, his remains were laid to rest in the Greyfriars' Churchyard, where reposes the dust of so many of Scotland's honoured dead.

[1] Kay's *Edinburgh Portraits*, Pop. ed., i. 36.

V

LORD BRAXFIELD

(1722–1799)

To Lord Braxfield belongs the unenviable reputation of being the most execrated judge in the annals of Scottish jurisprudence. Even Lord Advocate Mackenzie, whose cruelty to the Covenanters earned him the sobriquet of "Bluidy Mackenzie," was a scholar, a poet, and, some say, a gentleman; but the most ardent apologist for Braxfield is compelled to admit that his good qualities are not easily discoverable.

> Men's evil manners live in brass; their virtues
> We write in water.

The latter part of the Shakespearian dictum hardly applies to the "Hanging Judge," for the most charitable view of his career leads only to the conclusion that his virtues, if he ever had any, were distinctly elusive. He is popularly regarded as the counterpart of the "infamous Jeffreys"; but this hardly does him justice. When Cockburn dubbed him "the Jeffreys of Scotland," he was thinking more of his flagrant conduct in connection with the sedition trials of 1793–94 than of his general character. Brax-

Photo, Annan

LORD BRAXFIELD

From the Painting by Raeburn in Parliament Hall, Edinburgh

field, it must be acknowledged, was a shade better than the English judge. He was a sound and able lawyer, which Jeffreys was not, and he was no sycophant, which Jeffreys was. Nevertheless, no one who has studied in contemporary records the judicial part which he played at a critical period in Scottish affairs, and is familiar with the word-portrait which Cockburn drew from the life, can have any doubt that he came dangerously near being destitute of principle and character. Unscrupulous, tyrannical, coarse, dissipated, illiterate, he was morally almost featureless. He had a hard heart, a tainted mind, a cross-grained, domineering nature, and an uncouth exterior. A noble aspiration or a lofty motive he was incapable of appreciating. Without faith, without hope, without charity, he moved continually in a world of sordid interests and ignoble purposes.

Let it be admitted that Cockburn's ultra-Whiggism did colour to some extent his portrait of Braxfield, but the broad lineaments of the notorious Lord Justice-Clerk are unquestionably there. And what a repulsive portrait it is![1] "Strong built and dark, with rough eyebrows, powerful eyes, threatening lips, and a low growling voice, he was like a formidable blacksmith. . . . Illiterate and without any taste for refined enjoyment, strength of understanding, which gave him power without cultivation, only encouraged him to a more contemptuous disdain of all natures less coarse than his own. Despising the growing improvement of manners, he shocked

[1] *Memorials of his Time*, 1856, p. 113.

the feelings even of an age which, with more of the formality, had far less of the substance of decorum than our own. Thousands of his sayings have been preserved, and the staple of them is indecency; which he succeeded in making many people enjoy, or at least endure, by hearty laughter, energy of manner, and rough humour." [1]

The genius of Stevenson has familiarised an immense public with the odiousness of Braxfield's character—a public that Cockburn could not reach. The prototype of Weir of Hermiston was, as every one knows, no other than the redoubtable judge who sat at the head of the criminal court of Scotland in the closing years of the eighteenth century. "Mind you," wrote Stevenson in 1892 from far Vailima, "I expect *The Justice-Clerk* (afterwards changed to *Weir of Hermiston*) to be my masterpiece. My Braxfield is already a thing of beauty and a joy for ever, and, so far as he has gone, *far* my best character." [2] Of course, Stevenson, for the purposes of romance, added touches to his portraiture which are not to be found in the original; but as his description was mainly based on Cockburn's account, and from what he could glean from the Raeburn canvas, it is indisputable that the general characteristics of Weir of Hermiston faithfully reflect those of the truculent Braxfield. This judge had a strange fascination for Stevenson, to whom he makes more than one reference in his writings. Readers of *Virginibus Puerisque* [3] will recall his

[1] *Memorials of his Time*, 1856, p. 114.
[2] *Letters to his Family and Friends*, 1899, ii. 273.
[3] Stevenson's Works, 1895, *Miscellanies*, iii. 150-152.

graphic account of the impressions made upon him by the "Hanging Judge's" portrait when he saw it for the first time at the Raeburn Exhibition in Edinburgh in 1876.

Born in 1722, Robert Macqueen was mainly indebted to himself for his advancement in life, "being a man of no family and very small estate." [1] His paternal grandfather was gardener to Charles, Earl of Selkirk, and his son, John Macqueen, the father of the judge, was bred a writer, to qualify him to be baron-bailie to the Earl. He prospered in business, was sheriff-substitute of the Upper Ward of Lanarkshire, and in due season became the owner of a small property in the county, from which the future judge derived his legal title. His wife also belonged to Lanarkshire, being a daughter of John Hamilton of Gilderscleugh. Robert was the eldest son.

The family being large, and the means to support them small, John Macqueen could not afford to entertain exalted notions respecting the future of his children. Robert got a good, but not an expensive education, the father's intention being that he should succeed him. No stories have come down to us to show what manner of boy young Macqueen was when attending the grammar-school of Lanark, but at Edinburgh University, where he afterwards studied civil law, he seems to have created a favourable impression. At all events, there is the testimony of a class-fellow, Dr. Erskine, who affirms that the civil law students "would have fought for

[1] Ramsay's *Scotland and Scotsmen*, i 380

Robbie Macqueen, whose honesty and good nature made him a general favourite." [1]

Macqueen's ambition at first was to be a Writer to the Signet, and for some time he was an apprentice to an Edinburgh practitioner. When next we hear of him, he is in his father's office in Lanark. Here he came into contact with Dundas, afterwards the second President of that name, whose wife owned the estate of Bonnington. Dundas was struck by Macqueen's shrewdness and legal abilities, and urged him to qualify for the Scottish Bar. The advice was taken, and Macqueen set himself seriously to study for his new vocation. His industry was unflagging, and his enthusiasm great, and in 1744 he found himself wearing the gown of an advocate.

For a number of years he had the ordinary fate of young members of the Bar in having little to do, but gradually agents began to discover his merit, "which was not inaptly compared to a rough diamond." [2] When his friend, Dundas, became Lord Advocate, he was made one of his deputes, an office which, if it yielded little money, at least gave a young barrister an opportunity of showing of what stuff he was made. Macqueen had been a careful student of feudal law, and when the litigation arising out of the forfeitures consequent upon the Jacobite rebellion of 1745 came before the Court, he, as one of the counsel for the Crown, was found to be the right man in the right place. His extensive and accurate knowledge, and his clear and forcible exposition of the many com-

[1] Ramsay's *Scotland and Scotsmen*, i. 380 (*n.*).

[2] *Ibid.* i. 381.

plicated points at issue, called forth general admiration.

His good sense and sound law, his candour, his unfailing instinct for what was relevant, made both judges and agents overlook his ungainly presence, his rustic manners, his broad dialect, and his vulgarisms. Macqueen had none of the art of the rhetorician, indeed despised it. He mainly relied upon a vigorous understanding, a thorough mastery of legal principle, and the sheer driving power of a strong virile personality. Many brilliant lawyers there were at the Bar at this time, but ere long he was the rival of the foremost of them. When at the height of his fame he is reputed to have pled from fifteen to twenty causes in a single day. Boswell's lines in the "Court of Session Garland" is a reminder, too, that he was a proficient draughtsman.

> However, of our cause not being ashamed,
> Unto the whole Lords we straightway reclaimed;
> And our petition was appointed to be seen,
> Because it was drawn by Robbie Macqueen.

Macqueen's success at the Bar, conspicuous though it was, was eclipsed by his success in the tavern. Many outside Parliament House knew him to be a great lawyer, but many more recognised him as a great drinker. He early joined the claret-drinking, card-playing fraternity, and soon rose to be the ideal type of boon companion—coarse, boisterous, dissipated—a man who swore without provocation, "like an ensign of the last age in his teens,"[1] and who, when in high spirits and in congenial company, would

[1] Ramsay's *Scotland and Scotsmen*, i. 390.

exclaim in dubious English, "What a glorious thing is it to speak nonsense!"[1] As Stevenson says, "He was a convivial man, a lover of wine, and one who shone peculiarly at tavern meetings."[2] But though these drinking-bouts were neither infrequent nor slight, they seem hardly to have impaired his powers of work. "Bacchus," says Cockburn, "had never an easy victory over Macqueen." He is credited with having thriven on a "stintless regimen of beef, brandy, and claret," being firmly persuaded that a point of law will be more easily studied after drinking a bottle of the favourite beverage than by abstemiousness. It is a novel doctrine, but Macqueen seemed to lend countenance to the idea that it was true.

The character of this man appears to be almost humanly inscrutable. It defies all ordinary standards of comparison. His father is said to have been at much pains to give him a religious upbringing, and he himself, despite his deep potations and his love of strong expletives, took credit for being "a sincere Christian."[3] He would have indignantly repudiated any suggestion to the contrary. Of religion, Ramsay of Ochtertyre[4] deliciously remarks, "he retained all along a due sense, being thoroughly persuaded of its truth, though it did not always produce suitable fruits or make him set a watch on his lips."

He was illiterate to a degree hardly conceivable in a person occupying his exalted position. He

[1] Ramsay's *Scotland and Scotsmen*, i. 390.

[2] Stevenson's Works, 1895, *Miscellanies*, iii. 151.

[3] *Ibid.* i. 391.

[4] *Ibid.* i. 391.

had no interest in literature, or art, or philosophy. With the writings of the Dutch jurists he was tolerably familiar, and for the works of Lord Stair he showed all the reverence he possessed, but it is doubtful whether he ever read a book which did not bear directly upon his professional labours. He fully imbibed the spirit of Prior's lines :

> From ignorance our comfort flows,
> The only wretched are the wise.

The intellectual lustre of the Edinburgh of his day meant nothing to him. He preferred the joviality of the tavern to the learned talk of Monboddo's supper parties. While Kames was struggling hard to get his countrymen to speak and write "English undefiled," Braxfield was glorying in the vernacular and perpetrating the most outrageous Scotticisms. His humour was broad, but his speech was broader. "Hae ye ony coonsel, man ? " said he to Maurice Margarot, when placed at the bar on a charge of sedition. "No," was the laconic reply. "Dae ye want to hae ony appointit ? " continued the judge. "No," said Margarot sarcastically, "I only want an interpreter to make me understand what your lordship says." When Jeffrey, fresh from Oxford, began his career at the Scottish Bar, his speech gave his lordship much trouble. "The laddie," he remarked wittily, "has clean tint his Scotch and fund nae English."

After more than thirty years' exacting but eminently successful work as a pleader, Macqueen, in 1776, was raised to the Bench with the title of Lord Braxfield. This post he accepted only after the earnest solicitation of his old friend Dundas, for though it brought him honour, it implied substantial pecuniary loss. Four years later, he succeeded Lord Auchinleck, the father of Johnson's biographer, as a Lord of Justiciary. The appointment was not allowed to pass unnoticed. In the same year there was published an anonymous "Letter to Robert Macqueen, Lord Braxfield, on his Promotion to be one of the Judges of the High Court." Cockburn attributes this senseless pamphlet, for such it was, to Boswell. If he was really the author—and it is not difficult to imagine him in that capacity—then the publication may be set down as one of those "blazing indiscretions" for which the renowned biographer was so famous. Apart from the fact that he was the son of the retiring judge, it was highly presumptuous, if not something worse, to lecture the judges of the criminal court on their partiality, indecorum, and carelessness, as the writer of this pamphlet did in terms neither wise nor moderate. Moreover, it was surely very improper to address the "Letter" to Braxfield, who as yet had had no opportunities of committing the judicial sins complained of. The only construction that can be put upon the writer's action is that he was taking time by the forelock and warning Braxfield against a course of conduct to which his past record showed him peculiarly liable.

But whatever the explanation of this epistle, we may be sure that it did not hurt the new judge's feelings nor injure his prospects. As at the Bar so on the Bench, his forceful personality carried all before it. In 1788 he became Lord Justice-Clerk, in which capacity his most notorious deeds were done. It is impossible to understand what Braxfield was as a judge unless due allowance is made for his abnormal character—a character devoid of nearly every judicial virtue. He was coarse and jocular when he ought to have been dignified and circumspect; vindictive when he ought to have been dispassionate; cruel when he ought to have been just; boisterous and domineering when he ought to have been serenely calm.

"Judges," says Bacon,[1] "ought to be more learned than witty; more reverend than plausible; and more advised than confident." Braxfield ran counter to all three injunctions. He was a sort of swashbuckler of the Bench. It is true that he once declared (what is usually assumed on the part of a judge), "I am one of those who are always for giving fair-play to panels"; but this most excellent rule he honoured more in the breach than in the observance. He bullied prisoners, he bullied witnesses, he bullied young advocates if he thought them "Bar flunkies" (his term for fops), and, at times, he bullied his colleagues.

"It is impossible," writes Cockburn, "to condemn his conduct as a criminal judge too gravely, or too severely. It was a disgrace to the age. A dexterous and practical trier of ordinary cases, he was harsh to prisoners even in his jocularity, and to every counsel whom he chose to dislike. . . . It may be doubted if he was ever so much in his element as when

[1] *Essay on Judicature.*

tauntingly repelling the last despairing claim of a wretched culprit, and sending him to Botany Bay or the gallows with an insulting jest; over which he would chuckle the more from observing that correct people were shocked." [1]

And all the specimens of his lordship's *obiter dicta* that have been chronicled, bear out this amazing indictment by one who was himself a judge. Braxfield was indeed a "terror of the law." Lockhart, in his *Life of Scott*,[2] reports him as having said to an eloquent culprit at the bar: "Ye're a vera clever chiel, man, but ye wad be nane the waur o' a hangin'." When Muir, the political reformer, was being tried, Braxfield, parting with the last vestige of judicial honour, whispered to the father of Francis Horner (one of the Edinburgh Reviewers), as he entered the jury-box, "Come awa, Maister Horner, come awa, and help us to hang ane o' thae d—d scoondrels."[3] At a time when the procedure in criminal cases was more a mystery than it is now, and the line to be taken often seemed doubtful, Braxfield at all events was ready for any emergency. "Hoot! jist gie me Josie Norrie (a clerk of court well up in forms and precedents) and a gude jury, an' I'll do for the fallow"[4]—a typical example of his lordship's best judicial manner.

In ribaldry and coarseness, Braxfield would have offended the Lord Chesterfield of that day, a man by no means squeamish, if we are to judge by those flagitious letters he wrote to his son.

[1] *Memorials of his Time*, 1856, p. 115.
[2] Chap. xlviii.
[3] Cockburn's *Memorials*, p. 117.
[4] *Ibid.* p. 117.

Even the most sacred things were not immune from his ridicule. In one of the sedition trials, the prisoner, Gerrald, ventured to remark that all great men had been reformers, "even our Saviour Himself." "Muckle He made o' that; He was hangit"[1] was the profane reply of the man who prided himself upon being a "sincere Christian." On another occasion two young advocates, looking considerably the worse for a protracted orgy, were about to plead before his lordship when they were admonished in the following fashion: "Gentlemen, ye maun jist pack up yer papers and gang hame, for the tane o' ye's riftin' punch, and the ither's belching claret, and there'll be nae gude got oot o' ye the day."[2]

And where claret was concerned, Braxfield's opinion was not to be traduced. Being entertained once at Douglas Castle, and observing that port was the only wine produced after dinner, his lordship, with his customary rudeness, asked his host if "there was nae claret in the castle?" "I believe there is," was the reply, "but my butler tells me it is not good." "Let's pree't," said the senator. The claret having been produced and pronounced excellent, Braxfield, wishing to show that he was not ignorant of ecclesiastical phraseology, proposed that as a *fama clamosa* had gone forth against the wine, the parish minister (who was present) should "absolve" it. But his lordship had been a little foolhardy. "I know," said the clergyman, "that you are a very good judge in cases of civil and criminal law; but I see you do not

[1] Cockburn's *Memorials*, p. 117. [2] Kay's *Portraits*, Pop. ed., i. 122.

understand the laws of the Church. We never absolve till after three appearances." [1]

In the same year that Braxfield became Lord Justice-Clerk, he was called upon to play the principal judicial part in the trial of the notorious Deacon Brodie, who, for a time, was highly successful in his dual position of town councillor by day and burglar by night. In this, with the single exception of the Douglas Cause, the most famous Scottish trial of the eighteenth century, Braxfield was thoroughly in his element. It was a case well fitted to call forth all his sinister powers, and he made the most of his opportunities. Four other judges sat beside him, but he alone controlled the case.

John Clerk (afterwards Lord Eldin) was counsel for George Smith, one of the Deacon's confederates, and with this young and brilliant advocate Braxfield had several encounters. Clerk, it must be confessed, was rash and pugnacious, and just the type of man to ruffle the not too equable temper of the Lord Justice-Clerk. In the first encounter Clerk did not figure well. In language not very respectful, he charged the Court with admitting improper evidence. He was, of course, reproved, but he persisted in impugning the judgment of the Court, and in asserting that the jury were to judge of the law as well as the facts. "Sir, I tell you," exclaimed the infuriated Braxfield, "that the jury have nothing to do with the law, but to take it *simpliciter* from me." "That I deny," was Clerk's insolent answer. The Court

[1] Kay's *Edinburgh Portraits*, Pop. ed., i. 122.

was indignant, but Clerk held his ground, and once more affirmed that the jurors were judges of the whole case. " You are talking nonsense, sir," roared Braxfield. " My lord, you had better not snub me in this way," was the instant reply, whereupon his lordship merely said, " Proceed—gang on, sir." There followed more interruptions, and a tactful counsel would certainly have been more deferential, but Clerk never believed that discretion is the better part of valour. So he went on : " Gentlemen of the jury, I was just saying to you, when this outbreak on the Bench occurred, that you were the judges of the law and of the facts in this case." Braxfield : " We cannot tolerate this, sir. It is an indignity to this High Court—a very gross indignity, deserving of the severest reprobation." But Clerk would either address the jury in his own way, or not speak at all. Whereupon the Lord Justice-Clerk called upon the counsel for the prisoner, Brodie, to proceed with his address ; but the latter shook his head, as if declining to do so. The climax had now been reached. Braxfield was about to charge the jury when Clerk, starting to his feet, and raising a defiant fist to the Bench, shouted, " Hang my client if you daur, my lord, without hearing me in his defence ! " These words produced a great sensation, and the judges immediately retired to hold a consultation. On returning to the court, the Lord Justice-Clerk requested Clerk to resume his speech, which he did without further interruption.

Braxfield's address to the prisoners in passing sentence of death revealed the protean essence of his character. He was surely the last man in the world to reprove the vices of the age, and to point to the consolations of religion, but this he did in the case of Deacon Brodie. Here are his hypocritical words: "It is much to be lamented that those vices, which are called gentlemanly vices, are so favourably looked upon in the present age. They have been the source of your (Brodie's) ruin; and, whatever may be thought of them, they are such as assuredly lead to ruin. I hope you will improve the short time which you have now to live by reflecting upon your past conduct, and endeavouring to procure, by a sincere repentance, forgiveness for your many crimes. God always listens to those who seek Him with sincerity."[1] Not bad for a man who could make the Founder of Christianity the subject of a jest!

The most memorable episode in Braxfield's career—the episode which exhibits more clearly than any other his real characteristics, both personal and professional—was the part he played in the trials of Muir, Skirving, Margarot, and others who were charged with sedition in 1793–94. The judicial aspect of the matter, and particularly Braxfield's conduct, was exhaustively investigated by Cockburn in his *Examination of the Trials for Sedition in Scotland* (2 vols., 1888). It would not be difficult to convict Cockburn of bias. He was a staunch Whig, he himself was counsel for three prisoners who were tried for sedition in 1817–19, and he had the good fortune to live

[1] See *Trial of Deacon Brodie*, edited by Wm. Roughead ("Notable Scottish Trials" series), p. 209.

in later times when a loftier standard of ethics prevailed on the Bench. These circumstances were almost bound to influence his judgment, and influence it they did. To call the Lord Justice-Clerk "a coarse and dexterous ruffian"[1] was to betray a spirit which suggested anything but judicial serenity. Such a phrase Cockburn surely ought not to have used. But when every allowance has been made for his Whiggism, it cannot be said that his severe condemnation of Braxfield's methods is unmerited. The harsh, censorious, and avowedly partisan conduct of the Lord Justice-Clerk as revealed by the records of these trials is almost incredible to a person living in the twentieth century.

An attempt has been made to palliate Braxfield's wrongdoing by contending that such a judge as he was needed to curb the lawless spirit of the time. Braxfield may have crushed the lawless spirit; he certainly did not administer justice. Even when the trials were proceeding his judicial conduct was strongly criticised. The attention of Parliament was drawn to the matter, and Lord Advocate Dundas was compelled to inform him that representations had been made against the legality of the sentences on Muir and Palmer. But the Lord Justice-Clerk was utterly unrepentant. He affirmed that the sentences were legal, and gratuitously urged that the royal clemency should not be extended to either prisoner.

Only one influential voice was raised in Braxfield's defence—Lord Mansfield's. Unfortunately, it did not, on this occasion, count for

[1] Cockburn, *Sedition Trials in Scotland*, i. 86.

much since Mansfield admitted that he had no personal acquaintance with Braxfield, though he had "long heard the loud voice of fame that speaks of him as a man of pure and spotless integrity, of great talents, and of a transcendent knowledge of the laws of his country."[1]

How this man of "pure and spotless integrity" comported himself in the sedition trials of 1793–1794, we shall see presently. Meanwhile, it may be noted that Braxfield was a political partisan of the deepest dye. He was a disciple of Dundas, to whose "nod every man owed what he got, and looked for what he wished." And Dundas stood for a Toryism which spelt political degradation, and the triumph of the forces of reaction. Accordingly, Whigs, Radicals, French Revolutionists, and "siclike enemies o' the King and Constitution" were Braxfield's pet aversion. If he did not exactly hold with Dr. Johnson that "the first Whig was the Devil," he certainly made it his business both on and off the Bench to see that the "Whig dogs" did not get the best of it. Where politics were concerned, it was impossible to look for justice from Braxfield. "Bring me prisoners, and I'll find you law"[2] was his attitude during a period of intense political excitement. "His blameableness in these trials," says Cockburn, "far exceeds that of his brethren. They were weak; he was strong. They were frightened; he was not. They followed; he, the head of the Court, led."[3]

Braxfield's ruling principle in the sedition trials was to obtain a conviction, and having

[1] *Parl. Hist.* xxxi. 283. [2] *Sedition Trials*, ii. 87. [3] *Ibid.* ii. 87.

obtained it, to impose a sentence that would strike terror in the hearts of his political adversaries. The ethical sense had become so atrophied that he was prepared to go any length. Had not Dundas, who trembled lest the Lord Justice-Clerk's zeal for Toryism should carry him too far, counselled moderation, the situation might have been worse. But even as it stands, Braxfield's record is very black. Never, it may be confidently asserted, had the Scottish judiciary sunk so low, never had political passion so blinded judges who ought to have risen superior to all party feeling.

In the trial of Thomas Muir (1793), Braxfield accused the prisoner of trying to overturn "our present happy Constitution—the happiest, the best, and the most noble Constitution in the world."[1] Furthermore, he proclaimed the novel doctrine that to promote parliamentary reform was to be guilty of sedition. He also fulminated against the French as "monsters of human nature."[2] "Mr. Muir might have known that no attention could be paid (by Parliament) to such a rabble (the advocates of political reform). What right had they to representation? . . . A government in every country should be just like a corporation; and, in this country, it is made of the *landed interest, which alone has a right to be represented.*"[3]

This extraordinary outburst was severely commented upon in Parliament, but so many conflicting interests were at work that the judge was neither censured nor asked to retract. When

[1] Cockburn's *Sedition Trials*, i. 149. [2] *Ibid.* i. 176. [3] *Ibid.* i. 176

the jury unanimously found Muir guilty, Braxfield expressed his high approval of the verdict, declared that "transportation was the proper punishment," and "only hesitated whether it should be for life or for a term of fourteen years."[1] In such fashion was justice administered in Scotland in the closing years of the eighteenth century.

An equally violent display of political rancour occurred in connection with the trial of William Skirving (1794), Braxfield more than hinting that he expected the jury to acquit themselves as good party-men. All opposition to the predominant political mood of the hour was sedition. "I say, gentlemen, that the greatest union in this nation is necessary to support us under a war with a neighbouring nation, consisting of the most profligate monsters that ever disgraced humanity."[2] This tirade Braxfield wound up as follows: "It would be very difficult for me to conceive it possible that this man, now at the bar, can be found not guilty."[3] The jury did not misinterpret his meaning, and poor Skirving received the penalty of political contumacy.

Of all the political prisoners brought before Braxfield, Maurice Margarot gave, perhaps, the most trouble. During his trial (1794) a scene occurred to which it would be difficult to find a parallel in legal history. Margarot was no poltroon. Quite early in the trial he proved himself more than a match for the formidable Braxfield. Learning that the court was being filled with people who had paid the doorkeepers for

[1] Cockburn's *Sedition Trials*, i. 177. [2] *Ibid.* i. 281. [3] *Ibid.* i. 286.

admission, he demanded that the court should be open to all comers. "That you have no business with," was Braxfield's answer. Margarot said no more, but on entering upon his defence, he again threw down the gauntlet. The scene which then took place was so extraordinary that the passage-at-arms between the prisoner and the Lord Justice-Clerk may well be reproduced in full.[1]

"*Margarot.* Now, my lord, comes a very delicate matter indeed. I mean to call upon my Lord Justice-Clerk; and I hope that the questions and the answers will be given in the most solemn manner. I have received a piece of information which I shall lay before the Court in the course of my questions. First, my lord, are you on oath?

Braxfield. State your questions, and I will tell you whether I will answer them or not. If they are proper questions I will answer them.

Margarot. Did you dine at Mr. Rochead's at Inverleith in the course of last week?

Braxfield. And what have you to do with that, sir?

Margarot. Did any conversation take place with regard to my trial?

Braxfield. Go on, sir?

Margarot. Did you use these words: 'What should you think of giving him (Margarot) a hundred lashes together with Botany Bay,' or words to that effect?

Braxfield. Go on. Put your questions if you have any more.

Margarot. Did any person—did a lady say

[1] Cockburn's *Sedition Trials*, ii. 28-29.

to you that the mob would not allow you to whip me? And, my lord, did you not say that the mob would be the better for losing a little blood? These are the questions, my lord, that I wish to put to you at present in the presence of the Court. Deny them, or acknowledge them."

The consternation which this encounter—surely one of the most extraordinary that ever took place between a judge of the High Court and a prisoner—produced, may be more easily imagined than described. Braxfield appealed to his colleagues as to whether he should answer the questions; but, amazing to relate, all replied that they were irrelevant, and ought not to be answered. A more despicable piece of sophistry can hardly be conceived. Braxfield, at all events, knew that Margarot's questions were not only relevant, but that the story which gave rise to them was true. In a rash moment he had uttered the sentiments mentioned by Margarot at Mr. Rochead's house, and a lady had indiscreetly repeated them. In point of fact, his lordship never sought to deny the story. Moreover, at the subsequent trial of Joseph Gerrald, an offer was made to establish its truth by evidence independent of Braxfield, but the Court refused to allow the matter to be gone into—"a proceeding which," as Cockburn remarks, "it is difficult to reconcile with any hypothesis except one."[1]

Gerrald's trial came on in March 1794, and was conducted with all the severity and want of fair-play which had been displayed in the trials of Muir, Skirving, and Margarot. Judging by

[1] *Sedition Trials*, ii. 32.

Braxfield's summing-up, Gerrald's offence seems to have been one of nationality rather than of sedition. "Gentlemen," said his lordship, "Gerrald has no relation, nor the least property, in this country, but comes here to disturb the peace of the country, as a delegate from a society in England, to raise sedition in this country. I say he appears to me to be much more criminal than Muir, Palmer, and Skirving, because they were all natives of this country."[1] This statement was both irrelevant and untrue—irrelevant inasmuch as the circumstances of these men were not before the jury (Palmer had not even been tried before Braxfield), untrue, because Palmer, at any rate, was an Englishman.

Braxfield's valiant efforts to stem the rising tide of democratic sentiment gained him many friends who had no reason to be dissatisfied with the state of things which existed under the Dundas regime. But it was otherwise with the great mass of the people. The political animosity of Braxfield and his colleagues, and the remorseless way in which they transported men whose chief offence was that they were "Friends of the People," roused the most unruly passions. For a time Braxfield was quite as unpopular as Mansfield had been during the Gordon riots, though for a very different reason. In his very brief catalogue of virtues, courage occupied a prominent place. There was nothing clandestine about Braxfield. The man who told the Radicals to their faces that "they would a' be muckle the better o' being hangit"[2] might be lamentably

[1] Cockburn's *Sedition Trials*, ii. 90. [2] Kay's *Portraits*, Pop. ed., i. 122.

indiscreet, but was certainly no coward. As an instance of his great nerve, it is recorded that after the sedition trials were over, which was generally about midnight, he would walk to his house in George Square, alone and unprotected.

What kind of a domestic life Braxfield led it is impossible to say, but from what is known of his public character and of his habits, it is permissible to assume that the family circle would not be the brighter for his presence. He was twice married. His first wife, by whom he had two sons and two daughters, was a daughter of Major James Agnew of the 7th Dragoon Guards, and niece of Sir Andrew Agnew, Bart., of Lochnaw, Wigtownshire. He married, secondly, Elizabeth, daughter of Robert Ord, Lord Chief Baron of the Exchequer of Scotland, by whom he had no issue.

When Braxfield paid his addresses to this lady, he did so in a thoroughly business-like fashion. Having satisfied himself as to her suitability, he called upon her, and announced his mission with a brevity and point which all suitors will admire, though few can emulate. "Lizzy, I am looking out for a wife, and I thought you just the person that would suit me. Let me have your answer, off or on, the morn, and nae mair aboot it." It is pleasant to add that the lady was quite as business-like. Next day she returned a favourable answer, and the marriage took place with the minimum of delay. Ramsay of Ochtertyre relates [1] an anecdote of this lady upbraiding her husband for niggardliness. The

[1] *Scotland and Scotsmen*, i. 414 (*n.*).

story is to the effect that Lord Hailes and Braxfield were once entering a town where a circuit court was to be held, when Mrs. Macqueen remarked upon the shabbiness of their equipage compared with that of Hailes. "It is a shame," she said, "to have horses of different colours." "Never mind that, my dear," said her partner, "have we not a dog that he wants?"

Braxfield was a near neighbour of the father of Sir Walter Scott, the former residing at 28 and the latter at 25 George Square. Between the two families there appears to have been considerable intimacy; and it is interesting to recall that Scott's thesis on *The Title of the Pandects concerning the Disposal of the Dead Bodies of Criminals*, written in connection with his admission to the Faculty of Advocates, was dedicated to Braxfield—a tribute, no doubt, to the Lord Justice-Clerk's Toryism, which Scott shared to the full.

In his declining years Braxfield, no longer equal to the exacting pleasures of the tavern, became enamoured of the life of a country gentleman. Much of his leisure was passed at his Lanarkshire seat, "which he loved the more that he had gathered birds' nests there in his boyish years." [1] As a landed proprietor he did remarkably well. He devoted much time and attention to farming with excellent financial results, he improved and extended Braxfield, and he purchased "several valuable estates at a time when land was comparatively cheap." [2]

From his seventieth year onwards, Braxfield

[1] Ramsay's *Scotland and Scotsmen*, i. 392. [2] *Ibid.* i 392.

suffered much from ill-health, and for more than twelve months prior to his death he was unable to attend the Parliament House. He died at his town residence in 1799, and was buried at Lanark. "Regardless of the threats and invectives of a misled populace, Braxfield," wrote a contemporary, "discharged his duties with a manly firmness of mind, well-tempered intrepidity of conduct, and a wise and faithful application of the law, that must make his memory ever be gratefully remembered by his country." That so unrighteous a judge should have been graced with so fine an epitaph is one of the travesties of human life. "He has carried more sound law with him than he has left upon the Bench"[1] observed one of his ablest professional rivals on learning of his death. Posterity will prefer to think of Braxfield the lawyer rather than of Braxfield the judge, or of Braxfield the man.

[1] Ramsay's *Scotland and Scotsmen*, i. 393.

VI

LORD HAILES

(1726–1792)

With all its acknowledged ability and learning, the Scottish judiciary during the closing decades of the eighteenth century was hardly a theme for elation. Shining attainments there were, but the tone and atmosphere of the Bench did not lend much weight to Bacon's axiom that "the place of justice is a hallowed place,"[1] or to Coke's that "reason is the soul of the law."[2] A distinctive feature of the Supreme Court of Scotland of that day was its lapses from senatorial rectitude and dignity—the cruelty and grim humour of Braxfield, the coarseness and laxity of Kames, the astounding oddities of Monboddo and Gardenstone, the grotesque articulation and tedious irrelevancies of Eskgrove. Happily, there was at least one man on the Bench who set himself sternly to counteract so much judicial demoralisation.

Save in nationality, Lord Hailes had little affinity with his colleagues. A gentleman of rank and fortune, whom an Eton education had endowed with a polish and a width of outlook

[1] *Essay on Judicature* [2] Coke's *King's Bench Report*, p 7.

which was at enmity with parochialism in any shape or form, he strove persistently to exemplify the judicial virtues, and to redeem the Scottish Bench from the stigma of being the home of buffoons, cranks, roisterers, rabid politicians, and men of odd and clownish manners. Culture, sobriety of thought, conduct, and expression, and a keen moral sense were the things he most highly prized. Hailes's personality, it is true, lacks picturesqueness and dramatic attractiveness. A man who is vigilant about keeping the commandments, and doing the "correct thing," is, no doubt, a most edifying spectacle, but he does not present the best material for a really interesting and exhilarating study of human nature. In this sense the prim and dispassionate Hailes is the inferior of the harsh, bibulous, swearing Braxfield. Nevertheless, his career is well worth narrating if for no other reason than because Hailes had so little in common with those who sat with him on the judgment seat. His staid demeanour may well serve as a foil to set off the habitual unconventionality of his judicial brethren.

Born in Edinburgh in 1726, David Dalrymple was the eldest of sixteen children of Sir James Dalrymple, Bart., of New Hailes, Auditor of the Exchequer of Scotland, and of Lady Christian Hamilton. Not only did he come of distinguished lineage, but he could claim a hereditary connection with the Court of Session. His paternal grandfather, Sir David Dalrymple, was the youngest son of the first Viscount Stair, President of the Court of Session, and held the

LORD HAILES
From the Portrait by Kay

office of Lord Advocate for nineteen years. His mother, on the other hand, was a daughter of the sixth Earl of Haddington, the lineal descendant of the first Earl, who was Secretary for Scotland in the reign of James I. of England, and President of the Court of Session from 1616 till his death in 1637.

Both parents being supporters of the Union, and of the Hanoverian dynasty, and being anxious, too, that their eldest son should not contract that provincialism which many eminent Scots, a generation later, were painfully endeavouring to overcome, resolved to have him educated at Eton. This step, as will be seen later, bore most significantly on his career. Meanwhile, it is sufficient to point out that at this great public school he laid the foundations of that classical learning, the love of which was to last as long as life itself. At Eton, too, he acquired a "predilection for English modes and manners which marked his conduct and conversation in the after-part of life." [1]

His behaviour seems to have been exemplary; and at least one Eton boy never forgot his kindness. The story goes that an awkward country lad, named Hallam, who afterwards became Dean of Bristol and Canon of Windsor, came up to stand for a scholarship on the foundation. Lodged in the same house as Dalrymple, the latter became attached to him, and so materially helped him to pass his examinations that Hallam "confessed many years after, with tears in his eyes, that next to the providence of God, he

[1] Ramsay's *Scotland and Scotsmen*, i. 394.

owed all that he had to the philanthropy of Sir David Dalrymple."[1]

On leaving Eton, Dalrymple proceeded to Utrecht to study the civil law, a session under the famous Dutch masters of jurisprudence being then considered an indispensable qualification for every young man who wished to make his mark at the Scottish Bar. This was followed by a tour through France. In 1746 he arrived back in his native country after an absence of several years. He was now a young man of polish, culture, and refinement, with a partiality for things English, and speaking the tongue of the southron correctly.

The upheaval caused by the second Jacobite rebellion was now over, for which Dalrymple, a staunch Hanoverian and a lover of peace and concord, was devoutly thankful. In 1748 he was admitted a member of the Scottish Bar. For a man of talent, industry, and persuasive speech there were then excellent prospects, but Dalrymple did not quite realise the expectations of his friends. As an oral pleader he had only limited success. His knowledge of law was unquestioned, but a stiff, almost pompous, manner, a "weak ill-tuned voice" of English accent, a preference for legal minutiæ, and an impartiality more suited to the judge than the advocate, stood in the way of rapid promotion.

Much legal business, however, was then conducted by written pleadings, and here Dalrymple acquitted himself with more distinction. His documents were generally regarded as models of

[1] Ramsay's *Scotland and Scotsmen*, i. 393-394 (*n.*).

this form of legal writing. His defence of himself and the other guardians of the Countess of Sutherland against the aspersions of a lawyer of the same name has not yet lost its value, being still cited by lawyers desirous of proving the descent of the older Scottish titles to and through females.

Dalrymple was, in fact, one of the most noted genealogists of his time. He was the first man to proclaim the fact that there were flaws in the theory of the royal descent of the Douglases.[1] In a cogent dissertation, he demonstrated that the succession to the house of Douglas had gone into a wrong line with the accession of the third Earl in the middle of the fourteenth century, and that the meteoric career of the Douglases from that period down to 1488 was due to a genealogical blunder. In his view "the third and all subsequent Earls of Douglas were descended, not from the brother of the Good Sir James, who was supposed to have married Dornagilla Comyn, but illegitimately from Sir James himself."[2] Dalrymple was also convinced that "the mother of the Earl of Douglas, instead of being the fabled Dornagilla, was Beatrice, daughter of Sir David Lyndsay of Crauford."[3]

Though Dalrymple practised at the Bar for nearly twenty years, his earnings were not such as to cause him to hesitate when an offer of a seat on the Bench came his way. His awkward style and alien speech—for Parliament House

[1] Burton's *History of Scotland*, 1905, ii 419 (*n*)
[2] *Ibid* ii. 419 (*n*) [3] *Ibid.* ii 419 (*n*).

was still wedded to the vernacular—did not favour affluence. Accordingly, when in 1766, at the early age of forty, he mounted the Bench, he did so without any monetary sacrifice. He took the title of Lord Hailes, a name derived from the ancestral seat near Musselburgh, to which, together with the baronetcy and a small fortune, he had succeeded in 1750.

Possessing many of the qualities of a great judge, Hailes lent lustre to the Scottish Bench when its reputation was besmirched. Indeed, so profound were the differences of character and temperament between him and his brother judges that the wonder is that he should have been able to work with them for six-and-twenty years. He was humane when Kames could taunt Pitfour, who had an aversion to capital punishment, with being a very unworthy member of "our hanging court"; he had a deep sense of equity when blatant partisanship was in fashion; he was sedate and high-principled when jocoseness and ribaldry was a thing of everyday occurrence; he was painstaking and accurate when diligence was eschewed and patience was accounted no longer a virtue; and he was lucid and concise when clear thought and sententious speech were too often conspicuous by their absence. What marked Hailes off from most of his colleagues was his high moral worth, his unsullied honour. He would have scorned the slightest deflection from truth or equity. Thus he tried to give character, strength, and solidity to the Scottish judiciary when it was deficient in all three.

As a judge of the High Court of Justiciary, to

which he was appointed in 1776, he did his best to counteract those ugly features which, thanks chiefly to Kames and Braxfield, brought its proceedings into contempt. His industry and urbanity, and his studious avoidance of sensationalism were in marked contrast to the traditions of that Court. His manner in administering oaths and pronouncing sentences, especially upon prisoners doomed to die, was particularly impressive, while his "charges" to the jury were invariably those of a judge to whom "even-handed justice" was a thing of solemn import. But compassionate as he was, and loving mercy, he never forgot that the best interests of society could only be served by the rigorous punishment of crime.

His many estimable qualities notwithstanding, Hailes just missed being an ideal judge. Legal scholarship, integrity, exactitude, diligence, and an abiding sense of the majesty of justice, assuredly go a long way towards establishing judicial character of a high order; but Hailes had one serious deficiency. Braxfield revealed the weak point of his armour when, in reply to a remark that Hailes was a good judge, he declared in his vulgar way: "Him! he knows nothing but the nooks of a cause."[1] The "Hanging Judge" meant that Hailes was too much concerned about trivial points, too little about the central issues.

The complaint of a contemporary, that great lawyers thought the trifles of the law beneath their notice, was certainly not applicable to Hailes. Of a finical temperament, he was never

[1] Ramsay's *Scotland and Scotsmen*, i. 397 (*n.*).

more in his element than when contending for some infinitesimal point. It is said that he once dismissed a cause owing to a document having the word "justice" spelt without the final "e," an incident which James Boswell commemorated in the "Court of Session Garland," where Hailes is made to say:

> To judge of this matter, I cannot pretend,
> For justice, my Lord, wants an "E" at the end.

Such punctiliousness not unnaturally laid Hailes open to a charge of pedantry, though in reality he was far from assuming any such part. At the same time, his scrupulosity prevented him from taking broad views, and keeping a firm grasp of essentials.

And the microscopic propensity which marred his professional career, also robbed him of that position in literature to which his ability and learning entitled him. He was a born scholar. He had a capacity for protracted and recondite study which would have won him the admiration of a Casaubon or a Scaliger. Almost all his leisure was spent in poring over musty volumes, or in composition. His mind was essentially of the antiquarian order. He was an adept at throwing light on controverted points, the settlement of which depends upon wide knowledge, diligent research, and well-balanced judgment. Probably no man of his time exploded more fallacies, brushed away more cobwebs of fictitious history, dealt more stinging blows at hoary tradition. He was a terror to evil-doers in the literary as well as in the criminal sense.

His knowledge covered a wide field; and his pen was as indefatigable as his mind. Scarcely a year passed without the appearance of one or more of his publications, for he was constantly engaged in issuing pamphlets, mostly of a semi-theological order, writing brief biographies, editing chronicles, translating ancient poetry, or trying to galvanize into life forgotten authors. A list of forty-three works by Hailes is given in the *Dictionary of National Biography*; but this by no means represents the full measure of his literary activity, many of his lucubrations never being printed.

With the possible exception of the *Annals of Scotland*, Hailes did not produce a single work that survived his lifetime. He had no imagination, and very little literary sense. Instead of bracing himself for one supreme task, he frittered away his talents and his time in correcting other people's mistakes, or in exposing the hollowness of their theories. Doubtless, his labours gave pleasure to himself; but they were dull, stale, flat, and unprofitable to most people. Many of his writings were published at his own expense, for few read them, and fewer bought them. His lore was not appetising.

Hailes was a fervid Presbyterian, uncompromisingly orthodox, and with a taste for theological knight-errantry. When Gibbon wrote the famous chapters of his *Decline and Fall of the Roman Empire* in which he traces the development of early Christianity, Hailes felt that a fresh impetus had been given to the sceptical tendencies of the age, and like the dutiful son of the Church that he was, he resolved to break a lance with the great historian. This he did in a pamphlet entitled *Inquiry into the Secondary Causes which Mr. Gibbon has assigned for the rapid Growth of Christianity.* Of course this heroic effort brought joy to the hearts of the faithful. Hailes was represented as the youthful David slaying the giant Goliath. The whole bench of English bishops metaphorically fell on his neck, and even Gibbon himself admitted that he had found a "respectable adversary," though he fastened on the judge's weak point when he declared that "he scrutinises each separate passage of the two chapters with the dry minuteness of a special pleader." [1]

Gibbon, however, took the whole affair in good part. He confessed that Hailes's microscopical intelligence had possibly detected some flaw, and he generously praised his *Annals of Scotland* as the work of "a diligent collector and an accurate critic." [2] Hailes's strictures on the *Decline and Fall,* it must be admitted, were well founded. The conclusions of the historian regarding Christianity were, he contended, not only false but malicious—an opinion which has been substantiated by the whole trend of historical scholarship since Gibbon's day.

That Hailes should have been victorious in a controversy of this nature need cause no surprise. He was, in some respects, as Cosmo Innes said long ago,[3] "the very ideal of an historical inquirer. His mind was fair and dispassionate, and he reasoned with excellent logic. You will

[1] Gibbon's *Autobiography,* Hill's ed., p. 204. [2] *Ibid.* p. 204.
[3] *Lectures on Scotch Legal Antiquities,* 1872, p. 8.

seldom find a mistake in fact or a conclusion not warranted by the premises in Lord Hailes's *Annals*." But if he could sift and weigh material, and marshal facts most effectively, his style was poor. He had no moments of vision and power. He wrote history as he wrote a legal document—accurately and impartially, but without life and animation.

It is doubtful, however, whether Hailes wished to stake his reputation on his historical writings. He was proud of his burrowings in Christian antiquities, and most likely desired his many labours in that field to preserve his name from oblivion. Be that as it may, the modicum of renown which is his due, rests solely on his work as an historian. Posterity knows him, in Scott's apt phrase, as "the restorer of Scottish history." Lamenting the dearth of good general histories of Scotland, in a letter to Lord Montague, Scott remarked that the *Annals* was the "foundation-stone" of all such works—"an excellent book, though dryly written." [1]

With unerring insight, and pointedly, Scott indicates both the merit and the defect of this, the most important of all Hailes's writings. The *Annals of Scotland* was published in two instalments between the years 1776 and 1779. It is a work of moderate length, for, unlike Monboddo, the author was by no means addicted to verbosity. His original aim was "to exhibit a chronological view of the history of Scotland from the accession of Malcolm, surnamed Canmore, to the accession of Robert Bruce"; but

[1] Lockhart's *Scott*, new pop. ed., p. 502.

he ultimately brought the narrative down to the accession of the House of Stuart, and would have extended it further had not " various and invincible reasons " (*i.e.* the apathy of the public) obliged him to do otherwise.

The supreme interest and importance of the *Annals* consist in the fact that it was the first work dealing with the history of Scotland to be written on critical lines. While Robertson and Hume were writing glowing histories exhibiting the maximum of imaginative effort and the minimum of research, Hailes, in concise but bloodless diction, was narrating the history of Scotland during the Middle Ages after laboriously collating the original sources, and ruthlessly demolishing the fabric of legendary lore reared by Fordun, and embellished by Hector Boece and Buchanan. Clear and accurate knowledge, he rightly held, is always the best antidote to misconception and prejudice.

Hailes's courageous attempt to tell the story of Scotland along lines which did not do violence to the canons of sound historical criticism, was largely a thankless task. It implied the shattering of many a venerable tradition; and people preferred to be wrong with Blind Harry rather than be right with Hailes. An instance of the way in which Hailes's expurgated Scottish history was received, is recorded by Ramsay of Ochtertyre.[1] An old lady having applied to the latter for a romance, he, with a strange lack of humour, sent her the first volume of the *Annals*. The lady, who was well versed in the mythical

[1] *Scotland and Scotsmen*, i. 402 (*n.*).

story of her country, was so annoyed at the rejection of some popular stories of Wallace, that she informed Ramsay that if she were to come across Hailes, she would drive the powder out of the learned judge's wig.

The cold reception the *Annals* met with, hurt Hailes's feelings, and made him abandon further projects for the elucidation of the history of his native land. But the thoroughness and impartiality with which he executed his task are eloquently attested to by the fact that his work has been the text-book for all subsequent writers on this period. Much, of course, has come to light since Hailes's day, but the value of his narrative, as far as the facts were available to him, has never been impugned.

The footnotes of the *Annals* are packed full of well-digested information, and are often more illuminating than the text. In one of these, Hailes cautions his readers to discriminate between the Macbeth of Shakespeare's fancy and the Macbeth of history. "The genius of Shakespeare," he says, "gave such strength of colouring to the portrait, that the fictions of Boece assumed the form of historical realities. The weird sisters, the wood of Birnam advancing to Dunsinane, the prophecy that Macbeth should never be overcome by any one born of a woman, are incidents which the last age devoutly believed." He also upbraids Buchanan for heightening the process of illusionment by artfully softening the improbabilities of the tale of the weird sisters.

And along with sound and accurate scholarship, the *Annals* contains much shrewd observation expressed with epigrammatic terseness. Here is a truth which may seem commonplace nowadays, but in Hailes's time must have been very much the reverse. "Next to the passions of man, I know not anything which has so fatally checked the growth and progress of truth as that prejudice which tries every fact and custom related in history by the standard of our own manners. When we read of facts or customs dissimilar from what we see every day, we generally pronounce them to be fictitious. This is the brief decision of ignorance."

Hailes's connection with pure letters was slight. With the exception of some essays contributed to the *Mirror* and the *Gentleman's Magazine* (in one of which he detected the spuriousness of a portrait of Milton which had deceived Sir Joshua Reynolds), and some fugitive pieces, he wrote nothing entitling him to be called a man of letters. Nor was he particularly mindful of literary fame. He never sought to give the law in matters of taste and literature, as Kames did. So far as authorship was concerned, he was an historian of the antiquarian order, and, in a lesser degree, a classical scholar.

His attitude to the *literati* of Edinburgh was one of aloofness. A decided preference for English culture, a rigidity of principle, both religious and moral, and certain anti-social qualities were the main reasons why he did not fraternise with Hume, Adam Smith, Robertson, Blair, and the rest. His Eton education had given an English bent to his mind. He loved English ways and diligently cultivated English friendships. With Johnson, Burke, Warburton, Horace Walpole and many other literary magnates south of the Tweed, he was on intimate terms. He also numbered among his correspondents not a few of the dignitaries of the Church of England, but his Presbyterianism was never suspected.

Between Hailes and Hume there was some enmity. For this, his lordship was most to blame. In 1753, when Hailes was a young advocate, and quite unknown in the literary world, Hume asked him to revise his *Inquiry into the Human Mind*, but Hailes, who was a stickler for orthodoxy, declined. That the latter was able to withstand so flattering a compliment says much for his character and his religious convictions; but so friendly an act surely merited different treatment from that which Hailes subsequently meted out to Hume.

Some years later the amiable philosopher, in his capacity as Keeper of the Advocates' Library, placed on the shelves certain works of La Fontaine and Crébillon which Hailes, as a curator of the institution, thought impure. Not only did his lordship censure Hume, but he carried a resolution ordaining " that the said books be struck out of the catalogue of the Library, and removed from the shelves as indecent books, and unworthy of a place in a learned library." Thus Hailes vindicated his reputation for irreproachable morals, and maintained the pristine purity of the Advocates' Library. But if such action, which smells strongly of prudery, were necessary, surely his lordship might have gone about the matter with more circumspection, more especially as Hume had given genuine proof of his admiration of Hailes's abilities.

Hume never forgave the judge, whom he dubbed an "old wife," but judging by the references to him in his correspondence, he was not vindictive. In 1768 there was published anonymously a volume of philosophical essays in answer to Kames's *Essays on Morality and Natural Religion.* The work contained some severe criticisms of Hume, who conjectured that the author was Hailes, because the book was "wrote with tolerable neatness of style," though it contained "not so many attempts at humour as that pious gentleman would employ."[1] When informed of his mistake by Sir Gilbert Elliot, he replied with a playful hit at Hailes's English proclivities. "I thought," he wrote, "David had been the only Christian who could write English on the other side of the Tweed." But while Hailes disliked Hume, and dreaded his influence on religion, he was not intolerant. Vigorous defender of the faith though he was, he had discrimination and magnanimity to admire Hume's autobiographical fragment, which he translated into sonorous Latin.

The only literary Scotsman whom Hailes seems to have honoured with his friendship was James Boswell. How two such men could draw together is one of the problems of literary history. Certainly, they could hardly have been more dissimilar—Hailes, well-bred, refined, cultured, and almost obtrusively religious: Boswell, in-

[1] Hume's *Life and Correspondence*, ii. 414-415.

discreet, vulgar, bombastic, dissipated. But the fact remains—and a fact of outstanding importance it is—that but for Hailes, the immortal biography of Dr. Johnson might never have been written. Writes Boswell: "Sir David Dalrymple, now one of the judges of Scotland by the title of Lord Hailes, had contributed much to increase my high opinion of Johnson, on account of his writings, long before I attained to a personal acquaintance with him."[1]

The truth is, Hailes was one of the earliest and most cordial admirers of Johnson's writings. "He is one of the best moral writers which England has produced," he wrote in a letter congratulating Boswell on having obtained the great man's friendship. "I envy you," Hailes continues, "the free and undisguised converse with such a man. May I beg you to present my best respects to him, and to assure him of the veneration which I entertain for the author of the *Rambler*, and of *Rasselas*? Let me recommend this last work to you; with the *Rambler*, you certainly are acquainted. In *Rasselas* you will see a tender-hearted operator, who probes the wound only to heal it. Swift, on the contrary, mangles human nature."[2]

Johnson, to whom Boswell read Hailes's eulogium, was so much gratified that he drank a bumper to him as "a man of worth, a scholar, and a wit." "I have," said the Doctor, "never heard of him except from you; but let him know my opinion of him: for as he does not show himself much in the world, he should have the

[1] Boswell's *Johnson*, Hill's ed., i. 432. [2] *Ibid.* i. 432-433.

praise of the few who hear of him."[1] Thus began an acquaintanceship which quickly ripened into warm and enduring friendship. Johnson conceived a high opinion of the Scottish judge's learning and religious character, and was wont to say that he loved him "better than any man whom I know so little."[2]

When Johnson visited Scotland in 1773, Hailes was, of course, among those invited to meet him at Boswell's house in Edinburgh. The great biographer thus records his impressions of the occasion.[3] "This was one of Dr. Johnson's best days. He was quite in his element. All was literature and taste, without any interruption. Lord Hailes, who is one of the best philologists in Great Britain, who has written papers in the *World*, and a variety of other works in prose and in verse, both Latin and English, pleased him highly." Johnson was struck by his lordship's acumen. Among the topics discussed was Johnson's *Vanity of Human Wishes*. Hailes maintained that the author was mistaken in giving Vane and Sedley as examples of "unfortunate fair ones," in the following passage:

> The teeming mother, anxious for her race,
> Begs, for each birth, the fortune of a face:
> Yet Vane could tell, what ills from beauty spring;
> And Sedley curs'd the charms which pleas'd a king.

But whether the Doctor took up the challenge, or bowed to the superior wisdom of the judge, is not recorded. Hailes and Johnson also talked of the principles of biographic art, the latter

[1] Boswell's *Johnson*, Hill's ed., i. 451-452. [2] *Ibid.* ii. 293.
[3] *Ibid.* v. 48.

maintaining that "if a man is to write a panegyric, he may keep vices out of sight; but if he professes to write a Life, he must represent it really as it was."[1]

This meeting between the judge and the lexicographer—though the first and the last—was fraught with the happiest results. Johnson ever afterwards confided in Hailes's judgment. When the Ossian controversy was at its height, the Doctor anxiously asked Boswell, "Is Hailes on our side?"

Hailes, on the other hand, was careful that no important work of his should see the light without first receiving the imprimatur of Johnson. The Doctor was asked to revise the *Annals of Scotland*. The latter carried out the task very conscientiously, but found little to cavil at. Writing to Boswell in 1775, he says: "I have at last sent back Lord Hailes's sheets. I never think about returning them, because I alter nothing. You will see that I might as well have kept them."[2] Johnson, however, did make one emendation of which Hailes disapproved. In the account of the Scottish War of Independence his lordship had described his countrymen as a "free nation," but Johnson altered the adjective to "brave," a piece of English prejudice which Hailes could not tolerate. The latter, however, suggested that Johnson should draw from the material supplied by the *Annals* a character sketch of King Robert the Bruce, but the Doctor adroitly replied that it was unnecessary, though there were few things he would not do to oblige Hailes.[3]

[1] Boswell's *Johnson*, Hill's ed., iii. 155. [2] *Ibid.* ii. 293.
[3] *Ibid.* ii. 387.

Johnson praised the *Annals*, which he contrasted with the painted histories more to the taste of the age, a sly hit, no doubt, at Robertson and Hume.[1] "It is a book which will always sell, it has such a stability of dates, such a certainty of facts, and such a punctuality of citation. I never before read Scotch history with certainty."[2] Yet he frankly owns that the work contains "mere dry" particulars, and is to be regarded "as a Dictionary."[3]

Between the two men there seems to have been a pretty constant interchange of literary wares. Johnson sent Hailes some verses of his own on Inchkenneth, but, evidently not being particularly proud of them, with strict injunctions not to reveal the authorship. Hailes, on the other hand, presented Johnson with the fifth book of *Lactantius*, which he had published with Latin notes. He also furnished him with a few anecdotes for his sketch of James Thomson, the poet, and sent him verses on the somewhat uninspiring theme of the repair of Aberdeen University. Hailes thought that the effusion, which was from the pen of David Mallet, would please Johnson "as affording clear evidence that Mallet had appeared even as a literary character by the name of Malloch," his anglicising which had led Johnson to introduce him into his *Dictionary*, under the article "Alias."[4]

The broad lineaments of Hailes's character were plainly stamped on his outward appearance. Kay's etching[5] represents him as short and

[1] Boswell's *Johnson*, Hill's ed., iii. 58. [2] *Ibid.* iii. 58.
[3] *Ibid.* iii. 404. [4] *Ibid.* iv. 216-217. [5] *Edinburgh Portraits.*

corpulent, with a stolid countenance, in which there is not much suggestion of amiability. But the painting by Seton, which hangs in New Hailes House, is said to be much the truer likeness; and certainly from what is known of his character, and of his mode of living, this seems highly probable. Here the features are more refined, expressive, and intelligent, and indicate a man of high culture, dignified presence, and equable temper—one who is at peace with himself and with the world.

Hailes's lines were assuredly cast in pleasant places. Well-born, dowered with all the advantages of wealth, education, and high position, treading always the path of rectitude, and loving sober joys and simple ways, it was an even, tranquil, contemplative life that this old judge lived. But a man who is sedate, and reserved, and spends much time in "sessions of sweet silent thought," can hardly expect to be a social success. And Hailes was no exception to the rule. The haunts of frivolity, mirth, and dissipation knew him not. He could not have cut a pretty figure on the floor of the assembly to save his life, still less was he fitted to shine in the orgies and Rabelaisian humour of the tavern. Like Burke, he had an inborn stateliness of nature, which was continually warring against the low moral atmosphere of the age. Possessing the instincts of a gentleman and the spirit of a scholar, he saw clearly that the social customs of the time, especially hard drinking, high jinks, and eccentric habits, were inimical to both.

It is not difficult to understand how Hailes,

in later years, became virtually a stranger in his native city. So uncompromising an attitude to the prevailing tone and temper of Scottish society was bound to render him unpopular. At the same time it were wrong to suppose that because he had no liking for ceremonial dinners, suppers, and balls, and had no dealings with fellows of the baser sort, he was devoid of social gifts. Where the company was small, select, and thoroughly congenial, he could acquit himself creditably, if not brilliantly. He was an excellent host, kept a well-furnished table, and entertained handsomely. Though his conversational powers were mediocre, and his humour a negligible quantity, he generally could count on attentive listeners, for he had a richly stored mind, and a fund of entertaining anecdotes which he related most effectively. In entertaining at the circuit table, observes Ramsay of Ochtertyre, he was neither lavish nor sordid. "His equipage and table were handsome, and such as befitted his place; and if no drinker himself, he did not grudge his wine when the conversation took an interesting turn." [1]

Hailes was happiest when living the life of a country gentleman. He had a town house in New Street, off the Canongate, but its proximity to the bustle and turmoil of a densely crowded city, and the impossibility of obtaining that repose so essential to a man of studious habits, compelled him to seek a retreat "far from the madding crowd." During the later years of his life he lived almost permanently at New Hailes,

[1] *Scotland and Scotsmen*, i. 399.

a small but pleasantly situated estate skirting the Firth of Forth.

The half-dozen miles betwixt New Hailes and Edinburgh, his lordship traversed every morning during session in the family coach, which started before breakfast (that meal being served presumably on arrival in Edinburgh), and returned home in time for dinner. Being most economical of his time, his lordship, in his daily journeys to and from the capital, managed to combine recreation with business, for while he read his law papers, or pondered the theme of his next essay for the *Mirror*, or outlined a letter to Dr. Johnson, or read Horace, he was inhaling the sea breezes.

And very particular was Hailes about his health, though the methods he adopted to keep well were more rational than those of Monboddo, a fact of which that eccentric judge had once an unwelcome reminder. One winter day, while Hailes was warming himself at the fire in the Parliament House, he was joined by Monboddo. "What! my lord," said Hailes sarcastically, "do you require artificial heat like us mere moderns?" Monboddo looked annoyed, but made no answer. On Hailes returning to his seat on the Bench, however, Monboddo exclaimed, "Well said of him that leads the life of a bug!" [1]

Hailes's ideas of exercise were certainly not pretentious. A stroll through the fields around New Hailes, or a leisurely drive in his carriage was all the recreation he took. But he had his

[1] Ramsay's *Scotland and Scotsmen*, i. 412 (*n.*).

stated hours for exercise, as he had his stated hours for meals and study, and these were as unalterable as the laws of the Medes and the Persians.

Though rural life attracted him strongly, it was not because he evinced any interest in farming or gardening. He had none of the agricultural enthusiasm of Kames. Ramsay of Ochtertyre once spent a day at New Hailes, and, while walking through the fields, he asked his lordship if he was a farmer. Hailes's reply was decisive. "I once had a plough for six weeks, and was heartily tired of it."[1] Happily, his indifference to husbandry did not prevent him being an enlightened and considerate landlord.

The supreme value of country life, in Hailes's estimation, was that it gave a man of scholarly tastes that leisure and serenity without which laborious intellectual work is impossible. With infinite care, he reared at New Hailes an extensive library of rare and costly volumes. Here he passed much of his time in recondite study; in writing learned but arid disquisitions on Christian antiquities; in translating the Church Fathers with elaborate introductions dedicated to Anglican prelates; in annotating old Scottish songs and poems; and in investigating the arguments for the high antiquity of *Regiam Majestatem*.[2]

The tract which he wrote on the latter subject is, next to the *Annals*, perhaps the most important of his writings. It finally demolished a view which legal commentators and practical lawyers

[1] *Scotland and Scotsmen*, i. 412 (*n.*).
[2] Burton's *History of Scotland*, 1905, ii. 59.

had entertained for centuries, namely, that the collection of laws known as *Regiam Majestatem* were compiled by order of David I., "the Scots Justinian." Hailes demonstrated, on the contrary, that the work was little more than a transcript of the *Treatise on the Laws and Constitutions of England,* attributed to Randulph de Glanville, Chief Justice of England in the reign of Henry II. So implicitly did public faith in Scotland continue to rely upon *Regiam Majestatem* as a national treasure, that when Hailes published his tract, his destructive criticism "was received with a sort of surly discontent, as an unworthy effort to dispel a pleasing vision." [1] Assuredly, Hailes never ran any risk of being accused of patriotic prejudice. Indeed, several of his compositions were directed towards disillusioning his countrymen, and humbling their national pride.

"In private life Hailes was respectable and irreproachable—a dutiful son, a kind brother, an affectionate husband, and a tender parent." [2] He was twice married. His first wife, a daughter of the noted judge, Lord Coalston, died in childbirth. To her, Hailes was deeply attached, and he enshrined her memory in a Latin epitaph. His second wife was the daughter of another judge, Sir James Fergusson, Lord Kilkerran. There were two daughters, one born of each marriage, both of whom were a solace to their father in his declining years.

In an age characterised by attenuated faith and moral slackness, Hailes not only professed

[1] Burton's *History of Scotland,* 1905, ii. 59.
[2] Ramsay's *Scotland and Scotsmen,* i. 406.

but practised the Christian virtues. On one occasion he reprimanded an advocate for making a ludicrous application of a New Testament text. "Sir," said he, "you may take liberties with the Old Testament, but I will not suffer you to meddle with the New" [1]—an observation which throws some light upon his lordship's theological position. His piety was sincere, but it was free from any suspicion of moroseness or bigotry. His catholicity was such that he found no difficulty in reconciling loyalty to Presbyterianism with warm admiration of the Anglican Church, within whose borders were many of his dearest friends.

Hailes refrained from ecclesiastical as he refrained from secular politics, being rightly convinced that contention either in Church or State is incompatible with the position of a judge. With the leaders of the Church of Scotland he had little or no intimacy, but he made an exception in the case of Dr. Alexander Carlyle of Inveresk, upon whose ministrations he regularly waited. That incorrigible Moderate was in the habit of dining once a year at New Hailes, and came to the conclusion that nowhere did he get more good wine or more good "cracks" (talks).

When Hailes died in 1792 from apoplexy, the result of his too ardent devotion to study, Carlyle delivered a funeral oration in Inveresk Church which, if effusive, was substantially true. After referring to Hailes's "abhorrence of crimes, his tenderness for the criminals, his respect for the laws, and his reverential awe of the Omniscient

[1] Ramsay's *Scotland and Scotsmen*, i. 407 (*n.*).

Judge," he proceeded: "Affectionate to his family and relations, simple and mild in his manners, pure and conscientious in his morals, enlightened and entertaining in his conversation, he left society only to regret that, devoted as he was to more important employments, he had so little time to spare for intercourse with them." [1]

Hailes's merits were very considerable; his foibles were "few and venial." He had no humour, and could not have been facetious, even though it would have brought him "a world of happy days." His contemporaries respected rather than loved him, for his manner was distant, his speech immaculate, and his principles far too strict to please a wicked and a perverse generation. He could be mildly sarcastic at times, as the advocate, who had the pen of a ready writer, but no forensic ability, learned to his cost. Knowing the barrister's aversion to speaking at the Bar, Hailes would say: "Sir, that cause is somewhat out of my head; will you be pleased to recapitulate it?" [2] But irony rather than sarcasm was his forte. Once he was indignant about a plane tree being cut down by the magistrates of Stirling. Upon the Provost informing him that further vandalism was contemplated in the removal of Popish carvings from the parish church, Hailes remarked: "Since you have cut the tree you may also take away the trumpery." [3]

A scholar, a sound and learned lawyer, and a first-rate antiquary, Hailes was but an indifferent

[1] *Sermon on Lord Hailes's Death*, by Rev. Dr. Carlyle. Edin., 1792.

[2] Ramsay's *Scotland and Scotsmen*, i. 411 (*n.*).

[3] *Ibid.* i. 411 (*n.*).

author. He wrote enormously, but most of his writings had only to see the light of day to instantly perish. Not only was he without the gift of imagination and the graces of style, but he lavished his scholarship on themes which the most attractive writer would have found it hard to invest with human interest. He knew, however, what the writing of history on scientific lines meant; and it is his crowning achievement that he led the way in Scotland in showing that historical writing, if it is to be worthy of the name, must, in the first place, be based upon fact and not upon tradition. It was a great lesson that Hailes taught, but more than half a century was to elapse ere a new race of Scottish historians had learned its full significance.

VII

LORD ESKGROVE

(1729?–1804)

A CAREFUL study of the career of Lord Eskgrove, and of what his contemporaries said and wrote about him, suggests the unpleasant reflection that the qualifications demanded of a Scottish judge in the eighteenth century were somewhat slender. The most vivid impression one obtains is that of a lawyer who fought his way to judicial eminence with rather frail weapons. It is not easy to resist the conclusion that Eskgrove received a judgeship, not because of any manifestation of supreme intellect and character combined with legal acumen and learning, but by reason of eccentricities and foibles, and a grotesque appearance—all of which afforded endless amusement to the wits of Parliament House, and prevented Edinburgh society from becoming vacuous.

Eskgrove's character must have had some redeeming features, but Cockburn would have us believe that he was almost as black as he was painted. His lordship, we learn from that authority, was " an avaricious, indecent old wretch, whose habits and appearance supplied all Edinburgh with ludicrous and contemptuous anecdotes."[1] Was ever a more formidable indictment directed against the character of a judge? Cockburn, no doubt, was actuated to some extent by political prejudice; but even so, he would not have dared to write thus of one of his predecessors, unless there had been substantial grounds for doing so.

Nor, judging by the severity of Cockburn's criticism, does Eskgrove intellectually appear to have been far removed from Eskgrove morally. "Never once did he do or say anything which had the slightest claim to be remembered for any intrinsic merit. The value of all his words and actions consisted in their absurdity."[2] Cockburn, it is true, admits that he was "a very considerable lawyer; in mere knowledge probably Braxfield's superior."[3] He also says that Eskgrove was "cunning in old Scotch law." But he severely qualifies these assertions in another passage where he affirms that "Eskgrove's law was less connected with practical knowledge or common sense than, except for his example, could be believed."[4] Now, manifestly, if a judge despises practical knowledge and common sense, he is in a bad way. Probably the sober truth is that Eskgrove was not without legal erudition, but it was so mixed up with ludicrous ideas, and extravagant and ineffectual modes of exposition arising from certain temperamental peculiarities, as to rob it of any value.

Eskgrove's personal appearance was also cast

[1] *Introd. to Sedition Trials*, i. 86.
[2] Cockburn's *Memorials of his Time*, 1856, p. 119.
[3] *Ibid.* p. 118. [4] *Sedition Trials*, i. 15.

Photo, Swan Watson

LORD ESKGROVE

From the Painting by Raeburn
in Parliament Hall, Edinburgh

in the balance against him. Cockburn lays unnecessary stress on this point, since neither equity nor common sense decrees that a man shall be penalised simply because his countenance does not conform to the approved standard. Good looks are rarely the passport to positions of authority, least of all to a judgeship. But however that may be, it must be admitted that if Eskgrove's habits and sayings were odd, his personal appearance was odder still. A queerer or more ungainly person surely never sat upon the Scottish Bench.

Cockburn, who knew him in old age, describes him as of medium height, but bent and withered. "His face varied, according to circumstances, from a scurfy red to a scurfy blue; the nose was prodigious; the underlip enormous, and supported on a huge clumsy chin, which moved like the jaw of an exaggerated Dutch toy. He walked with a slow, stealthy step—something between a walk and a hirple, and helped himself on by short movements of his elbows, backwards and forwards, like fins. The voice was low and mumbling, and on the Bench was generally inaudible for some time after the movement of the lips showed that he had begun speaking; after which the first word that was let fairly out was generally the loudest of the whole discourse." "It is unfortunate," adds Cockburn, "that, without an idea of his voice and manner, mere narrative cannot describe his sayings and doings graphically." [1]

Judging by this word-portrait, Eskgrove, if

[1] *Memorials of his Time*, 1856, p. 119-120.

not an ogre, came perilously near being one. Assuredly, the culprits who had the misfortune to be brought before him had good reason to be awed by his presence for more reasons than one. Whatever notions they might entertain as to the majesty of the law, they would hardly be impressed by the majesty of the person who was called upon to administer it. Raeburn's portrait of this extraordinary judge, however, is more flattering than Cockburn's description.

The salient facts of the career of Sir David Rae, Lord Eskgrove, are soon told. He was born about 1729, and was the son of David Rae of St. Andrews, an Episcopal minister, by his wife Agnes, daughter of Sir David Forbes of Newhall, and niece of Duncan Forbes of Culloden, one of the ablest presidents the Court of Session ever had. After receiving the rudiments of his education at the grammar school of Haddington, he entered Edinburgh University, where he had as a fellow student the judicial colleague of his later years—the notorious Braxfield. How it fared with Rae at school and college we do not know, but if he was as whimsical then as he was in after life, it is doing him no injustice to infer that his record was undistinguished.

His career at the Scottish Bar, to which he was called at the age of twenty-seven, seems to have begun promisingly enough, for, in 1753, two years after his admission to the Faculty of Advocates, he was retained in an appeal to the House of Lords, where he not only distinguished himself, but made the acquaintance of Lord Hardwicke and his son, Charles Yorke. During the next dozen years, by industry and attentiveness rather than by any conspicuous talent, he built up a fair practice. Then the famous Douglas Cause came along, bringing in its train plenty of work for young advocates of fair ability. Rae was appointed one of the commissioners for collecting evidence, and in that capacity accompanied in 1764 two of his future colleagues on the Bench — Monboddo and Gardenstone — to France. It is equally noteworthy, as throwing light upon his attainments, that at a time when Robert Macqueen (afterwards Lord Braxfield), and several other supremely able men were at the Bar, Rae should have held for many years the position of leading advocate in the Scottish Court of Exchequer.

At the ripe age of fifty-eight, he succeeded Alexander Boswell, Lord Auchinleck, father of the biographer of Dr. Johnson, as an ordinary Lord of Session, assuming the title of Lord Eskgrove, a name derived from a small estate near Musselburgh, which he owned. His idiosyncrasies seem to have been no barrier to his promotion when once on the Bench. In 1785, only three years after his elevation, he was appointed a criminal judge, and in 1799 he succeeded Braxfield as Lord Justice-Clerk. Then he was created a baronet, but did not live to enjoy his honour long, for he died at Eskgrove in October 1804, barely five months after the distinction had been conferred upon him. He was then nearly eighty years of age, and had long been in a senile state. Eskgrove married in 1761 Margaret, youngest daughter of John Stuart of Blairhill,

Perthshire, by whom he had two sons and one daughter.

The eccentricities of Eskgrove suggest a comparison with Monboddo and Gardenstone. Unquestionably, the latter were formidable rivals where oddities were concerned, but they were men of much wider outlook, and of more conspicuous ability. Monboddo, though he wrote much elegant nonsense, was nevertheless an author of some repute, a classical scholar, and an anthropologist in the making. Gardenstone, on the other hand, busied himself with village-building, and with alleviating the lot of the valetudinarian.

But Eskgrove has his place in the book of remembrance largely on account of the fact that he was an absurd person who for two-and-twenty years administered the law in the Supreme Court of Scotland. His clumsy jokes, for his wit was extravagant rather than clever, were talked about and laughed over, until everybody in Edinburgh became aware that "Esky" had "perpetrated his latest." "People," says Cockburn,[1] "seemed to have nothing to do but to tell stories of this one man. To be able to give an anecdote by Eskgrove, with a proper imitation of his voice and manner, was a sort of fortune in society. Scott in those days was famous for this particularly. Whenever a knot of persons were seen listening in the Outer House to one who was talking slowly, with a low muttering voice and a projected chin, and then the listeners burst asunder in roars of laughter, nobody thought

[1] *Memorials of his Time*, 1856, p. 118.

of asking what the joke was. They were sure that it was a successful imitation of 'Esky'; and this was enough."

Eskgrove's judicial manner and speech, as well as his jokes, provided sport for the Philistines. His peculiarities were almost inexhaustible. Witnesses and juries never knew what indignity they might suffer at the hands of this eccentric judge. In the trial of Glengarry for murder, a lady of great beauty was called as a witness. She came into court wearing a veil, a circumstance which seemed to ruffle his lordship, who, before administering the oath, addressed the lady as follows: "Young woman! you will now consider yourself as in the presence of Almighty God, and of this High Court. Lift up your veil, throw off all modesty, and look me in the face." [1]

His behaviour towards juries was often insufferable. Sometimes he would "charge" for hours, brevity not being one of his judicial virtues. A lackadaisical person is never in a hurry, and Eskgrove's moralisings were frequently so protracted that a juryman unable to stand any longer (he insisted upon the jury standing during his address) would resume his seat. But woe betide the unfortunate juror who was caught in the act, for his lordship would sternly remind him that "these were not the times in which there should be shown any disrespect of this High Court, or even of the law." [2]

As an instance of some of the hardships inflicted on juries and prisoners by his lordship's

[1] Cockburn's *Memorials of his Time*, 1856, p. 122.

[2] *Ibid.* p. 123.

verbosity and irrelevancy, it is recorded that in a case in which three men were charged with having broken into Luss House, assaulted Sir James Colquhoun and others, and robbed them of a large sum of money, Eskgrove not only inflicted on the court an elaborate and learned disquisition on the nature of assault and robbery, but enlightened it as to the etymology of "hamesucken." Then he proceeded to remind the prisoners that they attacked the house and the persons in it, and robbed them. "All this you did," continued his lordship, "and God preserve us! joost when they were sitten doon to their denner!"

Cockburn has drawn[1] an amusing picture of the ordeal which awaited the unfortunate juror summoned to attend his lordship's court. "Often have I gone back to the court at midnight, and found Eskgrove, whom I had left mumbling hours before, still going on, with the smoky, unsnuffed tallow candles in greasy tin candlesticks, and the poor despairing jurymen, most of the audience having retired or being asleep; the wagging of his lordship's nose and chin being the chief signs that he was still 'charging.'"

And if Eskgrove's addresses to the jury were long and intolerably dull, the lot of the juryman was made still harder by the fact that they were badly spoken. It was not merely that his articulation was defective: his English was execrable. He cut a word of three syllables into two separate words, the first of two syllables and the last of one. Similarly, a word of two

[1] Cockburn's *Memorials of his Time*, 1856, p. 123.

syllables was divided into two words. Thus: "I met a young friend as I was walking in the Canongate," became, according to Eskgrove's elegant pronunciation, "I met one youngg friend as I was walking in the Canon-gate"—the pause between the syllables being always very decided. Juries were made familiar with jargon of this sort: "And so gentle-men, having shewn you that the pannell's argument is utterly impossibill, I shall now proceed for to shew you that it is extremely improbabill."

His lordship had also a weakness for adjectives, on the last syllable of which he bestowed particular attention. An exemplary person he would describe as "one excellent, and worthy, and amiabill, and agreeabill, and very good man." If restraint be the highest manifestation of art, then assuredly, where adjectives were concerned, Eskgrove was artless indeed.

Eskgrove did not revel in a "hangin' court," as did Kames and Braxfield, but he rather relished addressing a prisoner upon whom he had passed sentence of death. Not that he was specially fitted for the duty, for, unintentionally, he would mar the solemnity of the occasion by some ludicrous remark or unseemly gesture. His mode of address offered the unhappy man at the bar small consolation. Usually, he would wind up by assuring him in faulty English, barbarously pronounced, that "whatever your religi-ous persua-shon may be, or even if, as I suppose, you be of no persua-shon at all, there are plenty of rever-end gentle-men who will be most happy for to shew you the way to yeternal life."

Tedious, somnolent, dull, there were times when Eskgrove could display unwonted animation. Sir John Henderson of Fordell, an inveterate litigant, knew this to his cost. His lordship could never endure any imputation of bodily infirmity, and Sir John, who could never give the soft answer which turneth away wrath, rather imprudently, on one occasion, alluded to one of Eskgrove's vulnerable points. The Court was engaged in fixing the amount of some penalty that Sir John Henderson had incurred. Eskgrove, as usual, mumbled his opinion, though it was spoken loud enough to enable his brethren to hear that his view was that the fine ought to be £50. Sir John, however, could not hear, and begged his lordship to raise his voice, insolently adding that if the judges did not speak so as to be heard, they might as well not speak at all. This advice, however, was lost on Eskgrove, who asked his colleague, "What does the fellow say?" "He says that if you don't speak out you may as well hold your tongue," was the reply. "Oh! is that what he says?" continued Eskgrove. "My Lords, what I was sayingg was very simpell. I was only sayingg that in my humbell opinion, this fine could not be less than £250 sterlingg"—the amount of the fine being roared out.[1]

Eskgrove was not a born humorist, but he could be pawky. Lockhart tells a droll story[2] of how Scott, then a young advocate, pled before his lordship concerning a cow which his client was accused of selling while in an unsound

[1] Cockburn's *Memorials of his Time*, 1856, p. 123.
[2] *Life of Scott*, new pop. ed., p. 60.

condition. In opening his case, Scott maintained that the animal merely suffered from a cough. This was too much for Eskgrove's gravity, and he broke in with the remark, " I have had plenty healthy kye in my time, but I never heard o' ane o' them coughin'. A coughin' coo! that will never do." Scott lost his case, but had the satisfaction of knowing that a coughing cow was not the rarity his lordship imagined. A day or two later, he and a companion were on their way to Liddesdale when they saw in a field a fine young cow coughing lustily. " Ah," remarked Scott, " what a pity for my client that old Eskgrove had not taken Singdon (the name of the farm) on his way to the town. That bonny creature would have saved us :

> A Daniel come to judgment, yea a Daniel;
> O wise young judge, how I do honour thee!"

Cockburn shall tell another story. " I heard Eskgrove, in condemning a tailor to death for murdering a soldier by stabbing him, aggravate the offence thus: 'And not only did you murder him, whereby he was berea-ved of his life, but you did thrust, or push, or pierce, or project, or pro-pell, the le-thall weapon through the belly-band of his regimen-tal breeches, *which were his Majes-ty's*!' "[1]

Still another instance of Eskgrove's drollery may be given. In a cause relating to the game laws, the parties being the Earl of Breadalbane and Livingstone of Parkhall, the latter, who lost the case, propounded the novel doctrine that

[1] *Memorials of his Time*, 1856, p. 122.

in order to prevent noblemen from becoming effeminate, the legislature encouraged sportsmen to pursue their game wherever they could find it. Eskgrove fairly rose to the occasion by suggesting that Livingstone of Parkhall, and such as he, if they had no game to pursue within their own policies, should hunt upon the *highway*! "It will brace your nerves," added his lordship. As for the common people who felt the hunting instinct strong within them, he advocated the rolling of cannon balls as an excellent diversion. It would make them hardy without trespassing on their neighbour's property in pursuit of game.[1]

The wheels of justice ground slowly in Eskgrove's court. If he was not habitually indolent, he was at all events decidedly slow. Stupidity and ineptitude did not try his patience; but rhetoric and energy did. He did not like to be hurried, and when a brilliant and impetuous young advocate like Brougham was pleading before him, he felt uneasy. For more than a year Brougham was constantly appearing before his lordship, much to the discomfiture of the latter. One day it seemed as if he was not to be present, which made Eskgrove chuckle with delight. But his elation at being allowed to conduct the business of the Court in his easy-going fashion was short-lived, for before the day was far advanced Brougham duly appeared—ready and anxious for the fray. "I declare," said Eskgrove, "that man Broom or Brougham is the torment of my life." But Brougham, who

[1] Kay's *Edinburgh Portraits*, Pop. ed., ii. 23.

was not a man to be easily suppressed, proceeded forthwith to argue his case with many a rhetorical flourish. Eskgrove, however, usually had his revenge. In "charging" the jury, he would sneer at Brougham's eloquence, and call him "The Harangue." "Well gentle-men what did 'The Harangue' say next? Why it said this (mis-stating it); but here gentle-men, 'The Harangue' was most plainly wrongg, and not intelligibill."[1]

Eskgrove sat in most of the famous trials during the last two decades of the eighteenth century. But he was in great measure overshadowed by Braxfield's commanding personality. A man of little force of character, in whom the spirit of independence waxed feebly, Eskgrove was unfitted to play a strong part. He had little of Braxfield's practical sagacity and reasoning power. But he was of the same political school as the Lord Justice-Clerk and, in the sedition trials of 1793–94, he slavishly supported his chief. A high Tory, he regarded the regime of Dundas as the last word in good government. He who said anything to the contrary was both a fool and a knave. It was therefore incumbent upon his lordship to visit with the severest penalties all political reformers and French revolutionists, between whom he recognised no distinction.

In the various sedition trials, Eskgrove displayed the most flagrant ignorance and partisanship. In that of Palmer he anticipated the evidence by observing at the outset that "all

[1] Cockburn's *Memorials of his Time*, 1856, p. 122

nations are liable to have bad men among them." "I own," he continued, "I am little obliged to strangers who, coming here under the pretence of preaching what they call 'the gospel,' should preach sedition among the people." When Palmer's counsel tried to show the extent to which liberty of speech and discussion are tolerated in this country, by quoting Burke's saying that "kings are naturally lovers of low company," Eskgrove retorted, "Then low company should like kings"—a remark which, under other circumstances, would have been regarded as clever repartee, but which, in the present instance, was obviously intended to apply to the prisoner.

The judicial condition of Eskgrove's mind was further revealed in the trial of Skirving. That the prisoner should have dared to call "upon the *rabble* to remember their patriotic ancestors who shed their blood in the cause of freedom" was, in his lordship's eyes, an unpardonable political crime. His Toryism again spoke true in the case of Margarot. "It is not the province of such men as these (the advocates of political reform) to take upon themselves the amendment of the government. The intention of their meeting, they say, was to obtain universal suffrage or, in other words, to establish that every man living in this country is to have a vote to choose a representative in Parliament—a thing that never did obtain, and does not now obtain, and that never can obtain, in this country."

When Margarot put certain questions to

Braxfield[1] with the object of showing that he had pre-judged the case, Eskgrove was strongly opposed to the Lord Justice - Clerk answering them. His view was that what was said in a private company could not involve the fate of the trial. A more audacious attempt on the part of one judge to shield another can hardly be imagined. And it was clumsy as well as audacious, since Eskgrove might reasonably have objected to the questions being answered on the ground that the prisoner had refrained from making his allegations against Braxfield until the case had been partially heard. But he preferred to adopt a course which had neither law nor reason to support it—a course which created a strong suspicion that he knew that Margarot's allegations were true.

In the trial of Gerrald, Eskgrove suffered the humiliation of having to apologise to the prisoner. His lordship accused Gerrald of malevolence, and this led to a scene, the latter indignantly asserting that he came there not "to be the object of personal abuse, but to meet the justice of my country." Whereupon Eskgrove expressed regret for what he had said, and asked "the gentleman's pardon." He, however, maintained that Gerrald in proposing certain reforms (universal suffrage being among them), had acted criminally. It is almost incredible that a little more than a century ago, a Scottish judge should have been so ignorant of the inalienable rights of every Briton.

To call Eskgrove "a man of the greatest

[1] See p. 117.

integrity,"[1] is surely, in the light of these ugly facts, a curious perversion of the truth. His character, so far as we know it, does not heighten one's estimate of human nature. It was certainly not cast in the heroic mould. A man of limited outlook and culture, he was also mean, vulgar, obsequious. But for his amazing absurdities of speech and action, and his sadly attenuated judicial sense when trying political prisoners, he would have been forgotten.

His penuriousness was proverbial. The ingenuity which he displayed in cutting down the expenses of his circuit dinners, for which he received a fixed allowance, was marvellous. His butler had strict orders to check the bottles of wine by laying aside the corks. On one occasion, Eskgrove had the effrontery to go behind a screen, while his guests were still at table, and warmly reprimand his servant for being so liberal in his allowance of liquor. The conversation was overheard by the company, whose embarrassment must have been great, as his lordship maintained that it was "impossibill" they could have drunk so much. John, however, was positive, and Eskgrove, unable to improve the situation, put a handful of corks in his pocket, remarking that he must protect himself.[2] No doubt, his lordship found an odd moment in which to count the corks, and to mourn over the fact that his economy in the matter of circuit dinners had fallen below his expectations.

Eskgrove was unlettered, or nearly so. He

[1] Article in *Dictionary of National Biography*.

[2] Cockburn's *Memorials of his Time*, 1856, p. 121.

wrote no books, and read few. The *literati* of Edinburgh knew him not. He had no relish for "learned suppers," and he was as innocent of metaphysics and theology as he was of the essentials of good government. One slender link, however, bound him to literature. He edited the poems of Hamilton of Bangour, and wrote a short introduction. It was evidently a labour of love. Hamilton he had known intimately, and, after the poet's untimely death, he thought the best tribute he could pay to his memory was to bring out an edition of his poems. But it was a dubious service, the editor being, unhappily, a very unpoetical person. Probably, Eskgrove was not unconscious that he had taken upon him a task wholly beyond his powers. At all events he sheltered himself behind the appraisement of the *Caledonian Mercury*, which proclaimed Hamilton to be "in language, sentiment, and numbers a poet little (if at all) inferior to a Dryden, an Addison, or a Pope."

VIII

LORD BALMUTO

(1742–1824)

WITH the imposing names of Kames, Monboddo, and Hailes before us, it may seem as if there existed in the eighteenth century a tacit understanding whereby a Scottish judge should be, not merely a shining ornament of the law, but an ardent student of literature, philosophy, and the classics. It is well, however, to remember that there were judges in those days who evinced no interest in literature or scholarship, who had no yearning for authorship. Plain, blunt, honest men they were, living, it may be, inglorious, but not necessarily fruitless, lives. Though they never aroused suspicions as to their sanity nor countenanced the idea that copious libations to Bacchus constitute the sum of human happiness, many of them nevertheless furnish interesting studies in personality. Their characteristics were none the less sharply defined because their lives were lived on normal lines.

To this class belonged Claude Irvine Boswell, Lord Balmuto. A coarse-looking, strong-willed, passionate, boisterous man, with black hair and beetling eyebrows, he was by no means pre-

LORD BALMUTO
From the Portrait by Kay

possessing. His frame was tall, muscular, and extremely tough; but his mind was commonplace, his speech broad and harsh, his manners brusque, and his talents unexceptionable. He possessed some of the traits of Braxfield, but these did not include truculence and coarseness. He could sometimes be genial. He loved his joke, though he was wondrous slow in perceiving wit in others. He had an aristocrat's pride of family, and was lashed into fury when he learned that one of his daughters had eloped with her drawing-master. These and other traits, marked Balmuto as one of the last representatives of that school of Scottish judges who, flinging convention to the winds, kept life at the Parliament House from ever becoming prosaic.

Claude Irvine Boswell was born in 1742. He came of good stock, and was well brought up. His father, John Boswell of Balmuto, was the younger brother of James Boswell of Auchinleck, and was therefore a kinsman of the biographer of Dr. Johnson. He was a Writer to the Signet, and managed to amass sufficient wealth to purchase Balmuto, a small and rather bleak estate, a few miles north of Burntisland. He died, however, while his son, Claude, was still a child.

The education of the boy devolved upon the mother, who is said to have been a woman of uncommon mental energy, and extremely pious. At that time Mr. Barclay of Dalkeith was accounted the ablest and most successful of pedagogues in the vicinity of Edinburgh, and to his school many of the Scottish aristocracy sent their sons to receive the rudiments of education. It was this teacher's proud boast that he had had as a pupil—Lord Loughborough—one of the most illustrious of Lord Chancellors. To the Dalkeith school Boswell was sent at the age of six. Here he became acquainted with Henry Dundas, afterwards Lord Melville, and commenced a friendship which lasted until the latter's death in 1811.

At a later stage the lad was placed under Mr. Mundell, a well-known Edinburgh teacher. Nearly fifty years after, as a token of respect for this worthy man, a club was formed by his old scholars, who dined together at stated periods, when they tried to live their school-days over again, each being addressed by the name which he bore when he was one of the "schule laddies." So strict were members in the observance of this rule that any deviation was punished by a fine.

Boswell afterwards was a student at Edinburgh University, and was called to the Scottish Bar in 1766. In that year Sir David Dalrymple was elevated to the Bench as Lord Hailes, but Robert Macqueen was to enjoy a monopoly of the best things at the Bar for another ten years, before he was to achieve ignoble fame as Lord Braxfield. There were others, too, who had also attained to professional eminence. The times were therefore hardly propitious for a young advocate of mediocre talents and limited powers of application. But what Boswell could not win by ability, he obtained in a measure through family connections. His earnings, however, were never large, a circumstance which did not distress him, as he had neither the desire nor the incentive to work hard.

Much gaiety and frivolity were mixed up with the sober pursuit of the law. The son of an aristocratic family, and a beau and a wit besides, Boswell, of course, moved in the best circles of Edinburgh society. At the assemblies, his athletic figure and not unattractive gait captivated female hearts and made him an acceptable partner. In the tavern, too, he could make merry with congenial associates, for, although he never seems to have qualified as a toper, he thoroughly relished his claret, and the good cheer it brought in its train. He had also a taste for foreign travel, and when earnings were small, and fame a great way off, he spent a glorious six months on the Continent, drinking the cup of pleasure to its dregs. To a gay young man, Versailles had a special attraction. Thither Boswell bent his steps, and for a brief season was an eye-witness of what life was like at the French Court when the *ancien régime* was nearing its end, and the Revolution had already begun to cast its long shadows.

In 1780 he received his first promotion, being appointed Sheriff-Substitute of Fife and Kinross, a post which entailed hard work, no honour, and little pay. But it was the first rung of the legal ladder, and Boswell dare not despise it. For nineteen years he conscientiously discharged the duties, latterly made more harassing by reason of the political unrest caused by the upheaval in France. He, however, appears to have enjoyed the work, if one may judge from his habit, when he became a senator, of prefacing his decisions with the remark, "When I was Shirra' (Sheriff) of Fife"—a peculiarity reproduced in the celebrated "Diamond Beetle Case," to which reference will be made presently.[1] In the humbler office, he was a terror to evil-doers, particularly to the turbulent Fife boatmen.

With Monboddo's death in 1799 came his opportunity. He was raised to the Bench with the title of Lord Balmuto. For nearly three-and-twenty years he dispensed justice in the Parliament House. It was a period marking a distinct breach of continuity with the past. When Balmuto ascended the Bench, Braxfield had practically closed his sinister career, but the atmosphere of the Bench was still Braxfieldian. Judges still demeaned their position by coarse and dissolute habits, by indecorum, by eccentricity, and by the most barefaced political bias. But ere Balmuto had run his course a remarkable change for the better had been wrought. The Braxfieldian tradition had become but a shadow of its former self.

With the growing improvement of manners, there had come a higher standard of judicial rectitude. There were no more "characters" on the Bench, no more judges whose buffoonery or drinking performances were the talk of the town. The Monboddos, the Braxfields, and the Eskgroves had gone never to return. Their successors, though hardly superior to them in ability and learning, paid far more attention to judicial propriety. They were more refined,

[1] Kay's *Edinburgh Portraits*, Pop. ed., ii. 190.

more cultured, more sober-minded, more self-respecting. Living wise and well-ordered lives, they raised the tone and temper of the Scottish Bench. Life at the Parliament House under the new order of things might be less picturesque, less dramatic, less mirth-provoking, but the majesty of the law was upheld as it had not been upheld for many a year.

Balmuto entered into the heritage of the past. He had neither the character nor the capacity to bring about salutary changes. His elevation came too late in life to enable him to emancipate himself from the thraldom of a tradition that had dominated the Bench for more than a generation. But with him the tradition may be said to have died. As his career drew to a close the character of the judiciary had changed so much that he was rendered singular by his broad speech, his dry, clumsy humour, his oddities, and his flagrant breaches of decorum.

His style and peculiarities are, it is said, faithfully reproduced in the *jeu d'esprit* called the "Diamond Beetle Case," in which the manner and characteristics of several of the judges composing the "last sitting" of the old Court of Session (July 11, 1808) are imitated. This effusion, which is believed to have been written by George Cranstoun, afterwards Lord Corehouse, was much appreciated by those conversant with the ways of the *noblesse de la robe* who were pilloried. Cranstoun thus tried to parody Balmuto's style:[1] "A'm for refusing the petition. There's more Lice than Beetles in Fife. They ca'

[1] Kay's *Edinburgh Portraits*, Pop. ed., ii. 241.

them Beetle-clocks there. What they ca' a Beetle, is a thing as lang as my arm; thick at the one end and small at the other. I thought, when I read the petition, that the Beetle or Bittle had been the thing that the women have when they are washing towels or napery with—things for dadding them with; and I see the petitioner is a jeweller till his trade; and I thought he had ane o' thae Beetles, and set it all round with diamonds; and I thought it a foolish and extravagant idea; and I saw no resemblance it could have to a Louse. But I find I was mistaken, my Lord; and I find it only a Beetle-clock the petitioner has; but my opinion's the same it was before. I say, my Lords, A'm for refusing the petition."

This is a caricature of Balmuto's forensic oratory, but as caricature is but truth overstrained, the specimen may be accepted as conveying the essential characteristics of his style. And certainly it does not predispose one to the view that his lordship was either a man of vigorous understanding or of education. Balmuto was no credit to his teachers. He was illiterate to a degree hardly imaginable in the case of one occupying his position. Braxfield was unlettered, but he never left any one in doubt as to what he meant. Furthermore, he was shrewd and logical. Balmuto, on the other hand, was not only without virile qualities of mind, but his powers of expression were feeble in the extreme.

One wonders if Sydney Smith had Balmuto in mind when he made his oft-quoted observation about a surgical operation being required to get a joke into a Scotsman's head? His lordship was fond of joking on his own account, but he nearly always failed to appreciate the jokes of other people. His jocularity he carried with him to the Bench, but the specimens of his wit that have been recorded are distinguished by crudeness more than anything else. One day a young advocate, in addressing him, made a bold statement, and was drawn up with the remark, more candid than polite, "That's a lee, Jamie." "My Lord!" answered the astonished barrister. But Balmuto only added insult to injury. "Ay, ay, Jamie; I see by yer face you're leeing." "Indeed, my Lord, I am not," retorted outraged innocence. "Dinna tell me that; it's no in yer memorial (brief)—awa wi' ye." This was more than the counsel could stand, and he instantly left the Bar. Balmuto thereupon chuckled; and beckoning to an advocate's clerk, he inquired, "Are ye no Rabbie H——s man?" Receiving a reply in the affirmative, his lordship sought this clerk's endorsement of the view that "Jamie was leeing." But the clerk upheld "Jamie's" reputation for veracity. Balmuto did not pursue the matter further. He had had his joke, "made Jamie stare," and was perfectly satisfied. Accordingly, he closed the incident by requesting the clerk to write out what was wanted, and he would sign it.[1]

This is the kind of pranks that Balmuto loved to play on unoffending counsel. He was what would be called, in the parlance of to-day, "a

[1] Kay's *Edinburgh Portraits*, Pop. ed., ii. 190.

rough diamond." To cumbrous wit and uncouth speech, he added a turbulent temper. When past his eightieth year, his lordship bethought himself of retiring, though his eye was not dim nor his natural force abated. This step he took in the beginning of 1822, but he lived for other two years, dying at Balmuto in 1824, immediately on returning from several hours' exercise in the saddle. His last years were beclouded by the death, under his own roof, of his kinsman, Sir Alexander Boswell, of Auchinleck, from the effects of a wound received in a duel with James Stuart of Dunearn.

Balmuto married in 1783 Anne Irvine, who is described as having been "gentle and lady-like." [1] Mrs. Boswell, who became the heiress of Kingcausie, bore her husband one son and two daughters.

In private life the undesirable qualities which Balmuto displayed on the Bench seem to have been kept in strict subjection. He is spoken of as having been both amiable and benevolent. One of his intimate friends was the brilliant Henry Erskine, whom his lordship frequently accompanied in his walks in the Meadows after the Court had risen.

An interesting glimpse of the home life of this judge is afforded by that accomplished Scottish authoress, Mrs. Mary Somerville.[2] Balmuto in his youth had been a dancing companion of her mother's, who gave him the nickname of the "black bull of Norr' away," in allusion to the

[1] *Personal Recollections of Mary Somerville*, 1873, p. 55.
[2] *Ibid.* pp. 55-56.

northerly position of his estate. Mrs. Somerville was intimate with one of his lordship's daughters, whom she pities having to lead a dull life. Often she passed a whole winter " in that solitary place, Balmuto." But her life in Edinburgh was equally miserable, she being " much kept down by her father," and not allowed to associate much with people of her own age and station. The result was, as already indicated, she ran away with her drawing-master, " to the inexpressible rage and mortification of her father."

Once Mrs. Somerville visited Balmuto, the occasion being signalised by a mad experiment that nearly terminated the career of his lordship and his son. The latter had a turn for chemistry, and his father being rather proud of the fact, took Mrs. Somerville to see his son's laboratory. The lady had never heard the word before, and not being reconciled to the " curiously-shaped glass things," and suspicious of the nature of the son's experiments, she beat a hasty retreat. Hardly had she left the room when " there was a very loud report, followed by a violent crash." On returning she found that the young man had been knocked down, that his father was trembling from head to foot, and that the apparatus had been smashed.

When Balmuto died, there passed away a Scots judge of the old school—honest, droll, and good-natured, but culture was not the poorer, nor law.

IX

LORD NEWTON

(1747–1811)

A LITTLE more than one hundred years ago, there might have been seen sitting on the judgment seat in the Parliament House an excessively, corpulent man with lustrous eyes, and a countenance as crimson as the robes he wore. His general demeanour was suggestive of listlessness and torpor rather than of mental vigour, and the sober and dignified graces of the law. Usually his massive head reclined on his chest or rested on his hands, which were crossed on the bench. To all appearance he looked as if he enjoyed, while wearing his robes, many hours of peaceful slumber. Yet this drowsy judge, who seemed to claim kinship with the Seven Sleepers of Ephesus, had both a quick ear and an agile intellect. Nothing that was of importance escaped him. Let counsel say something arresting, and instantly the head was upraised, and an eagle eye was upon him. But once the speaker had resumed platitudinising, down sank the head, and his lordship dozed until the next significant remark.

To those unacquainted with his lordship's

Photo, Swan Watson

LORD NEWTON

From the Painting by Raeburn in Scottish National Gallery, Edinburgh

methods of discharging his duties, it seemed hopeless to expect justice at his hands; but it was all a mistake, as an inexperienced advocate once learned to his cost. He was pleading very earnestly when he suddenly stopped, and remarked that it was unnecessary to go on as his lordship was fast asleep. But he was soon disillusioned. "Ay, ay," exclaimed his lordship, "you will have proof of that by and by." And so the young advocate had, for the somnolent judge luminously reviewed the case, and entered an emphatic and elaborate judgment against him.[1]

This senator, who seemed so singularly to combine lethargy with vigilance, was Charles Hay, Lord Newton, a man famed for "law, paunch, whist, claret, and worth."[2] His rubicund visage and slumberous disposition were directly attributable to the fact that he took copious draughts of liquor, being accounted one of the "profoundest drinkers" of his day.[3] His bibulous performances were really remarkable at a time when drinking records were not easily established. He could quaff three large bottles of claret at a sitting, and immediately thereafter dictate sixty pages of an important law paper without a hitch. He was a grave senator by day, and a reveller by night, and from all accounts he played this difficult part supremely well.

In Newton's case, the limits of physical endurance appear never to have been reached. His carousals were of the most protracted description. Often, after a night of hard drinking, he would

[1] Kay's *Edinburgh Portraits*, Pop. ed., i. 145.
[2] Cockburn's *Memorials of his Time*, 1856, p. 223.
[3] Kay's *Edinburgh Portraits*, Pop. ed., i. 145.

drive home about seven in the morning, sleep a couple of hours, and mount the bench at the usual time, looking the very picture of sobriety. A good story is told of a French visitor to Edinburgh who, on stepping one morning into the Parliament House, was amazed to see, in the dignified capacity of a judge, the gentleman from whom he had parted only an hour before in a state of intoxication.[1]

Newton's "daily and flowing cups," remarks Cockburn, "raised him far above the evil days of sobriety on which he had fallen, and made him worthy of having quaffed with the Scandinavian heroes."[2] But if Newton was a hard drinker, he partially redeemed himself by being a quiet drinker. So at least some of his contemporaries thought. His libations were attended by no quarrelling, no horseplay, no loquacity. The more he drank, the more amiable he became. What saturnine qualities lurked in his nature speedily vanished, and he became more subdued, winsome, and even circumspect than he was when sober. He had a pet notion that conversation, at least when it is of a sort that excites admiration, spoils good company. Consequently, he preferred to do homage to Bacchus by maintaining a respectful silence. Indeed, the only thing capable of ruffling his serenity on such occasions was the spectacle of a fellow-convivialist not taking as many or as full bumpers as himself.

This jovial, hard-drinking, lethargic, but very able judge was the son of James Hay of Cocklaw,

[1] Kay's *Edinburgh Portraits*, Pop. ed., i. 145.
[2] *Memorials of his Time*, 1856, p. 223.

a well-known Edinburgh Writer to the Signet. He was born in 1747, and, after an education befitting his station and future profession, he became an advocate at the early age of twenty-one. This precocity was due as much to natural ability as to industry. Hay's knowledge of the law when not much beyond his teens was such that he used to declare that he was then as good a lawyer as he was at any future period of his career. Besides extensive knowledge, he had the talents of an effective pleader. Eschewing everything showy or meretricious, he relied mainly upon the compelling power of a disciplined and vigorous mind.

Accomplished, shrewd, diligent, sociable, Hay was in high favour at the Bar; and in many of the famous cases of the last quarter of the eighteenth century, he played a worthy part. When Deacon Brodie found himself entangled in the meshes of the law through breaking into the Excise Office, Hay was employed as junior counsel. He also saw the Deacon expiate his crime on the gallows.

Hay had practised at the Bar for nearly forty years before a judgeship came his way. This tardiness was not due to lack of ability or experience, nor even to his foibles. What kept him back was the fact that he was a zealous Whig when Toryism seemed to have gained a permanent ascendancy. There was only one appointment to a Scottish judgeship made during the reign of "The Talents," and it fell to Hay, a circumstance of which he was not unnaturally proud. In 1806 he was raised to the Bench by the Fox

Administration, succeeding Lord Methven. His judicial title was Lord Newton, but in private life he was known as the "Mighty Goth,"[1] an appellation which may have had something to do with his enormous bulk, but more probably with his vehement espousal of the Whig cause.

Despite his somnolence, his inordinate love of strong drink, his oddities, and his miscellaneous shortcomings, Newton had more of the makings of a judge in him than some of his colleagues whose character for rectitude and industry was unimpeachable. What they would discover only after long and laborious excogitation, he would discover intuitively. His knowledge, insight, and judgment were eminently praiseworthy, and no one doubted the judicial temper of his mind.

And his heart was as sound as his head. He had a genius for friendship. Many detested his politics, but all admired him personally. He was unswervingly loyal, good-natured, fond of cracking a joke, relished lively but not too intellectual talk, and was the soul of a convivial gathering. He was an enthusiastic card-player. Indeed, it was sarcastically remarked of him that "cards were his profession, and the law only his amusement."[2] The only diversion which he positively disliked was punning, a practice invariably resorted to by his friends when they wished to tease him. He had also a marked antipathy to pompous and rhetorical persons; but he viewed eccentricity in every shape and form with a sublime toleration.

Nor is this to be wondered at since he himself

[1] Kay's *Edinburgh Portraits*, Pop. ed., i. 146. [2] *Ibid.* i. 145.

was much given to whimsicality. When an advocate, he wore the gown of Lockhart, afterwards Lord Covington. At last the garment became a thing of shreds and patches, and he was compelled to get a new one; but as he still wished to be thought the wearer of "Covington's gown," he hit upon the ingenious plan of having a portion of the original garment sewn with the new.[1]

He took delight, too, in pleasantry. On one occasion an advocate, unwilling to forgo a day's curling, failed to appear in a case for which he had been "briefed." The opposing barrister insisted on taking decree, but Newton refused to take this course. "No, no," said the kindly judge, "the cause may wait till to-morrow, but there is no security that the frost will wait for Mr. Millar."

Newton had no taste for literature, or for the society of those who were addicted to writing. He had also an unconquerable aversion to philosophers, and he was not enamoured of poets, save Burns, of whom more anon. Plain living and high thinking, he considered a drab existence. The height of human bliss was the company of wits who could make merry for hours over the wine-cup. It almost goes without saying that he was a member of every Edinburgh club where drinking and epicureanism were held in high esteem.

Chief of these was the "Crochallan Fencibles," a club which met in "Dawney" Douglas's tavern in Anchor Close, a place famed for good claret,

[1] Kay's *Edinburgh Portraits*, Pop. ed., i. 146.

uproarious mirth, and all manner of buffoonery—the scene, too, of the daily and nightly orgies of the Pleydells, the Fairfords, and the Crosbies. This tavern was "a good specimen of those profound retreats which have been spoken of as valued in the inverse ratio of the amount of daylight which visited them." [1]

"Dawney" Douglas, the keeper, was, like his patrons, a very jolly person, and was specially noted for his singing of a Gaelic song called "Crochallan" (*i.e.* Colin's Cattle). Hence the first half of the club's title. The other half was derived from a company of volunteers, which was raised to defend the country when the regular army was in America. The members of the club, which owed its inception to William Smellie, who printed the Edinburgh edition of Burns's poems, were each given some military title. Newton, fittingly enough, was Major and Muster-Master General of the corps. The latter office entailed the drilling of recruits. It was no easy matter to become a member of the Crochallan Fencibles, the custom being to subject candidates for admission to a species of horseplay by way of testing their tempers.

Newton discharged the duties of his office not wisely but too well. Burns, on being introduced to the Crochallans in 1787, declared that he had never been so abominably thrashed in his life.[2] The bard, however, stood the ordeal with wonderful equanimity, and commemorated the occasion in an extemporaneous effusion

[1] Chambers's *Traditions of Edinburgh*, new ed., p. 179.

[2] Chambers's *Life of Burns*, new ed., ii. 53.

descriptive of Smellie, who held the somewhat gruesome office of "hangman" to the corps.

Between Newton and Burns a warm friendship sprang up, though, probably, it was based upon the fact that they were fellow-Crochallans, rather than upon any literary interests. His lordship, however, was not wholly inappreciative of Burns the poet, for when Lord President Dundas, the elder brother of Viscount Melville, died in 1787, he urged the bard to mark the melancholy event by writing some verses.[1] Burns complied, but, as he himself admitted in a letter[2] to Newton enclosing the verses, the effort was not in his happiest vein. Be that as it may, Newton is entitled to the credit, along with Alexander Wood, surgeon, of having induced Burns to indite the elegy beginning:

> Lone on the bleaky hills, the straying flocks
> Shun the fierce storms among the sheltering rocks.

Newton was also a leading spirit of the *Ante-Manum* Club, "a jovial institution which contained, and helped to kill, most of the eminent topers of Edinburgh for about sixty years preceding 1818, when the degenerate temperance of the age (*sic*) at last destroyed it."[3] So writes Cockburn, who, along with Jeffrey, joined the club a few years before it expired, merely to get some idea of what a toper of the last age was like. Newton assiduously attended the meetings of this club during many long years, and when he died, the members, true to their principles, drank a

[1] Chambers's *Life of Burns*, new ed., ii. 222. [2] *Ibid.* ii. 224.
[3] Cockburn's *Memorials of his Time*, 1856, p. 224.

full bumper to the memory of their departed chief, and bowed reverently to his portrait, which was appropriately hung in the place where he passed so many nights of revelry. One ought not to omit to add that the *Ante-Manum* derived its name from a most excellent rule, and, looking to the state of hopeless inebriety in which most of the members found themselves when the hour of departure drew nigh, a most necessary precaution—namely, that all bills be settled in advance.

Though he was the fortunate possessor of two estates, Newton and Faichfield, a country life had few attractions for his lordship. It was too slow, too solitary, too melancholy. What signified the sober joys of the country, or the glories of a noble landscape to a town-bred man wedded to the riotous distractions provided by a tavern in one of the dark wynds of Edinburgh? Newton had his gods, but they had feet of clay.

Consequently, he never played the part of country gentleman with any zest. It is said that he gave some attention to improving the methods of husbandry, but he had scanty knowledge of farming. Being shown one day a field of unusually large turnips, his only remark was that those grown on his own land were no bigger than "gouf ba's" (golf balls)—an expression which his friends did not forget, his lordship being continually pestered with the question as to how his "gouf ba's" were thriving.[1]

Newton died at Powrie in Forfarshire in 1811. His earthly pilgrimage had lasted sixty-four years,

[1] Kay's *Edinburgh Portraits*, Pop. ed., i. 146.

which, considering that few men of his time quaffed more bumpers, spoke volumes for the toughness of his constitution. Newton was an eminent lawyer, an impartial judge, an honest, true-hearted man; but posterity, alas! thinks of him only as a wine-bibber, or, mindful of Raeburn's portrait, identifies him with the man "just awakened from clandestine slumber on the bench" (to quote Stevenson's description of the painting). So it rings true throughout the ages that—

> The evil that men do lives after them;
> The good is oft interred with their bones.

X

LORD HERMAND

(1743?–1827)

GEORGE FERGUSSON, better known by his judicial title of Lord Hermand, was one of the most extraordinary persons who ever attained the rank of a Scottish judge. His legal talents were admittedly unexceptionable. Neither at the Bar nor on the Bench did he rise above respectable mediocrity. What celebrity he had was almost entirely due to extraneous circumstances. By a strange irony his reputation as a judge is overshadowed by his reputation as a toper. Newton and Hermand "were great 'cronies,' and had many convivial meetings together";[1] but Newton, as has been shown, was an able judge and an admirable lawyer, as well as a noted drinker. Hermand, on the other hand, did not sustain the dual reputation. Incredible though it may appear, he is remembered more by his bacchanalian performances than by his labours on the Bench.

Cockburn, who married one of Hermand's nieces, and had therefore good reasons for minimising, if not screening his foibles, is even constrained to admit that this crazy judge "acted

[1] Kay's *Edinburgh Portraits*, Pop. ed., ii. 37.

LORD HERMAND
From the Portrait by Kay

in more of the severest scenes of old Scotch drinking than any man at last living."[1] What has been said of Lord Newton's predilection for card-playing might almost with equal truth be said of Hermand's filial devotion to Bacchus: Drink was his profession, and the law only his amusement. To quote again his candid relative: "Commonplace topers think drinking a pleasure; but with Hermand it was a virtue."[2] In his view there was something wrong with the man who dared to set limits to his capacity for bacchanalian enjoyment. A person who could not, or would not, drink whole-heartedly, was a person to be shunned by all who were concerned about the maintenance of human fellowship.

In his maturer years, Hermand unfeignedly lamented the fact that the business of drinking was no longer taken seriously, and did his best, more by example than by precept, to preserve a pastime (as he conceived it) that had been falling into disrepute. When some youths of a later age aspired to moderate drinking, Hermand was full of lamentation: "What shall we come to at last? I believe I shall be left alone on the face of the earth—drinking claret!"[3]

Nor was there anything forced or unreal in Hermand's pathetic solicitude for the cause of strong drink. He sincerely believed that a man would acquit himself better in all the human relationships, if he had respect for drinking. Liquor was a necessity of his being; without it, he was a poor, miserable creature. His lordship

[1] *Memorials of his Time*, 1856, p. 134.
[2] *Ibid.* p. 134.
[3] *Ibid.* p. 225.

was so convinced that alcohol was intellectually stimulating that he was confident that he could have converted the Pope if he could only have got his Eminence to sup with him. "And certainly," adds Cockburn, "his Holiness would have been hard to persuade, if he could have withstood Hermand about the middle of his second tumbler." [1]

Numerous anecdotes have been recorded, which shed a strong light upon his attitude towards drinking. Two young men, after spending many hours over the punch-bowl, had a quarrel, which resulted in one stabbing the other to death. The survivor was convicted of culpable homicide, but received only a lenient sentence, much, however, against Hermand's will. He felt that an injury had been done the cause of drinking, and was strongly in favour of transportation. "We are told," he said, "that there was no malice, and that the prisoner must have been in liquor. In liquor! Why, he was drunk! And yet he murdered the very man who had been drinking with him! They had been carousing the whole night, and yet he stabbed him after drinking a whole bottle of rum with him! Good God, my Laards,[2] *if he will do this when he's drunk what will he not do when he's sober?*" [3] This is just such a judgment as one would expect from a member of the notorious *Ante-Manum* Club.

With Hermand, says Cockburn, "the jollity of the Circuit was the only thing respectable

[1] Cockburn's *Memorials of his Time*, 1856, p. 135.

[2] Hermand thus pronounced "Lords."

[3] Cockburn's *Memorials*, p. 140.

about it. Nothing made it contemptible, even judicially, except sobriety. I once heard the servant of his serene colleague, Pitmilly, who had a strong taste for decorum and law, and none whatever for laughter or liquor, tell the chambermaid at Perth to bring his master a large kettle of warm water. Hermand, who was passing to his dinner at midnight, said, 'God bless me, sir, is he going to make a whole kettle of punch,—and before supper, too!' 'No, no, my Lord, he's going to his bed, but he wants to bathe his feet first!' 'Feet, sir!' exclaimed Hermand, 'what ails his feet? Tell him to put some *rum* among it, and to give it all to his stomach!'"[1]

It is consolatory to learn that Hermand's worship of Bacchus was, like that of his colleague, Newton, well-bred. It was characterised by no violence or coarseness, and by very little noise. But the amazing thing is that a man who indulged with unfailing regularity in copious libations should have lived to a patriarchal age. And not only lived, but worked, for he retained his judgeship until he was considerably beyond four-score years. Hermand would have proved a formidable problem to the temperance advocate of to-day. Drinking seemed to agree with him. At any rate, he had never any serious illness, and it was only rarely that he was muddled. The deeper the potation, the sounder he slept, and the fresher he rose.

But it is time to say something biographically of this remarkable man who saw nothing incompatible in the wearer of judicial robes being an

[1] *Circuit Journeys*, 2nd ed., p. 73.

out-and-out convivialist. George Fergusson was the eighth son of Sir James Fergusson of Kilkerran, the title being derived from the ancestral seat, situated among highly romantic scenery in the parish of Dailly, Ayrshire. Sir James married Lady Jean Maitland, the only child of Lord Maitland, eldest son of John, Earl of Lauderdale. Blue blood coursed, therefore, in Hermand's veins; and, despite all his devotion to the bottle, he never forgot that he was an aristocrat, a circumstance always duly betokened by his manner and dress, if not by his tastes and speech. Though born near the middle of the century—the year of his birth is usually given as 1743—he generally spoke broad Scots.

In 1765 Fergusson was called to the Scottish Bar. For the long period of thirty-four years he trod the floor of the Parliament House, but his practice was never large. In his earlier days, he was a fairly diligent student, though his reading was anything but systematic. As a pleader his career was distinguished by nothing uncommon, and gave token of nothing remarkable. But lack of knowledge, and only average mental ability were counterbalanced to some extent by intense earnestness. Temperamentally, he was the sworn foe of the phlegmatic and the lackadaisical. He never did things by halves. A man of tremendous energy, he rarely knew the delights of repose—except in bed. Whatever cause he espoused—be it strong drink, Calvinism, or the superiority of Scots law over English—he espoused with all his might. His characteristic restlessness evoked the witty remark that if he had made the heavens, he would have permitted no fixed stars.[1]

It was to the passionate intensity of his nature that Hermand owed what measure of success he obtained at the Bar. He made the cause of his clients his own. They deserved to win because they had put their trust in the abilities of George Fergusson. With quite exceptional force and zeal, he would drive home his view as the only tenable one. Indeed, such was the exuberance and the impetuosity of his eloquence that he literally foamed at the mouth, occasionally with unpleasant results to those who chanced to be near him. When he was pleading in the House of Lords once, the Duke of Gloucester, who was a considerable distance from the Bar, rose and said with pretended gravity, "I shall be much obliged to the learned gentleman if he will be so good as to refrain from spitting in my face."[2]

On Braxfield's death in 1799, Fergusson ascended the Bench as Lord Hermand, the title being derived from a small estate which he owned about sixteen miles west of Edinburgh. In 1808 he was appointed a Lord of Justiciary, in which capacity he was best known to the public. It is conceded that, as a judge, Hermand was conscientious and well-intentioned, but these qualities of themselves are sufficient to give him only a second-rate place among Scottish jurisconsults. Moreover, what merits he had were neutralised, to a considerable extent, by dogmatism, intemperate

[1] Cockburn's *Memorials of his Time*, 1856, p. 132.
[2] *Ibid.* p. 136.

speech, and overbearance. A finely-balanced judgment, which sees clearly the arguments of both sides and is slow to decide, he could not appreciate. Lord President Campbell was much given to halting between two opinions. This ruffled Hermand, who, on one occasion, in following Campbell, commenced his opinion with the significant remark, "My Laards, thank God, I never doubted!"[1]

This was the weakness of Hermand's position as a judge. It is conceivable, as Lord Morley says somewhere, that everlasting neutrality may degenerate into a tiresome affectation. At the same time positiveness is surely the last infirmity of the judicial mind. Had Hermand doubted, or at least hesitated more, his record would have been more brilliant than it is. But a fierce impetuosity and an intractable will drove him strange lengths. It was also against him that he had little respect for authority, and none for tradition. His contumacy was proverbial. He was a man of law who was pretty much a law unto himself—manifestly a most dangerous person. His law was not got from books; he brought it forth from the depths of his own wayward understanding. He was wont to say with more rhyme than reason, "My Laards, I *feel* my law—*here*, my Laards," striking his heart.[2] He was quite equal to rebelling against the high authority of an Act of Parliament when it happened to conflict with his own prejudices. Let a statute be quoted against him, and

[1] Cockburn's *Memorials of his Time*, 1856, p. 136.
[2] *Ibid.* p. 137.

he would exclaim vehemently: "A statute! What's a statute? Words, mere words! And am I to be tied down by words? No, my Laards, I go by the law of right reason." [1]

The "law of right reason" is all very well, but Hermand ought to have known, indeed, must have known, that nothing, not even the peerless wisdom of a judge, can override the force of a statute. Lord Holland called attention to this extraordinary outburst in the House of Lords, a fact of which Hermand was apprised by his colleague, Lord Gillies, who was always ready for some banter at Hermand's expense. But by this time the latter had either forgotten his ebullition, or did not choose to remember it. At all events, he endorsed Lord Holland's opinion, and talked glibly about the Court suffering from "the rashness of fools." But Gillies was not to be baulked of his prey. "Well, my Lord, but who could Lord Holland be alluding to?" "Alluding to?" said the wily Hermand, "who can it be but that creature Meadowbank?" [2]

Arrogant and capricious, Hermand was continually warring against all who dared to question the soundness of his judgments. For the Supreme Court of Appeal he had a marked antipathy. Once the House of Lords sustained the validity of a qualification to vote for a member of Parliament. Hermand denounced this judgment as not only bad, but so bad that "I defy Omnipotence to make it good." [3] But it would be foolish to take too seriously the opinions of a man who

[1] Cockburn's *Memorials of his Time*, 1856, p. 137.
[2] *Ibid.* p. 138. [3] *Ibid.* p. 138.

had no difficulty "in conceiving a world where twice three was not six."[1]

Another wrangle with the House of Lords occurred in connection with a case about a lease. The Court of Session believed it had the power to make a new contract for parties, different from the one which the parties had made for themselves, but Lord Chancellor Eldon and his colleagues thought otherwise, and requested the Scottish judges to reconsider the matter. Hermand's reconsideration took this form: "Why, my Lords, I beg to put a very simple question to the House of Lords. Suppose that the tenant had engaged to hang himself at the end of the lease, would their Lordships enforce that?" But Eldon was not to be caught. When the case came again before the House of Lords, the Lord Chancellor, after reading aloud Hermand's question, remarked, with the utmost gravity, "that he would endeavour to make up his mind upon the very important question put when the case should come before their Lordships in regular form." This, Eldon followed up by recalling old times when his friend, George Fergusson, and he "used to do battle at this bar in Scotch causes," adding, with a touch of raillery, that his learned friend had not then the admiration of the Court of Session which he seemed to have acquired since. Hermand, when he heard of this incident, exclaimed, with more candour than discretion, "If he knew the truth, sir—though this is a secret—he would find that I had not got it yet."[2]

Eldon's allusion to his early friendship with

[1] Cockburn's *Memorials*, 1856, p. 138. [2] *Ibid.* p. 139.

Hermand was quite apposite. They were frequently coadjutors, though it does not appear that the latter rated the talents of the future Lord Chancellor very highly. They were counsel once in an important Scotch entail case in the House of Lords. It was Eldon's first appearance before that august tribunal over which he was one day to preside, and he felt rather nervous. So he resorted to the doubtful expedient of writing his speech, and then reading it over to Hermand to see if it would do. "Do, sir!" said Hermand, "it is delightful—absolutely delightful! I could listen to it for ever. It is so beautifully written, and so beautifully read! But, sir, it's the greatest nonsense. It may do very well for an English Chancellor; but it would disgrace a clerk with us." [1]

But if Hermand had a caustic tongue and a defiant manner, it is none the less true that his bark was worse than his bite. He attracted more than he repelled. Under a rough exterior there beat a warm heart. He was thoroughly human, and all his excesses and peculiarities of speech and action only added piquancy to his character. With the members of the Bar he was a favourite, despite the fact that many of them could recount rather trying ordeals when he was on the war-path.

Hermand's forceful and quixotic personality appealed to the public far more than that of any other Scottish judge of his time. His doings and sayings were talked about and laughed over as those of a "public character." His unconventionality, his tempestuous spirit, his indis-

[1] Cockburn's *Memorials of his Time*, 1856, p. 137.

cretions, his astounding extravagances, his wild manner and wilder habits—all these invested his individuality with an element of interest, even of charm, which appealed to all sorts and conditions of men. "Was he in an argument, or at whist, or over his wine; in court, or at an election, or a road meeting; consulting with a ploughman, or talking with a child; he was sure to blaze out in a style that nobody could have fancied, or could resist enjoying."[1] The broad humanity of the man was overpowering.

Always a "good hater" (to use Dr. Johnson's phrase), there was yet no enemy to which his heart, under propitious conditions, would not soften. No love was lost between Hermand and his colleague, Lord Cullen. For several years they did not meet socially, but once, being on circuit duty in the West of Scotland, they renewed acquaintance, by compulsion rather than by choice, at the supper table of an inn on the shores of Loch Fyne. The ice was hard to break, but copious supplies of liquor did what was needful. Soon the mirth grew fast and furious, and, after several hours' carousing, the two judges embraced and vowed eternal friendship, toasted wives, and delighted the younger legal members of the company by imitating the oddities of their judicial brethren. Cockburn, who was an eye-witness of this strange spectacle, says Cullen was compelled to keep his bed next day as the result of his potation; "but the immortal head of Hermand was clear and cool in the morning by six; and after a short time of business and a

[1] Cockburn's *Memorials of his Time*, 1856, p. 133.

long sail, he returned to the charge at dinner with a picturesque and cordial exuberance of spirits which the concentrated kindness and gaiety of all Argyllshire could not have equalled."[1]

If more proof were needed of Hermand's soundness of heart, we should find it in his passionate fondness for the young. He thoroughly understood children. His way with grown-up people was not exactly winsome, but where children were concerned, his manner was altogether different. To know Hermand at his best, one had to see him talking gaily to a group of boys. And age never weakened the bond of sympathy. When he had reached fourscore years, he was wont to engage his grand-nephew, aged ten, in a game of bowls. "No wonder," he said, "that that little fellow and I are such friends. There are just seventy years between us."[2]

"Crabbed age and youth," says the great dramatist, cannot live together. Hermand's case provided a singular instance to the contrary. An English midshipman having killed a much bigger lad in self-defence, was tried at Glasgow before his lordship. The sight of a sailor boy wearing his uniform at once touched the compassionate heart of the judge. He at first refused "to try a child," but when he found this position untenable, he sought refuge in another. The indictment, which bore that the prisoner had killed the deceased "wickedly and feloniously," having been read, Hermand said, "Well, my

[1] *Circuit Journeys*, p. 88.
[2] Cockburn's *Memorials of his Time*, 1856, p. 140.

young friend, this is not true, is it? Are you guilty or not guilty?" "Not guilty, my Lord," came the reassuring reply. "I'll be sworn you're not." The remark did credit to Hermand's goodness of heart; but it was highly improper, and reflected only too accurately the spirit in which he tried the case. But, despite his sympathy, the guilt of the young midshipman was fully established. The sentence, however, was of the most lenient description, the lad being sent to prison for only a few days.[1]

Hermand, like his predecessor, Braxfield, was a strong Tory. He was one of the judges in the trial of Baird and M'Laren, who were convicted at Edinburgh in 1817 of having delivered seditious speeches near Kilmarnock, and sentenced to six months' imprisonment. But though he felt keenly on political matters, and had grave misgivings about reform, he does not appear to have tarnished his judicial reputation in the way that Braxfield did. He did not allow his Toryism to blind his judgment or to do violence to his sense of justice. He could even keep a corner of his heart for certain Whigs whom he found good men and true, though despicable politicians. Lord President Blair he did not like, partly because he was not fond of claret and whist, and partly because of his politics; but when that great jurist died, Hermand wept like a child.

With all his imperfections, Hermand accounted himself a man of religion. He attempted to reconcile the irreconcilable—piety and inordinate affection for the wine-cup—and, in his own eyes,

[1] Cockburn's *Memorials of his Time*, 1856, p. 141.

he succeeded. He saw nothing inconsistent in a man drinking hard all week, and going regularly to church on Sundays. Of course, it might be argued that so hardened a toper had all the more need of religious instruction: they that are whole need no physician, but they that are sick. But Hermand was conscious of no backsliding; his penitential moments were few and far between. He believed himself to be a good Presbyterian, "with a taste for Calvinism, under the creed of which he deemed himself extremely *pious, with the indulgence of every social propensity*."[1] Nobody, of course, marvelled that this judge should unite within himself zeal for religion and an insatiable longing for good claret. It was Lord Hermand who did those things, and that was sufficient.

The truth is, Hermand put on his religion as he put on his coat—when it suited him. In the General Assembly of the Church of Scotland he was a familiar figure, and few important debates took place in which his voice was not heard. Cockburn has drawn a vivid picture of him declaiming in the Assembly against infidelity and religious doubt. "What a figure! as he stood on the floor, declaiming and screaming, amidst the divines—the tall man, with his thin powdered locks and long pig-tail, the long Court of Session cravat flaccid and streaming with the heat, and the obtrusive linen!" Addressing the Moderator, he declared, with the confidence of unimpeachable orthodoxy, "Sir, I sucked in the being and attributes of God with my mother's

[1] Cockburn's *Memorials of his Time*, 1856, p. 135.

milk." His love for his mother "exceeded the devotion of any Indian for his idol"; and under this feeling he told the Assembly that there was no apology for infidelity, or even for religious doubt, because no good or sensible man had anything to do except to be of the religion of his mother; which, be it what it might, was always the best. "A sceptic, sir," he added with righteous indignation, "I hate. With my whole heart I detest him. But, Moderator, *I love a Turk!*"[1] Yet this staunch Presbyterian, who would have extirpated heresy with all the zeal and fanaticism of a Torquemada, was himself not above doing very unorthodox things. On one occasion he interrupted a clergyman who was offering up a prayer at the opening of a Circuit Court, and requested him to be as concise as possible, as there was a great deal of business to be done.[2]

Probably the reason why Hermand lived so long and vigorously was not, as he himself foolishly supposed, because he drank so much, but because he took plenty of open-air exercise. Though, like that other bibulous law lord, Newton, he was inured to the miasmatic atmosphere of courts and taverns, he could fully appreciate the delights of the country, which Newton could not do. To Cowper's saying that "God made the country, but man made the town," he would not have demurred. Nothing pleased him more when the vacation came round than to retire to his estate, and live the life of a country gentleman. Hermand was situated in a rather bleak and

[1] Cockburn's *Memorials of his Time*, 1856, p. 208.
[2] Cockburn's *Circuit Journeys*, p. 42.

inhospitable country, but it was paradise to his lordship. There, dressed in deep " rig-and-fur," with black-and-white striped woollen stockings, a grey felt hat on his head, stout shoes on his feet, and a weeding hoe in his hand, he might be seen going forth, with " shining morning face," for a long summer day's work on his farm. He was an enthusiastic agriculturist, and spent much time and money in improving the lands of Hermand. He was also a generous landlord, and was at great pains to cultivate good relations with those employed upon his estate.

On Sundays he occupied the Hermand pew in the parish church. Seated beside him was his favourite Newfoundland dog, Dolphin, whose paws rested unceremoniously on the book-board. Dolphin was most exemplary in his church attendance, for whether his master went to the kirk or not, he at any rate was there. Indeed, such was Dolphin's appetite for sermons that when there was no service in the parish church, he did not disdain the humble meeting-house of the Dissenter.[1]

Hermand generally employed himself on his way to the parish church in switching down obnoxious weeds, which he performed with a cane to which a bill-hook was attached. One Sunday he found so many weeds that when the church was reached the service was over. " Dear me! is't a' owre already ? " said Hermand to the first group of homeward-bound worshippers he met. " I may just gang my way back again."[2]

Hermand was not a man to be trifled with,

[1] Kay's *Edinburgh Portraits*, Pop. ed., ii. 40. [2] *Ibid.* ii. 40.

least of all on the Bench. There were probably more "scenes" in his court than in that of any of his colleagues. He had peculiar ideas, and more peculiar ways of enforcing them, with the result that judicial decorum was often entirely lost sight of. He was presiding once at a trial, in which life and death were at stake, when the solemnity of the proceedings was suddenly disturbed by a musical box giving forth the air of "Jack's Alive." His lordship was furious. "Macer," he shouted, "what in the name of—— is that?" The officer, however, could not solve the mystery any more than his lordship, and was frantically looking round for the offender, when a person sitting in court answered, "It's 'Jack's Alive,' my Lord." "Dead or alive, put him out this moment," roared the enraged judge. "We canna grup him, my Lord," was the reply. "If he has the art of h——, let every man assist to arraign him before me, that I may commit him for this outrage and contempt," rejoined Hermand. By this time the tune had ceased, and the macer blandly informed his lordship that the offender had escaped. Hermand was, of course, indignant, but not being able to improve matters, the trial was resumed. In a little, however, the strains of "Jack's Alive" were again heard. "Is he there again?" thundered his lordship, whose anger was now fanned to a white heat. "By all that's sacred, he shall not escape me this time. Fence, bolt, bar the doors of the court; and, at your peril, let a man living or dead escape." The court was now in an uproar, and there was a general search for the author of the unseemly disturbance, but, as before, all in vain. Whereupon his lordship declared, in more subdued tones, that he was now inclined to think that the sound was too ethereal for this world—" a *deceptio auris*, absolute delusion, necromancy, phantasmagoria." [1] Hermand never fathomed the mystery of how the jovial strains of " Jack's Alive " came to be heard in his court that day.

Hardly less characteristic is an incident which occurred in the Justiciary Court. Hermand having been disturbed by a noise asked the court officer the cause of it. " It's a man, my Lord," was the rather vague reply. " What does he want ? " " He wants in, my Lord." " Keep him out." But the man got in, and the noise was renewed. Again his lordship demanded an explanation of the renewal of the disturbance. " It's the same man, my Lord." " What does he want now ? " " He wants out, my Lord." " Then keep him in. I say, keep him in." [2]

Off the Bench, Hermand's irascibility frequently afforded much amusement to his friends, if torture to his victims. A waiter having smashed a decanter at a dinner-party, his lordship chased the man out of the room, jumping over chairs and other obstacles in his effort to capture his victim. The incident caused roars of laughter, and the dinner-party had hardly regained its composure when his lordship returned from the pursuit and resumed his seat as if nothing had happened.[3]

[1] Kay's *Edinburgh Portraits*, Pop. ed., ii. 39.
[2] *Ibid.* ii. 38. [3] *Ibid.* ii. 41.

Even more ludicrous is the story of how Hermand received the defeat of the Pitt Administration. He was proceeding to the Parliament House, and had reached the Mound, when he was informed that the Government had been ejected. Unmindful of where he was, his lordship gave vent to his feelings by shouting out, "They are out—by the —— they are all out, every mother's son of them." A lady, who happened to be passing, thinking that it was the inmates of a menagerie in the vicinity that Hermand was referring to, seized the judge in her arms and screamed, "Good ——! we shall then be all devoured." [1]

Cockburn speaks of Hermand being a great reader in his early days; but the remark applies rather to law than to literature. As life advanced his studious habits did not become stronger, for most of his leisure was spent either on his estate, where he indulged to the full in an out-of-doors life, or in convivial company, which was not calculated to increase his zest or his capacity for learning. Hermand, therefore, was not much of a bookman. Nevertheless, be it said to his honour, that he was one of the first admirers of the novels of Sir Walter Scott, though the romancist was the "Great Unknown" as long as Hermand lived. When *Guy Mannering* came out, he "was so much delighted with the picture of the life of the old Scottish lawyers in that most charming novel, that he could talk of nothing else but Pleydell, Dandie, and the high-jinks, for many weeks. He usually carried one volume of

[1] Kay's *Edinburgh Portraits*, Pop. ed., ii. 40.

the book about with him; and one morning, on the Bench, his love for it so completely got the better of him, that he lugged in the subject, head and shoulders, into the midst of a speech about some most dry point of law; nay, getting warmer every moment he spoke of it, he at last fairly plucked the volume from his pocket and, in spite of the remonstrances of all his brethren, insisted upon reading aloud the whole passage for their edification. He went through the task with his wonted vivacity, gave great effect to every speech, and most appropriate expression to every joke." During the whole scene, Sir Walter Scott was present, seated, indeed, in his official capacity, close under the judge.[1]

In private life Hermand was very popular. Turbulent and cynical though he was, his friends were many. They might laugh over his frailties, his uproarious animal spirits, his eccentricities, but convinced they were that, at bottom, he was the soul of honour. And, as has already been more than hinted, he was sociable, too. No convivial gathering was complete without him, for not only were his drinking powers very considerable, but he had a fund of pleasant humour and varied entertainment, which could keep a whole tavern merry for hours. He was "a prince of good fellows."

Outwardly, he had not the appearance of a roisterer. He was tall and slight, with bright grey eyes, thin and powdered hair which flowed down into a long gentlemanly pig-tail, and a keen expressive countenance. While his air and

[1] *Peter's Letters to his Kinsfolk*, ii. 121-122.

manner were those of a well-born and well-bred gentleman, his dress was antique. It was difficult to tell, as he trudged up the High Street of Edinburgh, whether he was a lawyer or a farmer, the garments pertaining to both being usually found upon his person. His dress, says Cockburn, was reminiscent of the days "when trousers would have insulted any company, and braces were deemed an impeachment of nature."[1] A narrow strip of muslin barely concealed his long neck, his coat sleeves were ridiculously short, while there was an undesirable display of linen consequent upon his upper and lower garments declining to meet. His legs were swathed in black-and-white striped woollen stockings, and shoes of uncouth make covered his feet. Sartorially, he was a curious compound of a hurriedly-dressed aristocrat and a happy-go-lucky rustic.

But Hermand was no old fogey, feeble in body and still feebler in mind, sentimentally doting upon the past, and everlastingly reiterating that the former days were better than these. He seemed to have discovered the elixir of life, the secret of perpetual youth. His mind was ever receptive of new ideas, and welcomed the progress of invention. When stricken in years he would talk fondly of the manners and customs of a time long since vanished, but he was of too buoyant a nature not to be mindful of the present, and keenly interested in the future. A vein of cheery optimism kept him from entertaining that unwelcome visitor of our mellow years—a morbid

[1] Cockburn's *Memorials of his Time*, 1856, p. 131.

interest in the "might have beens." "Let us drink and be merry, for to-morrow we die," is not a very exalted or helpful view of life; but Hermand, at any rate, was satisfied with it. No doubt, it was a fool's paradise; but then he had been playing the fool for so long that he could scarcely conceive of another, far less wish for it.

A bibulous man is usually scantily equipped with the domestic virtues, but Hermand seems to have been an exception to the rule. Cockburn, who had good reason to know his family life intimately, alludes to his "revering household." Hermand married Miss Graham M'Dowall, daughter of William M'Dowall of Garthland, who, after a long wedded life, survived her husband several years. There were no children. But while rather monotonous, his home life was far from unhappy, a fact which presumably was due more to the merits of his wife than to his own, for manifestly his mode of life was hardly conducive to his growth in domestic grace.

Hermand was mercifully preserved from that pitiless foe of old age—mental atrophy. His mind remained almost unimpaired up to the very end, while, physically, a slower walk and a more tranquil manner were all the marks that senility had stamped upon him. Scott remembered that when Hermand began to fail in his limbs, he was wont to observe that Lord Succoth came to court earlier than usual, whereas the simple fact was that his lordship himself took longer to walk to the Parliament House.[1] In 1826, after

[1] Lockhart's *Life of Scott*, new pop. ed., p. 584.

more than a quarter of a century of judicial work, he resigned his judgeship. His retirement was brief, for in the following year he died at Hermand, having reached the respectable age of eighty-four years.

XI

LORD ELDIN

(1757–1832)

As Lord Eldin had an irrepressible love of paradox, there can be no injustice in emphasising the view that his own career was a supreme instance of paradox. His record as an advocate was long, brilliant, and extraordinarily lucrative; his record as a judge, brief and impotent. It was assuredly not an auspicious day when John Clerk became Lord Eldin. The lustre of his achievement lay behind; the future had nothing in store, save five years of judicial barrenness, of decrepitude, mental as well as physical. If we mention Lord Eldin, the judge, it is only to point the way to John Clerk, the superb advocate, whose professional income for twenty years was never less than £5000 a year. The pleader far excelled the judge.

Born in 1757, John Clerk came of a family distinguished for "talent, caprice, obstinacy, worth, kindness, and oddity."[1] He was the eldest son of John Clerk of Eldin, who owned a small estate in the parish of Lasswade, Midlothian. Old Clerk fully maintained the

[1] Cockburn's *Memorials of his Time*, 1856, p. 272.

reputation of the family for ability and dogged determination. He was a man of many accomplishments—a skilful draughtsman, an etcher on copper, a pioneer in geology, in which capacity he frequently accompanied the celebrated Dr. James Hutton on his excursions. But he was best known as the author of an *Essay on Naval Tactics*, which is said to have helped Rodney to his triumph off Dominica, and to have deeply influenced Nelson himself. Clerk's claim to have first suggested the idea of breaking the enemy's line in naval warfare has been disputed, but there is no doubt that his ideas materially contributed to British naval success during the spacious days of Nelson. Seldom, indeed, does a landsman become an authority on naval strategy. Clerk, however, could maintain that while his theories were not based on practical knowledge, his life-long interest in sea warfare had been quickened by the fact that several members of the Eldin family had served with distinction in His Majesty's Navy. His son, John, though he had little enthusiasm for the subject, was proud of the *Essay on Naval Tactics*. It was a striking reminder that his family had brains. In 1803 he prevailed upon his father to publish a new edition on any conditions which Archibald Constable considered "fair and proper." [1]

Old Clerk took a deep interest in the brilliant career of his son, and was wont to say in his old age: "I remember the time when people seeing John limping on the street, used to ask, 'What lame lad is that?' and the answer would be,

[1] *Archibald Constable and his Correspondents*, i. 59.

Photo, Annan

LORD ELDIN

From the Painting by Colvin Smith, R.S.A., in Parliament Hall, Edinburgh

'That's the son of Clerk of Eldin.' But now, when I myself am passing, I hear them saying, 'What auld grey-headed man is that?' and the answer is, 'That's the faither o' John Clerk.'"[1]

On the maternal side, Clerk could also boast of distinguished lineage. His mother was Susannah Adam, whose brothers were the celebrated architects of that name. It was the mother of Robert Adam who had a horror of David Hume, "the atheist," until one evening her son brought him to supper, when her antipathy speedily vanished. After "the atheist" had gone, the old lady, in blissful ignorance of the identity of her son's guest, complimented Robert on the company he kept, and said she liked the "large jolly man." Nothing could have excelled the exquisite courtesy of her reply on learning that the "large jolly man" was none other than the arch-heretic himself. "Well, you may bring him here as much as you please, for he is the most innocent, agreeable, and facetious man I ever met."[2]

Clerk originally intended to enter the Indian Civil Service, but just then his friends descried ominous signs in the political horizon, with the result that his thoughts were turned in the direction of the law, the only other profession suitable at that time to a young man of rank and talent. Accordingly, after serving his apprenticeship in the office of a Writer to the Signet, and practising for a year or two as an accountant, he in 1785 was called to the Scottish Bar, and soon

[1] Cockburn's *Memorials of his Time*, 1856, p. 273.
[2] Alex. Carlyle's *Autobiography*, 3rd ed., p. 272.

was fairly launched on a career which was to bring him both fame and fortune.

Indomitable energy, intense zeal, wide and exact knowledge of the law, brilliant forensic gifts, and unfailing resourcefulness were the main factors of Clerk's success. He was not eloquent, nor emotional, nor profound; but he was usually shrewd, practical, relevant. No Scots lawyer of his time was more finely equipped with all the essentials of a great pleader. His coolness and self-possession, born of an unwavering belief that John Clerk was endowed with superlative gifts, amazed everybody, and, at times, probably himself. No rebuff deflected him from the even tenor of his way, no amount of legal hair-splitting confused him. He would neither be banned, cajoled, nor allured.

Cockburn notes particularly his uncommon zeal. "He did not take his fee, plead the cause well, hear the result, and have done with it; but gave the client his temper, his perspiration, his nights, his reason, his whole body and soul, and very often the fee to boot." [1] Clerk was no hireling plying his trade perfunctorily, and having his eye only on the filthy lucre. Like a good Cromwellian soldier, he made the cause he espoused a thing of conscience.

In *Peter's Letters to his Kinsfolk*,[2] Lockhart says that "by the unanimous consent of his brethren, Mr. John Clerk is the present coryphæus of the Bar. . . . Others there are that surpass him in a few particular points both of learning and of practice, but, on the whole, his

[1] *Life of Jeffrey*, i. 202. [2] ii. 44.

superiority is entirely unrivalled and undisputed. . . . Never was any man less of a quack than Mr. Clerk; the very essence of his character is scorn of ornament, and utter loathing of affectation. He is the plainest, the shrewdest, and the most sarcastic of men."

While Clerk's merits were undeniably great, his defects were by no means trifling. As he stood at the Bar, a diminutive, wizened figure with searching blue eyes, intellectual face, massive forehead (on which usually rested heavy-rimmed spectacles), and grizzly hair, always in disorder, he looked every inch a pugnacious person. Cockburn likens his face and head to that of a "thorough-bred shaggy terrier."[1] Carlyle, some hours after his arrival in Edinburgh for the first time, visited the Parliament House, where the only figure that impressed him was that of Clerk, "veritably hitching about, whose grim strong countenance with its black, far-projecting brows and look of great sagacity fixed him in my memory."[2]

It was Clerk's driving power, his intense eagerness that not seldom led to his undoing. He was foolhardy, censorious, violent. When there was nothing to thwart his purpose, he was orderly, sensible, and natural, but when obstacles were thrown in his path, he was a tornado, and was heedless of consequences. He would bully witnesses, insult opposing counsel, and even defy the judges. His attitude was that of a man who has taken up a cause, and must hew his way to victory with what implements lie readiest to his

[1] *Life of Jeffrey*, i. 200. [2] *Reminiscences*, ii. 224.

hands. Clerk was the gladiator of the Bar, and was there to win against all comers.

That he should find himself the hero of professional brawls was only to be expected. "His whole session was one keen and truceless conflict, in which more irritating matter was introduced than could have been ventured upon by any one except himself, whose worth was known, and whose intensity was laughed at as one of the shows of the court."[1]

Clerk had not much intellectual respect for the Bench. Lord President Blair was the only judge who elicited his admiration. He did not see eye to eye with Blair politically, but he knew a great lawyer when he saw him. After hearing the Lord President in a few crisp sentences demolish an argument which had caused him (Clerk) much trouble to rear, and which he believed to be unassailable, Clerk is said to have bitterly ruminated on his failure, and then to have muttered, "My man, God Almighty spared nae pains when He made your brains."[2]

His bickerings with the judges would fill a small volume. The line he generally took was that the judge who dared to be adverse was not merely defeating the ends of justice, but opposing him. It is difficult to know which to marvel at most—the monstrous attitude of Clerk, or the pusillanimity of the judges. There was the maximum of insolence, but only the minimum of reproof. Clerk was allowed to address the Bench pretty much as he pleased, and if he

[1] *Life of Jeffrey*, i. 202.

[2] *Peter's Letters to his Kinsfolk*, ii. 42.

chanced to be deficient in respect and courtesy, nobody regarded his misconduct too seriously.

Clerk was counsel for the prisoner, George Smith, in the trial of Deacon Brodie, and how he comported himself towards the judges, particularly to Braxfield (who ought surely to have been a match for him), has already been recorded.[1] An even more glaring instance of the liberties he took with the Bench was his altercation with Lord Glenlee, which created a scene fortunately rarely witnessed in a court of justice. The Court was in the act of deciding a commonplace cause, and Glenlee was speaking, when Clerk, who was counsel for one of the parties, attempted to interpose a remark. Glenlee, however, declined to give way. "Na, Mr. Clerk," he said, "I'm not to be interrupted. That's really impertinent." The remark lashed Clerk into fury. "Impertinent! I wish you would say that anywhere else." Glenlee, who in his young days was dexterous with the small-sword, instantly took up the challenge. "I'll say it wherever you like." The consternation which this angry encounter caused may be imagined.

Lord Justice-Clerk Boyle severely censured Clerk, and demanded an instant and ample apology. "My Lord," said the recalcitrant Clerk, "I'll make no apology." The brutal frankness of this reply only added fuel to the flames. Now came a peremptory demand for an apology from the united Bench. "Very well, my Lords, since your Lordships will have it, I'll make an apology. But it shall be an apology

[1] See pp. 110-111.

to the Court. I'll make no apology to my Lord Glenlee." This, says Cockburn, who was an eye-witness of the scene, "made bad worse; and there was a more positive order for an instant apology to Lord Glenlee. Then came the triumph of Clerk's skill. Drawing himself up, full length, on his sound leg, and surveying all the judges, as a terrier does a rat that he means to worry at a bite, calmly and scornfully, and with a half-smiling leer at what he knew he was going to do, he said, steadily and coolly, 'Very well, my Lords, since your Lordships insist upon it, I now make an apology to Lord Glenlee, *in respect of your Lordships' commands.*' These last words were spoken with the utmost scorn—as much as to say, 'What the better are ye of that, my Lord.' And everybody felt that the insult was repeated; but the Court was thankful to get out of the affair on any decent pretext, and I felt relieved when the scene was over." [1]

There were other qualities which did not tend to soften the asperity of this *enfant terrible* of the Bar. Conscientious, diligent, well-meaning, loyal, Clerk's character was yet not strong enough to cast out jealousy. He was inclined to be spiteful, and not above resorting to sharp practice, when those who were running the professional race with him seemed to be drawing abreast.

And his influence, great though it was, might have been greater, had he given less rein to paradox, and a biting humour. Both wounded his friends and increased the bitterness of his enemies. Lastly, but this is a venial fault—he

[1] Cockburn's *Journal*, ii. 207-210.

was vain. Cockburn thinks this too strong a word, but a person who dotes upon his own achievements, expatiates upon his own virtues, and proclaims by his actions, if not always by his words, that he is a very superior person, must not complain if he is taunted with being vain. Clerk was a very clever person, and he had the misfortune to know it, and to trade upon it. But clients were not inclined to lay too much stress upon his shortcomings. It was sufficient for them if he could win their case, and win their case he often did in most brilliant fashion. Consequently, briefs showered upon him, and when at his best, he had nearly one-half of the business of the Court of Session in his hands.

In 1806 Clerk was appointed Solicitor-General for Scotland. He was a keen Whig, and as in law, so in politics, he did not believe in half measures. On the acquittal of Lord Melville, Edinburgh was illuminated, though Clerk tried hard to rob the Tories of their triumph. The Lord Advocate being absent, he, as Solicitor-General, wrote to the Lord Provost, and warned him that if any demonstration took place it would probably lead to a popular outbreak, for which the Town Council would be held responsible. The Lord Provost took the hint, had Clerk's letter read aloud in the streets, and issued a proclamation that, in consequence of the Solicitor-General's objection, the magistrates trusted that the citizens would refrain from publicly testifying their delight at the acquittal of Lord Melville. But Edinburgh was illuminated, in spite of the Solicitor-General, though the display would have been on a more elaborate scale had Clerk not conspired against it.

In 1823 Clerk was raised to the Bench, and took the title of Lord Eldin. That the brilliant pleader should elect to sit among the judges whom he had so often treated with scornful contempt, fairly baffled the popular intelligence. On the day on which Clerk took his seat an old agent, mindful of John's resplendent past, was overheard saying, "Eh! is he gaain' up amang them?"[1] It was almost impossible to think of Clerk "except as a man who was born to tear and snarl at judges. In the wiry, uncombed locks, breaking out from below the wig, and the shrewd, sensible face, the contracted limb, and the strong arms, they saw the traces of a thousand tough battles, and could not believe that these were all over, and that John was henceforth only to be seated, decorously, on a high place."[2]

Clerk entered upon his duties with a severe handicap. He had attained the age of sixty-five, and was practically a worn-out man. Thirty-eight crowded years at the Bar had impaired his mental powers, and wrought havoc on his physical frame. Moreover, he was in financial straits. True, he had earned more money than any counsel of his time, but then he had a genius for spending it. Costly pictures, rare books, lavish hospitality, charity, and unbusiness-like habits were the sum of his improvidence. He therefore mounted the Bench rather by compulsion than by choice.

[1] Cockburn's *Memorials of his Time*, 1856, p. 408.

[2] *Ibid.* p. 407.

But even supposing his health had been good, Clerk was temperamentally unfitted for his new position. Many of the qualities that had distinguished him as an advocate were a hindrance to him as a judge. His erratic and volatile nature, and his liability to frequent gusts of passion were not conducive to success on the Bench. To add to his difficulties, his memory became defective, and ultimately failed altogether. On one occasion, a debate had been partly heard before him one day, and concluded the next. But in the later stages he forgot entirely what had been argued in the earlier, and actually proposed that the debate should be recommenced.[1]

After eking out an inglorious judicial existence of barely five years, Eldin resigned in 1828, and henceforth devoted himself to his pictures, his prints, his books, and his cats. He was passionately fond of the fine arts, and spent immense sums on pictures. A fee of one hundred guineas was once paid him. Next day, the agent who had employed him happened to call at his house, when Clerk said, "John, where do you think your fee is?" The agent pleaded ignorance, and then Clerk, with an air of triumph, pointed to a small painting of a cat.[2]

Eldin was not only a good judge of pictures and of sculpture, but he drew and etched cleverly, and was in the habit of gratifying his fondness for the ludicrous by pencilling any object that struck his fancy. It is said [3] that he furnished

[1] Kay's *Edinburgh Portraits*, Pop. ed., ii. 266. [2] *Ibid.* p. 267.
[3] Kay's *Edinburgh Portraits*, 1837 ii. 440 (*n*).

Kay with the original sketch of the "Three Legal Devotees" for his *Original Edinburgh Portraits*. He was a life-long friend of Sir Henry Raeburn, his acquaintance with the great portrait-painter dating from the days when he was a law student. As Clerk "had some skill of hand in the art of painting," he invited Raeburn frequently to his rooms, where learned discussions on "high art" took place. Of one of these occasions, Allan Cunningham [1] tells an amusing story. Raeburn happened to arrive at his friend's lodgings when the landlady was placing two dishes on the table, one containing three herrings and the other three potatoes. "Did I not tell ye, woman," said Clerk, "that a gentleman was to dine with me, and that ye were to get *six* herrings and *six* potatoes?"

Though he never had leanings towards authorship, Eldin had a genuine taste for literature. He was a well-read man in the best sense, and would surprise and delight his friends by the readiness and accuracy with which he ranged over a wide field of literary topics. Next to buying pictures, nothing gave him more pleasure than to buy rare books. An enthusiastic bibliophile, he kept a vigilant eye on the booksellers' catalogues, attended the dispersal of valuable private libraries, and revelled in literary treasures.

In 1801 Archibald Constable acquired the Gordonstoun library for a very small sum, and sold it shortly after to Eldin for not much more. Constable, who was not often caught napping,

[1] *Lives of British Painters*, rev. ed., ii. 261.

ultimately discovered that he had parted with the library at a ridiculously low figure, and offered Eldin £1000 and a pipe of port wine for the recovery of it. The latter, finding that he had not sufficient room in which to house so large a collection of books, agreed to the proposal, and the library once more passed into the hands of Constable.[1] The Gordonstoun library, which, it is interesting to add, was sold by auction for £1530 in 1816, was founded by Sir Robert Gordonstoun, one of the Gentlemen of the Bedchamber to James VI. and Charles I., and premier baronet of Scotland. His library was principally formed between 1600 and 1656, and contained a representative selection of the best authors of ancient and modern times, together with first editions of Shakespeare's plays. When purchased by Eldin the library was almost intact.[2]

Eldin was a connoisseur of no ordinary type. His house in Picardy Place, Edinburgh, was literally a museum of paintings, rare prints, etchings, sculpture, old china, and musty but expensive tomes. His consulting room, according to Cockburn, presented an extraordinary scene. "Walls covered with books and pictures, of both of which he had a large collection; the floor encumbered by little ill-placed tables, each with a piece of old china on it; strange boxes, bits of sculpture, curious screens and chairs, cats and dogs . . . and all manner of trash, dead and living, and all in confusion—John himself sitting in the midst of this museum, in a red worsted

[1] *Archibald Constable and his Correspondents*, i. 400-403.

[2] *Ibid.* i. 400.

nightcap, his crippled limb resting horizontally on a tripod stool, and many pairs of spectacles and antique snuff-boxes on a small table at his right hand." [1]

While the world was unanimous in praising the high quality of Clerk's brains, it was as decided in maintaining that his person was without form or comeliness. He was about as plain a looking man as one would meet in a day's march; and to his plainness, a contracted limb, which only admitted of his standing erect when he poised it in the air, added a touch of the grotesque. As he hirpled home one day, he overheard a young lady say to her companion, "That's Johnnie Clerk, the lame lawyer." Whereupon Clerk turned round and said, "No, madam, I may be a lame man, *but not a lame lawyer*." [2] And if Eldin was grotesque in appearance, he was slovenly in dress. He wore the oddest of garments. He looked like a man who, having lain too long in bed, had rushed to his wardrobe, and seized what clothes lay readiest to his hand. But, sartorially, much may be forgiven a bachelor.

Eldin lavished his affection on cats, as his predecessor, Gardenstone, had lavished his on pigs. Instead of a wife to grace his hearth, he preferred half a dozen cats. When a client called, Clerk would generally be found seated in his study with one of his feline companions perched upon his shoulder. But cats are not always the best friends when business has to be done,

[1] Cockburn's *Life of Jeffrey*, i. 204.
[2] Kay's *Edinburgh Portraits*, pop. ed., ii. 266.

and Eldin's affection for those animals was often sorely strained. One day, when pondering a law paper, a feline disturbance occurred at the back of his house, and so great was the commotion that he threw up the window, and tried *viva voce* to quell the row. This method, however, completely failed, but before resorting to stronger measures, Eldin magnanimously resolved to give the cats the full benefit of law as provided in the case of rebellious human beings. His lordship then slowly and solemnly read the Riot Act. The cats, however, remained obdurate, and it was not until the judge had fired a pistol among them that the animals scampered off.[1]

To see Clerk at the Bar or on the Bench was to behold an irritable, morose, and highly contentious man. But once beyond the precincts of the Parliament House, it did not take long to discover that there was another and more genial side to his character. His social capacity was great. He cut a pretty respectable figure in Edinburgh society, frequented the company of wits and men of fashion, was fond of clever, lively talk, and by no means despised the good cheer provided by the tavern. He had not the bacchanalian talents of a Hermand, but he often drank to excess. His most imposing orgy was the annual dinner of the Bannatyne Club, which he invariably attended, always to the pleasure of the company, but generally with disastrous consequences to himself. At the termination of one of those feasts, over which Sir Walter Scott usually presided, Eldin, while proceeding to his

[1] Kay's *Edinburgh Portraits*, 1837, ii. 441 (*n*.).

carriage, tumbled downstairs and broke his nose, an accident which compelled him for a time to live the life of a recluse. When he reappeared in Court, his nose was almost hidden by healing plaster, which, naturally, did not improve a countenance never regarded as attractive. Some one who indiscreetly asked how he came by his injuries, got for reply that they had been caused by his lordship's studies. "Studies!" exclaimed the bewildered inquirer. "Yes," continued Eldin. "Ye've heard, nae doot, about 'Coke upon Littleton,' but I suppose you never heard of 'Clerk upon *Stair*'"—a joke which the juridical student greatly relished.[1]

Eldin's last days were sunless. There are few sadder spectacles than the decay of a fine intellect; and this, with the corresponding attrition of his physical powers, and money anxieties, was the burden which Eldin was called upon to bear during his declining years. Well would it have been had a man of his restless energy died in harness. But his life was prolonged for five years after his retirement from the Bench. He died at his house in Picardy Place in 1832—the year also of the passing of his great contemporary, Scott.

Eldin had reached his seventy-sixth year—a good old age, but his pilgrimage might have been even longer, certainly happier, had he toiled less strenuously, kept a stricter check upon the turbulent forces of his nature, and been less extravagant. But if Eldin failed, he was a brilliant failure.

[1] Kay's *Edinburgh Portraits*, Pop. ed., ii. 268.

XII

LORD JEFFREY

(1773–1850)

Sir Sidney Lee has defined biographic talent as the power to transmit personality. Judged by this standard, Cockburn's *Life of Jeffrey* does not stand high. No doubt Cockburn's narrative makes excellent reading. He sheds a steady light upon this side of Jeffrey's career and upon that; he tells us much that is of interest and value about the early days of the *Edinburgh Review*; he draws a graphic picture of the political thraldom of Scotland in pre-Reform days; but, biographically, he lacks the one thing needful—the power to transmit personality. The *Life of Jeffrey* is defective both in conception and execution. We get glimpses of the "famous little gentleman" whom Carlyle, not very felicitously, dubbed the "Scotch Voltaire"; but no more than glimpses. In vain do we try to discover in Cockburn's pages the man Jeffrey in his true proportions—the prince of Edinburgh Reviewers, the deep-dyed Whig who fought desperately to overthrow a political system for which his Tory father would have laid down his life, the embodiment, if not always of senatorial wisdom and learning, at all events of senatorial dignity.

What Walter Pater said of a much more competent literary craftsman, may be said of Cockburn, "He stood in need of technique, of a formed taste in literature, of a literary architecture." His sins for the most part are those of omission rather than commission. There are immense gaps in his narrative. Many important aspects of Jeffrey's character and achievement, notably the magnitude of his literary labours, are either inadequately dealt with or ignored altogether. This arose from no lack of knowledge or of veneration, but solely from his deficiencies as a biographer. He was simply, as Dr. Johnson said of Tom Birch, "a dead hand at a life."

It may, therefore, be safely asserted that the biography of Jeffrey still remains to be written. And the wonder is that no competent hand has essayed the task, since there cannot be any question that the elusive personality, shining talents, and manifold labours—literary, political, legal—of Jeffrey form a fit biographic theme. It is true that he was not a star of the first magnitude. A man of genius he certainly was not. Nor was he a thinker or a scholar. Nevertheless he holds a secure and commanding position in literary history. It is possible to assert as much without assenting to Cockburn's preposterous notion that he was "the greatest of British critics."[1] A man who failed to discern the true inwardness of the Romantic movement, and whose shallow view of the functions of criticism

[1] *Life of Jeffrey*, i. 1.

Photo, Swan Watson

LORD JEFFREY

From the Painting by Colvin Smith, R.S.A., in Scottish National Portrait Gallery, Edinburgh

spurred him to indiscriminate abuse of the "Lakemen," had not the vestige of a claim to any such title.

But no one can attempt an impartial survey of Jeffrey's twenty-seven years' labours in connection with the *Edinburgh Review* without being impressed by two things. The first is that he was a literary workman who had no reason to feel ashamed. The agility of his mind, the brilliance of his style, the multifariousness of his knowledge are fully attested by the two hundred articles which he wrote for his periodical. He plied a facile, lively, and amazingly versatile pen. Hazlitt tersely and neatly summed up Jeffrey's literary merits when he said, "He is a master of the foils; he makes an exulting display of the dazzling fence of wit and argument."[1]

The other truth is that Jeffrey made the *Edinburgh Review* a most powerful organ of public opinion. Brougham's saying that a better editor could not have been found in Europe is believable. Probably no editor ever gathered round him so much distinguished talent. The mere mention of the *Edinburgh Review* in its palmy days recalls such Titans as Scott, Coleridge, Hazlitt, Macaulay, Chalmers, Carlyle, the two Mills, and many others.

Francis Jeffrey was born in Edinburgh in 1773, two years after the birth of Walter Scott. His father, George Jeffrey, was one of the Depute Clerks of the Court of Session. He is described as having been sensible "and very respectable," but of a gloomy temper. A bigoted Tory,

[1] *Spirit of the Age*, 4th ed., p. 246.

Henry Dundas was, in his eyes, the soundest of administrators. When his son entered upon his university career, his sole concern was that he should not become tainted with Whig principles. He even went the length of forbidding him to attend the lectures of a brilliant teacher who was known to have dipped himself " deep in witty Whiggery." But, alas ! all his fond hopes were blasted ; and he lived long enough to experience the mortification of seeing his son become a zealous and active champion of the political creed which to him was anathema.

Jeffrey's mother was Henrietta Louden, daughter of John Louden, a " stickit minister," who ultimately found his true vocation in farming. Mrs. Jeffrey died when her son was only thirteen. She had " all the maternal virtues and was greatly beloved by her family," [1] which consisted of two sons (Francis being the elder) and three daughters.

While robust, Francis was slight and diminutive. Before he was nine he was a tolerably good dancer, but no other form of recreation, except walking, had any attraction for him. He learned his letters at home, and John Cockburn, " who had a school in the abyss of Bailie Fyfe's Close, taught him to put them together." [2] At the age of eight he was sent to the High School of Edinburgh, which was then at the summit of its fame. The rector was the celebrated Dr. Adam, a most estimable man, who was born " to teach Latin, some Greek, and all virtue." [3] Dr. Adam

[1] *Life of Jeffrey*, i. 2. [2] *Ibid.* i. 3.
[3] Cockburn's *Memorials of his Time*, 1856, p. 5.

lived for his school. Even on his death-bed his mind wandered to the familiar scene, his last words being, "But it grows dark, boys: you may go." Scott, who was one of his pupils, says, "It was from this respectable man that I first learned the value of the knowledge I had hitherto considered only as a burdensome task."[1]

Jeffrey's record at the High School was distinctly better than Scott's. He was recollected "as a little, clever, anxious boy, always near the top of the class, and who never lost a place without shedding tears."[2] His diligence and precocity were astonishing. Besides his school lessons, he was absorbed in books of travel and of natural history, and revelled in Hume's *History of England* and Middleton's *Life of Cicero*.

And he was making the acquaintance of authors as well as of books. One day in the winter of 1786–87, while sauntering down the High Street of Edinburgh, he stopped to look at a man whose appearance struck him as uncommon. A shopkeeper, noticing the incident, tapped him on the shoulder and said, "Aye, laddie! ye may weel look at that man. That's Robert Burns."[3] Shortly afterwards, he had the dubious honour of assisting to carry the biographer of Dr. Johnson to bed in a state of helpless intoxication. Boswell, on learning next morning who had been his bearers, patted young Jeffrey on the head, told him that he was a promising lad, and held out the hope that if he

[1] *Autobiography*. [2] *Life of Jeffrey*, i. 6. [3] *Ibid*. i. 8.

went on as he had begun, he might live to be a Bozzy himself.[1]

At the age of fourteen Jeffrey was sent to Glasgow University, where he remained two winter sessions. Though he does not appear to have won any honours, he was marvellously industrious. He took copious notes of the lectures, wrote long and elegant essays on the Immortality of the Soul, the Benevolent Affections, the Law of Primogeniture, and other exalted themes; tried his hand at poetry, story-writing, and literary criticism; won distinction in a debating society; wrote to his old teacher, Adam, proposing a philosophical correspondence, and, had the university authorities not forbidden the piece, would have acted Sigismunda in Thomson's *Tancred and Sigismunda.*

He also found time to harangue his fellow-students on Glasgow Green against voting for Adam Smith as Lord Rector, a proceeding dictated not by any personal antipathy to the author of the *Wealth of Nations*, but simply by that contrariness so dear to the student heart. The professors were in favour of Smith, and, of course, their wishes must be opposed. Jeffrey, on the whole, seems to have been a favourite with his class-mates, though they could not abide his "whim of cherishing a premature moustache, very black, and covering the whole of his upper lip." [2]

Returning to Edinburgh, he spent the next two years in attending law classes, in literary composition, and in browsing in the well-stocked

[1] *Life of Jeffrey*, i. 34.   [2] *Ibid.* i. 12.

library of his uncle, William Morehead, to whose seat in Stirlingshire he frequently repaired. Self-culture had now become a passion, and in the "dear, retired, adored little window"[1] of his garret in the Lawnmarket, he passed many hours in this commendable pursuit. He translated Cicero, summarised a history of Greece, indited a poem on dreaming, drew up an elaborate survey of ancient and modern learning, tried to refute Lavater, and wrote sixty essays, hoping thereby to emulate Addison, Steele, and Johnson.

Subsequently, he became convinced that "this sort of trivial writing" accomplished very little in the way of mental improvement, and he resolved to write no more. The essays treat of all manner of subjects, and while the thought is generally crude and the style commonplace, they are evidence of a degree of culture and a taste for recondite study unusual in a man so young. For example, one paper entitled "My Opinions of Some Authors," consists of a collection of fifty criticisms of noted English and French authors. But the most curious production of all is an analysis of his own character, which he found of such absorbing interest and importance, that the theme could not be compressed into less than seventy folio pages.

Meanwhile his passion for knowledge had suffered a check. In 1791 he entered Queen's College, Oxford, with high hopes. He conceived the University to be a great seat of learning: he found it only a place of "praying and drinking." Within a week of his arrival he writes of

[1] *Life of Jeffrey*, i. 21.

his fellow-students as "pedants, coxcombs, and strangers";[1] laments the "blank parties—the quintessence of insipidity; the conversation dying from lip to lip, every countenance lengthening and obscuring in the shade of mutual lassitude";[2] and conjures up visions of happiness at the Scottish Bar.

But sadly disappointed as he was with the atmosphere of Oxford, he did not regard the year spent there as wholly lost. If he did not drink deeply of the spirit of the place, he could at least console himself with the fact that Oxford had helped him to get rid of his "habitual Scotch," an object very near his heart. The success, however, was only partial, for, as Lord Holland wittily put it, "If Jeffrey had lost the broad Scotch at Oxford, he had only gained the narrow English."[3] Oxford had this further advantage that it gave him leisure in which to translate the *Life of Agricola*; to write essays on the philosophy of Happiness, and on Beauty (the latter subsequently enlarged for the *Encyclopædia Britannica*); and to compose a sermon, a form of literary exercise to which he was rather addicted.

Jeffrey was now nineteen, and had to bethink himself seriously of a profession. Some one had suggested that he should become a merchant, but he shuddered at the thought. While at Oxford he had had visions of making a living by poetry. "I feel," he wrote to his sister, "I shall never be a great man unless it be as a poet."[4] And certainly if industry could make a man a

[1] *Life of Jeffrey*, i. 35.
[2] *Ibid.* i. 38.
[3] *Ibid.* i. 47.
[4] *Ibid.* i. 69.

poet, then Jeffrey ought to have been one of the foremost. Unweariedly did he strive to scale the heights of Parnassus; but notwithstanding all his efforts, he wrote despairingly in 1792 that his poetry was not improving, and that if he could find it in his heart to abandon writing verses, he would be the better of it. Unfortunately, the seduction was too great, and he continued for several years longer to pour out odes, sonnets, elegies, tragedies, with a fatal facility. One of his poems, entitled "Dreaming," was in blank verse, and ran to about 1800 lines. He also entertained thoughts of publishing a translation in the style of Cowper's *Homer*, of the *Argonautica* of Apollonius.

But his poetic ambitions gradually waned in face of the stern necessities of everyday life. It was plain that he must don the gown of an advocate, and walk the floor of the Parliament House. That the law was his destiny was to some extent shown by his dialectical skill at the meetings of the Speculative Society, of which he became a member in 1792. He shone in nearly every debate, crossed swords with opponents like Brougham and Francis Horner, and read five papers in which he discussed, among other topics, the influence on Europe of the discovery of America, the authenticity of the Ossian poems, and the character of commercial nations.

Admitted to the Scottish Bar in 1794, Jeffrey began his legal career inauspiciously. Encouraged by the genial influence of his uncle, Morehead, he had imbibed Whig principles, and to be a Whig in the days when Henry Dundas was in the zenith of his power, and Braxfield was ruthlessly transporting men for having dared to advocate political reform, was practically to court social ostracism, and to completely bar the road of professional advancement.

Nowhere was the demarcation line of party politics more sharply drawn than in Edinburgh. The man who talked there of the sacred principle of freedom and of the supersession of Tory oligarchies had to be prepared for many hard blows. That Jeffrey should have turned pessimist is scarcely to be wondered at, the oppressiveness of his situation being such that he was glad for a time to quit his native city. "It is now," he writes dolefully, "nearly two months since I have been in Edinburgh, and I do not yet know how long it may be before I return to it. There are few places which have less hold upon my affections, and few in which I feel myself so truly solitary." [1]

We cannot but admire Jeffrey's steadfastness to principle in face of so much stern and relentless opposition. Had he only accepted unmurmuringly the old-fashioned Toryism which his father was so anxious he should fall heir to, his path to preferment would have been comparatively easy, for besides obliging patrons, he had considerable legal attainments. But his political faith was dearer to him than all else. Whatever others might do, he, at all events, must hold fast to the tenets of philosophical Whiggism.

Having come to look upon "a slow, obscure, and philosophical starvation at the Scotch Bar

[1] *Life of Jeffrey*, i. 63.

as a destiny not to be submitted to," [1] Jeffrey thought of trying to earn his bread by literature and journalism. He interviewed some London editors, but they did not give him much encouragement, and he returned to Edinburgh sorely dejected. An unsuccessful attempt to obtain a minor legal appointment still further confirmed him in his resolution to desert the law. The fight was no doubt a hard one, but Jeffrey probably was desiring more success than could be reasonably looked for. He had only been half a dozen years at the Bar, a period much too short in which to build up a remunerative practice, even assuming that his talents had been of the first order, and his politics of the most approved pattern.

Jeffrey's fortunes seemed to have reached their lowest ebb when an incident happened which was fraught with momentous consequences. Between 1797 and 1800 several young men of talent and social position settled in Edinburgh. Among them were Sydney Smith, a young English curate both witty and wise; Lord Webb Seymour, brother of the Duke of Somerset, who came to Edinburgh to study geology and mathematics with Playfair; and James Grahame, author of *The Sabbath,* "sepulchral Grahame," as Byron called him. These young men being sturdy Whigs were drawn to each other by the bonds of a common political faith. By and by they coalesced with the Edinburgh group of Whigs represented by, among others, Jeffrey, Brougham, Thomas Thomson, Cockburn, and Francis

[1] *Life of Jeffrey,* i. 105.

Horner who, according to Sydney Smith, "loved truth so much that he could never bear any jesting upon important subjects." At frugal suppers in humble lodgings, the party would foregather of an evening, when Jeffrey's talk, Brougham's high jinks, Grahame's Jacobite songs, and Richardson's flute helped to pass many a pleasant hour. But it was not all jollification. Daring spirits these young men were, and they had serious business on hand. They aimed at nothing less than breaking the fetters which bound them to a scheme of things—political, social, literary—that they considered had long been obsolete.

One stormy night in March 1802, the group met in the house of Jeffrey in Buccleuch Place, when Sydney Smith proposed that they should start a high-class magazine. This was agreed to with acclamation. Whereupon the resourceful Sydney suggested that the motto of the periodical should be *Tenui musam meditamur avena* ("We cultivate literature on a little oatmeal"); but as this was too near the truth to require emphasis, it was decided that a sober maxim from Publius Cyrus would serve the purpose more effectually.

Such was the genesis of the *Edinburgh Review*, the fortunes of which Jeffrey was to control for the next twenty-seven years. On October 10, 1802, the promoters of the magazine, in fear and trembling, launched their first "blue-and-yellow." The number makes curious reading nowadays. The extreme diversity of its contents, as well as the ability with which each subject is treated, and the high literary level maintained throughout, cannot but excite admiration; but criticism might have been as well served had the articles not been so unconscionably long. Literature, science, theology, travel, politics, economics, medicine are all represented. A glance, however, at the imposing but very unappetising list of articles suggests the melancholy reflection that the writers were expending a vast amount of critical acumen on literary trash. Jeffrey's review of Southey's *Thalaba,* covering twenty closely-printed pages, is the only contribution of any note. Who, to-day, has the courage to read Mrs. Opie's poems, or can summon up sufficient interest in Olivier's *Travels* or Dr. Haggarth's *Views on the Prevention of Infectious Fevers*?

But with all its blemishes, the first number of the *Edinburgh* abundantly showed that a new era in periodical criticism had dawned, and that the doom of the Grub Street fraternity was sealed. The journal was an instant success, and Jeffrey was compelled to admit that his gloomy prognostications as to its future were wide of the mark. "It is impossible," writes Cockburn, "for those who did not live at the time and in the heart of the scene to feel or almost to understand the impression made by the new luminary, or the anxiety with which its motions were observed." [1]

The success of the *Edinburgh* was mainly due to two factors. The first was that the founders of the journal, by insisting that the editor alone should be responsible for what appeared in its

[1] *Life of Jeffrey*, i. 131.

pages, prevented it from becoming, like its predecessors, the servile instrument of the bookseller. The other factor was the handsome, one might almost say lavish, payment of contributors, thus securing the best talent. At first remuneration was regarded as of no moment. It was, in Cockburn's phrase, "to be all gentlemen and no pay." But there came a rude awakening, and when Jeffrey took over the editorial reins after the first number, he told Constable, the publisher, to allow ten guineas a sheet. Not long after the minimum was raised to sixteen guineas, though two-thirds of the articles were paid at a much higher rate. The editor, on the other hand, received £50 a number, but when his duties became more burdensome, his salary was largely increased.

Although started as a Whig organ, the *Edinburgh* at the outset was by no means rabid in its political views. Even a high Tory like Scott found it nowise inconsistent with his principles to contribute largely to its pages. Gradually, however, Whig opinions came more prominently to the front, and Tory readers became fewer. With the publication of the twenty-sixth number, containing the famous Cevallos article, a climax was reached. So incensed was the Earl of Buchan by that article, that the noble lord, in order to relieve his feelings, kicked the obnoxious magazine into the middle of the street. The Cevallos article, which was mainly the work of Jeffrey, expressed grave doubts as to the success of British arms in Spain, and was regarded as highly unpatriotic. The indignation of Tory readers knew no bounds, and, as a matter of course, they stopped their subscriptions, a step which was speedily followed by the establishment of a new magazine, the *Quarterly Review*, more in harmony with their views.

And if Tory politicians were estranged, so were many influential authors. Sydney Smith wished the magazine to become "able, intrepid, and independent." In the matter of literary criticism, it became all three, and, unfortunately, vituperative as well. Those were the palmy days of slashing criticism, when to be candid was to be brutal. Byron, Scott, Wordsworth, Southey, Moore all came in for a share of rhetorical abuse. After reading the review of his *Hours of Idleness*, Byron is said to have instantly drunk three bottles of claret, and begun *English Bards and Scotch Reviewers*, which will remain an enduring memorial of the *Edinburgh's* diatribes. The irate poet, as every reader of the satire knows, did not fail to pay the journal back in its own coin. Who does not remember the lines upon the hapless editor ?—

> The Tolbooth [1] felt defrauded of her charms
> If Jeffrey died except within her arms.

But Byron lived to repent this youthful folly, for we find him writing to Jeffrey in 1815 to the effect that he would be "most happy to obtain and preserve whatever portion of your regard you may allot to me," and expressing the hope that they would soon meet.[2]

But perhaps the most notable of the numerous

[1] An Edinburgh prison. [2] *Life of Jeffrey*, i. 416.

literary feuds arising out of the acrimonious tone of the *Edinburgh* was that in which Jeffrey and Tom Moore were the protagonists. Reviewing *Epistles and Odes*, Jeffrey referred to the Irish poet as " the most licentious of modern versifiers, and the most poetical of those who in our times have devoted their talents to the propagation of immorality." This was more than Celtic blood could stand. Moore challenged his traducer to a duel. The challenge was accepted, and the pair, armed with pistols, met in a field near London, and, but for the timely intervention of the police, would probably have decided the merits of the quarrel most effectually. Like Byron, the Irish poet afterwards became a friend, and more than once in later years did he regale a company assembled under Jeffrey's roof with song and story. So often did he sing his song " Ship ahoy " that " the upland echoes of Craigcrook ought long to have had its burden by heart."

As early as 1807 Scott complained bitterly of the *Edinburgh's* politics, and the breach was further widened by Jeffrey's review of *Marmion*, his main stricture (which was grossly untrue) being that the poet had neglected Scottish feelings. Scott, like the noble man that he was, showed no resentment, and begged the man who had criticised *Marmion* so unfairly, to dine with him. Jeffrey went, and the evening passed pleasantly enough, but when the reviewer rose to go, Mrs. Scott, who had taken the critique keenly to heart, could not resist a parting shot. " Well, good-night, Mr. Jeffrey," she said, " dey tell me that you have abused Scott in de *Review*, and I hope

Mr. Constable has paid you very well for writing it."[1] In later years, Jeffrey saw that "the tomahawk style of criticism" was a mistake, and was generous enough to admit having said petulant things about Southey, and written "rather too bitterly and confidently of the faults of Mr. Wordsworth's poetry."

But if Jeffrey applied a rigid and superficial code of critical rules in a narrow and mechanical way, it must be placed to his credit that he introduced through the pages of the *Edinburgh* not a few brilliant writers. Carlyle's connection with the magazine began in 1827, and for some years Jeffrey and he were intimate. Jeffrey paid more than one visit to Craigenputtock, and Carlyle was a frequent caller at Craigcrook. But their temperaments were too dissimilar to permit of warm and sympathetic friendship, and there were frequent disagreements, if never an open rupture. Jeffrey complained of Carlyle being "so dreadfully in earnest," and Carlyle confessed that he did not find Jeffrey's "the highest kind of insight in regard to any province whatever. . . . In Literature he had a respectable range of reading, but discovered little serious study. . . . On all subjects I had to refuse him the title of 'deep.'"[2] The two men had long discussions and "argumentative parryings and thrustings," Jeffrey trying all the while to turn Carlyle from "German mysticism" to "dead Edinburgh Whiggism, Scepticism, and Materialism"—a "for ever impossible enterprise."

[1] Lockhart's *Life of Scott*, new pop. ed., p. 154.

[2] Carlyle's *Reminiscences*, ii. 252.

Carlyle at this time, however, was almost unknown, and Jeffrey was an "immense acquisition" to him. After the first interview, "the poor paper on Jean Paul" appeared in the next number of the *Edinburgh*, and caused "a sensation among the Edinburgh buckrams," which was subsequently heightened by the more elaborate and grave article on German Literature.

Macaulay was another of Jeffrey's "discoveries." In 1825 appeared the famous essay on Milton, which drew from the editor the memorable words: "The more I think of it, the less I can perceive where you picked up that style." For the next twenty years Macaulay was the mainstay of the *Edinburgh*, and would have become its editor had the magazine's headquarters been removed to London. There was no friend of his declining years for whom Jeffrey had a greater regard than for Macaulay, and this goodwill was fully reciprocated. One of the last pieces of literary work that Jeffrey did was to revise the proof-sheets of Macaulay's *History of England*—a task which he performed "with the diligence and minute care of a corrector of the press." [1]

Hazlitt's relations with the *Edinburgh* were not so cordial as those of Macaulay. Though he contributed frequently from 1814 till his death in 1830, he never was admitted to the inner circle. Nor did he add much to his reputation by his contributions to the magazine. Jeffrey and Hazlitt, though sharply divided by politics, were always good friends, and when the master

[1] *Life of Jeffrey*, i. 402.

of epigram was nearing his end, his quondam editor did him a turn which revealed the nobler side of his character. While on a visit to Carlyle at Craigenputtock, Jeffrey one morning received a brief and piteous note from his old contributor. It ran as follows: "Dear Sir,—I am dying: can you send me £10, and so consummate your many kindnesses to me?—W. Hazlitt." Jeffrey at once sent a cheque for £50 and, in Carlyle's words, "poor Hazlitt died in peace from duns at least."[1] Carlyle himself was a beneficiary. At a critical moment Jeffrey lent him £100, and on another occasion offered to settle upon him an annuity for the same amount.

Jeffrey's own labours in connection with the *Edinburgh* were truly herculean; and what makes them all the more wonderful is the fact that they were carried on for many years in conjunction with a large practice at the Bar, and an endless round of social and public engagements. During the twenty-seven years of his editorship, he wrote some two hundred articles. While they were neither profound nor original, as Cockburn alleges, they were generally very readable. Jeffrey had a wide range of subject. There was hardly a department of human knowledge into which he did not venture. Probably had he been less discursive, he would have been more weighty.

It is surprising that Jeffrey's contributors were so docile, for he took liberties with their manuscripts which no reputable author nowadays would tolerate. Once assured of their compe-

[1] Carlyle's *Reminiscences*, ii. 250-251.

tence, the modern editor allows his contributors pretty much a free hand. Not so, Jeffrey. He believed in rigorous editing, no matter who the writer was. In a letter to Macvey Napier, his successor in the editorial chair, he wrote: "I fear Carlyle will not do, that is, if you do not take the liberties and the pains with him that I did, by striking out freely, and writing in occasionally."[1]

Jeffrey used his editorial powers to the full, making, in some cases, so many emendations of one kind and another that when a proof reached the author, he hardly knew his own work. This incessant application of the blue pencil necessarily increased the editorial labour enormously; and it is open to question whether, in the end, it had all the value Jeffrey ascribed to it. In many instances, it is to be feared that the revision did justice neither to his contributor nor to himself.

In 1829 Jeffrey severed his connection with the *Edinburgh* on his unanimous election to the Deanship of the Faculty of Advocates. He thought it was "not quite fitting that the official head of a great law corporation should continue to be the conductor of what might be fairly enough represented as in many respects a party journal,"[2] and he was doubtless right. At the same time it is fairly chargeable against Jeffrey that he adopted a patronising tone towards literature when he began to rise in the legal profession. Indeed, he once confessed to a fear

[1] Macvey Napier's *Correspondence*, p. 126.

[2] *Life of Jeffrey*, i. 284.

lest he should be considered as "fairly articled to a trade that is not perhaps the most respectable"; and when, in 1827, he was hankering after the "dignified ease of a Baron of Exchequer, and his connection with the *Edinburgh* was whispered as an objection," he priggishly replied that from the very first he had "been anxious to keep clear of any tradesmanlike concern in the *Review* and to confine myself pretty strictly to intercourse *with gentlemen only*, even as contributors." [1] All this came rather badly from a man who, in his early years, found in literature almost his sole support.

Jeffrey is chiefly remembered as the first and most brilliant editor of the *Edinburgh Review*, though he himself would have preferred to win his crown of glory as a lawyer. Journalism was a congenial and withal lucrative occupation, but the law was his profession. So, while immersed in the affairs of the great Whig organ, he was sedulously cultivating closer acquaintance with the business of Parliament House. When Francis Horner removed to London, shortly after the starting of the *Edinburgh*, he left his barrister's wig to Jeffrey. After a fortnight's trial, the latter wrote: "Your wig attracts great admiration, and I hope in time it will attract great fees also." [2] The wish was gratified, though only after many lean and anxious years. In 1803 his professional income was only £240, and he thought of accepting a Chair of Moral and Political Science at Calcutta. But his talents as a pleader, his high (if somewhat austere) character, and his

[1] *Life of Jeffrey*, i. 280. [2] *Ibid.* i. 146.

literary renown all helped to overcome the deep dislike of his Whiggism. "His steerage," says Cockburn, "was that of a first-rate legal pilot." He was well versed in legal principle, understood the rules and philosophy of evidence, and was persuasive if rather voluble in his speech. By 1812 Jeffrey was enjoying a large practice.

Carlyle in his *Reminiscences* presents a pleasing picture of Jeffrey as he appeared in the Parliament House when he was rising into fame. His form was short and wiry, and the face, though neither keen nor handsome, was far from expressionless. The hair was black and bushy, and rather closely cropped. His head was usually wigless, for he maintained that no wig would fit it. He had a clear, sonorous voice, and there was unwonted vivacity in all his motions and gestures. He had not much humour, but he was an excellent mimic. Carlyle says that he became famous as an advocate by his saving from the gallows one, Nell Kennedy, a country lass who had shocked all Scotland by a wholesale murder, "done on her next neighbour and all his household in mass, in the most cold-blooded and atrocious manner conceivable to the oldest artist in such horrors. . . . Jeffrey by such a display of advocacy as was never seen before, bewildered the poor jury into temporary deliquium, or loss of wits . . . and brought Nell clear off." [1]

This performance brought Jeffrey almost more fame than he wished. He rose into "higher and higher professional repute from this time, and to the last was very celebrated as what his satirists

[1] *Reminiscences*, ii. 226-227.

might have called a 'Felon's Friend.'" He also made his mark as a pleader before the General Assembly of the Church of Scotland. Carlyle saw him in this capacity in 1814, and was impressed by his cleverness, vivacity, and "free-flowing ingenuity." On one occasion, however, he nearly lost caste. In defending a clerical client against a charge of drunkenness, he first contested the evidence, and then assuming its sufficiency, tried to extenuate the offence. "Was there," he asked, "a single reverend gentleman in the House who could lay his hand on his heart and say that he had never been overtaken by the same infirmity?" Instantly there were loud protestations, but these Jeffrey dexterously silenced by saying: "I beg your pardon, Moderator. It was entirely my ignorance of the habits of the Church," whereat members of Assembly laughed heartily.[1]

Jeffrey's domestic life was particularly happy. In 1801, when not earning £100 a year, he married Catherine, the dowerless daughter of the Rev. Dr. Wilson, Professor of Church History in St. Andrews University. The lady, who was a second cousin of his own, he describes as not showy or remarkable in person or character, but having "good sense, good manners, good temper, and good hands, and, above all, I am perfectly sure that she has a good heart, and that it is mine without reluctance or division."[2] Jeffrey and his bride took up residence in a five-storied tenement in Buccleuch Place, Edinburgh. Their means were small, but their love was great, and

[1] *Life of Jeffrey*, i. 183. [2] *Ibid.* i. 118.

during their brief union, for his wife died prematurely, Jeffrey experienced unalloyed happiness.

In 1810 his literary earnings enabled him to remove to a more commodious house at 92 George Street, which was his town residence until his final removal to 24 Moray Place. Here he received a visit from M. Simond, a French refugee, whose wife was a sister of Charles Wilkes of New York, a nephew of the notorious John Wilkes. The Simonds were accompanied by their niece, Charlotte, daughter of Charles Wilkes, with whom Jeffrey speedily fell in love. In 1813 he went to America to claim her as his bride. It was a tedious and stormy voyage, and Jeffrey had his full share of sea-sickness. Columbus himself, he told his friends, could not have been more delighted than he was when land was sighted. After his marriage he visited some of the principal cities of the United States, met many notable Americans, and had more than one political interview with President Madison.

The union with Miss Wilkes lasted thirty-four years, and, like his former marriage, was attended by much happiness. Carlyle frequently met the second Mrs. Jeffrey, of whom he has left a characteristic portrait. "She was a roundish-featured, not pretty but comely, sincere, and hearty kind of woman, with a great deal of clear natural insight, often sarcastically turned; to which a certain nervous tic or jerk of the head gave new emphasis or singularity; for her talk went roving about in a loose, random way, and hit down, like a flail, unexpectedly on this and that, with the jerk for accompaniment, in a really genial fashion. She and I were mutual favourites; she liked my sincerity, as I hers." [1]

Mrs. Jeffrey accompanied her husband on his visits to Craigenputtock. Once the Carlyles met them by appointment in Dumfries, where a day was passed. Jeffrey and Mrs. Carlyle went to visit a Mrs. Richardson, "authoress of some novels," and, Carlyle adds, "an old flame of Jeffrey's, perhaps twenty-five or thirty years before." Mrs. Jeffrey, who seems to have been cognisant of this fact, remarked "with easy sarcasm" to Carlyle, after the pair had gone, "These old loves don't do." [2]

From the start of the *Edinburgh Review* the circle of Jeffrey's acquaintances had gradually widened, and, shortly before his second marriage, he had lived down the animosity to his politics sufficiently to mix somewhat freely in Edinburgh society. Though not exactly a genial man, he had a certain charm of manner which even his literary adversaries could not resist. The man who could transform rancour, as in the case of Moore and Byron, into unstinted admiration, must have been possessed of some magnetic influence. Jeffrey, said Hazlitt, "is a Scotchman without one particle of hypocrisy, of cant, of servility, or selfishness in his composition." [3] But these qualities of themselves would not account for his capacity for comradeship. What attracted was his kindliness, sincerity, and charity. The truth is there were two Jeffreys. There was Jeffrey the critic, who found his keenest

[1] *Reminiscences*, ii. 248. [2] *Ibid.* ii. 247.
[3] *Spirit of the Age*, 4th ed., p. 250.

enjoyment in using the scalping knife, and there was the Jeffrey of private life—warm-hearted, chivalrous, and much given to hospitality.

He shone in mixed company, being an excellent talker, though a bad listener. He had no talent for anecdote, and was a poor hand at repartee. Hazlitt says [1] Jeffrey's difficulty was not to speak, but to be silent; and Lockhart, emphasising the copiousness and fullness of his conversation, confesses that it acted upon him "like the first delightful hour after taking opium." [2] Carlyle, on the other hand, thought his mimicry better than his talk. In the *Reminiscences*, he recalls how Jeffrey enlivened an evening in the drawing-room at Craigenputtock by mimicking certain public speakers. "The little man strutted about, full of electric fire, with attitudes, with gesticulations, still more with winged words, often broken-winged, amid our admiring laughter; gave us the windy-grandiloquent specimen, the ponderous-stupid, the airy-ditto, various specimens, as the talk, chiefly his own, spontaneously suggested them." [3]

Though a town-bred man, Jeffrey had a genuine love of country life. In 1812 he became tenant of Hatton, a small estate about nine miles west of Edinburgh. Here he passed three successive summers, and was supremely happy in entertaining his friends, in romping with children, and in drinking in the tranquil beauty of the place. Hatton was exchanged in 1815 for Craigcrook, a more pretentious seat pleasantly

[1] *Spirit of the Age*, 4th ed., p. 248.
[2] *Peter's Letters to his Kinsfolk*, i. 68. [3] *Reminiscences*, ii. 249.

situated at the foot of Corstorphine Hill, and within walking distance of Edinburgh. The house, which had been previously occupied by Archibald Constable, the "grand Napoleon of the realms of print," was merely an oblong keep with irregular projections, and a large round tower at one end, surrounded by "a bad kitchen garden" hemmed in by high and massive walls. During the thirty-five summers that he spent at Craigcrook, Jeffrey largely transformed the place, and made it at last a thing of beauty. Alterations and additions were from time to time carried out on the house, while the garden, which is supposed to have been in Scott's mind when he described the garden of "Tully-Veolan" in *Waverley*, was extended and remodelled.

With the acquisition of Craigcrook, Jeffrey's social instincts developed apace, and he began to entertain on a much more lavish scale. Not only his Edinburgh friends, but distinguished visitors to Scotland enjoyed his hospitality. "With the exception of Abbotsford," says Cockburn, "there were more interesting strangers at Craigcrook than in any house in Scotland."[1] On Saturday afternoons, during the summer months, well-known members of the Scottish Bar with their families might be seen wending their way along the spacious Queensferry road, intent on spending a few hours under the hospitable roof of the laird of Craigcrook. The company usually assembled about three, and after an informal reception, the guests would betake themselves to various forms of recreation. Some

[1] *Life of Jeffrey*, i. 236.

would climb the hill to obtain a magnificent view of the Firth of Forth and the Fifeshire hills; others would saunter in the garden and feast their eyes upon a wide expanse of glorious yellow roses; while a third party, of which the host was generally one, would enjoy themselves to their hearts' content on the bowling-green. And when evening shadows fell, the company would assemble round the festive board, where with good wine and good talk, mirth and song, the joyous day was brought to a close.

Comely Bank, where Carlyle took up house after his marriage, is not more than a couple of miles from Craigcrook, and when Jeffrey and the Sage became intimate, there was much coming and going between the two houses. In returning from town, Jeffrey frequently rode by Comely Bank. Here Carlyle would meet him, and the two men—Jeffrey on horseback and Carlyle on foot—would enliven the rest of the journey to Craigcrook by discussing German mysticism, or the virtues of the Whigs, or the last number of the *Edinburgh.* Sometimes these discussions were prolonged at Craigcrook till two or three o'clock in the morning, Carlyle, who was never awed by Jeffrey's intellectuality, more than holding his own. On Sundays they would wander about the woods in the vicinity of Craigcrook, or climb the hill to admire the glorious panorama of sea and land to be seen from that vantage-ground. Then, as the day closed, Jeffrey would accompany Carlyle most of the way back to Comely Bank, engaging all the while in the most lively talk.

The Craigcrook days were the brightest in Jeffrey's life. He loved his country home with all the affection with which Scott loved Abbotsford. It was a haven of rest, of gladness, where nerves were braced and energies restored. Regretfully he quitted it when the autumn was far spent; joyfully did he return to it when the time of the singing of birds had come. And if he was happiest at Craigcrook, he was probably most miserable when parliamentary duties necessitated a long stay in London. Though he went much into society, was feasted and lionised, and met many celebrities, he remained an alien in the great city to the last. Of Jeffrey's life in London Carlyle has left us two pictures. The one exhibits an over-worked, much-worried Government official, with impaired digestion and irascible temper, exclaiming, "I am made a mere post office of," because, forsooth, some letters addressed to his house, and which he opened, were not intended for him. The other picture shows Jeffrey baffled by the maze of London streets, and Carlyle coming to the rescue.

One pleasant incident was his dining with Wordsworth in the spring of 1831, when, despite the hard things Jeffrey had said about the poet, the two became "great friends." Wordsworth, he writes, "is not in the very least Lakish now, or even in any degree poetical, but rather a hard and a sensible, worldly sort of a man."[1] At Holland House he met Talleyrand, whom he found more natural, plain, and reasonable than he had expected. The Frenchman "did not eat

[1] *Life of Jeffrey*, i. 322.

much, nor talk much about eating, except only that he inquired very earnestly into the nature of 'cocky-leeky' (a Scotch soup), and wished to know whether prunes were essential."[1]

It usually caused Jeffrey some effort to unbend, but where children were concerned he had no difficulty whatever. He understood the child nature, and wherever youngsters foregathered, he readily entered into all their frolics. Calling one day, unexpectedly, on Sydney Smith, he found his friend absent, but his children playing in the garden. He immediately joined in their sport, mounted their donkey, and was proceeding in triumph round the garden, to the infinite delight of the children, when Sydney Smith and his wife appeared at the door. So ludicrous a scene fairly convulsed Smith, who, as he shook hands with his old friend, broke forth into the following impromptu :

> Witty as Horatius Flaccus
> As great a democrat as Gracchus :
> As short, but not so fat as Bacchus—
> Here rides Jeffrey on his jack-ass.[2]

Writing to his father-in-law in 1822, Jeffrey, aged forty-nine, laments the absence in London of the four or five houses "into which you can go at all hours, and the seven or eight women with whom you are quite familiar, and with whom you can go and sit and talk at your ease, dressed or undressed, morning or evening, whenever you have any leisure, or indisposition to be busy. In London I have only visiting acquaintances, at least among that sex, and that does

[1] *Life of Jeffrey*, i. 328. [2] *Memoir of Sydney Smith*, pp. 103-104.

not suit or satisfy me."[1] If the truth must be told, Jeffrey was rather partial to philandering. Carlyle makes this abundantly clear. "He was much taken with my little Jeannie, as he well might be. . . . He became, in a sort, her would-be openly declared friend and quasi-lover; as was his way in such cases. He had much the habit of flirting about with women, especially pretty women, much more the both pretty and clever; all in a weakish, mostly dramatic, and wholly theoretic way (his age now fifty gone); would daintily kiss their hands in bidding good-morning, offer his due homage, as he phrased it; trip about half like a lap-dog, half like a human adorer, with speeches pretty and witty, always of trifling import. I have known some women (not the prettiest) take offence at it, and awkwardly draw themselves up—but without in the least putting him out. The most took it quietly, kindly; and found an entertainment to themselves in cleverly answering it, as he did in pertly offering it;—pertly, yet with something of real reverence, and always in a dextrous light way."[2]

Among all his lady friends probably no one stood higher than Miss Clementina Stirling Graham, whose talent for impersonation and mimicry was the talk and the wonder of fashionable Edinburgh people at the beginning of last century. Jeffrey, as has been indicated, was himself a reputable mimic, but this excellent Scottish lady was more than a match for him. She would don clothes suitable to the character she intended to portray, generally that of a

[1] *Life of Jeffrey*, ii. 201. [2] *Reminiscences*, ii. 238.

whimsical Scottish lady of uncertain age, and would then proceed to "mystify" all those of her friends who were not in the secret. Jeffrey was one of her victims, and those who wish to know how he was "taken in" by the imaginary "Lady Pitlyal," one of Miss Graham's favourite characters, may read the whole story in her amusing volume, entitled *Mystifications*.

Jeffrey was not much of a traveller. His visit to America was mainly for the purpose of claiming a wife. In 1815 he ventured as far as the Continent, wandering through Holland and Flanders, and spending some time in Paris. But the interest of the tour lay in his visit to the field of Waterloo only four months after the battle. There he picked up a piece of cloth and a bridle as relics of the memorable fight, the evidences of which were even then being fast obliterated. He found almost nothing marking the scene of so much havoc and desolation. "The people were ploughing and reaping, and old men were following their old occupations, in their old fields, as if sixty thousand youths had not fallen to manure them within these six months." In 1823, in the company of the Wilkeses, he made a more extended Continental tour, visiting Germany, Switzerland, and northern Italy, and returning home by Paris.

Two years later he got what he calls "a glimpse of Ireland," where he saw Daniel O'Connell, by whom he was favourably impressed. But most of his holidays, when he was not at Craigcrook, were spent by the shores of Loch Lomond, which had a great fascination for him. For several years he put up at an inn, but in 1822 he became acquainted with the proprietor of Stuckgown who, observing his attachment to the district, generously invited him and his family to take up their quarters in the mansion whenever they came to Loch Lomond. The invitation was gratefully accepted, and the visits to the neighbourhood were renewed almost annually until the year 1838. On Loch Lomondside the days passed pleasantly in walking, climbing, and boating.

In Jeffrey's day the politician was anything but a type of "sweet reasonableness." The ethical aspect of things hardly came within his line of vision. The man who pursued the *via media,* who drew distinctions, who refused to consign all his political opponents to perdition, was irrecoverably lost. The Tories thought nothing too bad for the Whigs, and the Whigs were not slow to return the compliment. Nowhere was exacerbated political feeling more rife than in Scotland. What Macaulay wrote of the Romans "in the brave days of old" had no significance there :

> Then none was for a party ;
> Then all were for the state ;
> Then the great man helped the poor,
> And the poor man loved the great.[1]

The country was seething with partisanship of the most blatant kind. Jeffrey was a Whig, therefore he must be identified with what was revolutionary in the ideas of 1789. But nothing

[1] Macaulay's *Horatius,* st. 32.

can be farther from the truth than to represent Jeffrey as a rabid democrat or a full-blown republican intent on upsetting the whole body politic, and introducing the worse extravagances of the French Revolution. It is true that he found fault with the Whigs for being too aristocratic in their leanings, and too much disposed to leave out of account the people as a direct political element; but it is also true that he despised Radicalism, both popular and philosophical. Cobbett and Bentham were, in his view, frail repositories of political truth. Jeffrey was a thorough-going reformer like the rest of them, and both by tongue and pen sought to annihilate a political system not much removed from serfdom; but, as regards the attainment of his object, he had all a lawyer's love for what was constitutional and moderate. He had no belief in short cuts to political emancipation.

What Jeffrey did was to act as a restraining influence when the political passions of the people had almost reached a white heat. Convinced that the cause of reform was bound to triumph, he was resolved that zeal should be tempered by discretion. His policy was one of caution, though it never lacked courage. From 1816 onwards until the passing of the first Reform Bill in 1832, no political gathering of any importance was held in Edinburgh in which he did not take part. In 1816 he spoke in favour of the abolition of the income tax, and four years later he made a speech at the memorable "Pantheon meeting" which caused a great commotion in Tory quarters. Between 1821 and 1826 he was the principal speaker at a series of political meetings, when he tried to concentrate attention on general principles, and not on the triumph of party. All that pertained to the political and social well-being of the people was shrewdly and temperately discussed. Even industrialism, which was then in its infancy, came in for skilful handling. A speech of Jeffrey's explaining the "dangers and follies of unions and strikes by workmen" was published as a pamphlet, and 8000 copies were quickly sold.

Jeffrey's splendid work for political reform made his claims for legal preferment irresistible. Accordingly, when towards the close of 1830 the Whigs came into office, he was made Lord Advocate. "I wish my father," he wrote, "had lived to see this day . . . for the triumph I should have had over all his sad predictions of the ruin I was bringing on my prospects by my Whig politics."[1] It was a great honour, but it entailed much sacrifice and endless worry. It meant the forsaking of a comparatively tranquil and sedentary life, considerable pecuniary loss, and a bustling and harassing official career in London. So drastic an upheaval in the life of a man who had reached the mature age of fifty-seven was not to be lightly considered. Jeffrey, however, did not flinch. He entered enthusiastically upon his electioneering campaign, and such was the rapacity of the pre-Reform elector that in eighteen months he managed to dispose of £10,000 in trying to secure a seat.

He was first chosen for the Forfarshire Burghs,

[1] *Life of Jeffrey*, i. 306.

but was unseated owing to a flaw in the procedure. In April 1831 he sought refuge in Lord Fitzwilliam's pocket borough of Malton, where he had personally to visit six hundred people, deliver an oration on horseback, and pay £500 "for feeding this punctilious constituency." Three months later, on Parliament being dissolved, he was again elected for Malton. In December 1832, however, his wish to be returned to the first Reformed Parliament by his native city, was gratified.

Jeffrey was not a success in Parliament, which, considering the lateness of his entering it, is not surprising. Moreover, his official position prevented him from acting with that freedom and independence which are the privilege of the private member. His speeches were dull and formal, and were often spoken in a scarcely audible voice. One notable exception was a speech on Reform in March 1831, which was praised by Sir James Mackintosh, and published "at the request of the Government."

His parliamentary reputation rests on his skilful piloting through the House of Commons of the measures for parliamentary and burgh reform in Scotland. To Lord Holland he wrote hinting that there would be another rebellion if they were not placed on the statute book. This letter was shown to William IV., who was not at all alarmed, his only remark being that Jeffrey in using the word "mis-give" for "fail" had perpetrated a Scotticism, whereat His Majesty's Lord Advocate was much chagrined.

In 1834 Jeffrey resigned his office, and betook

himself to "the venerable functions of a judge." His leave-taking of parliamentary life was tinged with joy rather than with regret, since he felt himself being relieved of duties for which neither his health nor his temperament fitted him. Often had he pined "for shades and leisure, and the Doric sounds of my mother's tongue," and now his "bright vision of leisure, reason, and happiness" was to be realised. Before leaving London the Scottish members of Parliament entertained him to a "jolly dinner," at which "they staid till one o'clock, and were not all sober";[1] while the Press patted him on the back, and congratulated him upon returning to Edinburgh "with perfectly clean hands," his upright and honourable nature scorning jobbery.

Breathing once more the congenial atmosphere of the Parliament House, Jeffrey obtained a new lease of life. He cast all politics aside (a practice more novel then than it is now) and would not have bestirred himself at an election to help his best friend. His time was now almost wholly passed in the discharge of his judicial functions, and in the diligent cultivation of the society of his friends. The circle of his older acquaintances was alas! painfully small, and scarcely a year passed in which he had not to mourn the loss of some dear friend of his early manhood.

Scott's death in 1832 was a great blow, for in spite of many a feud, both literary and political, the two men never ceased to regard each other as friends. Their intimacy dated back to that wintry

[1] *Life of Jeffrey*, i. 355.

night in 1792 when, newly admitted a member of the Speculative Society, Jeffrey beheld the strange spectacle of a young man in a huge woollen nightcap reading an essay on ballads. This turned out to be Scott, who happened to be suffering from toothache. Jeffrey was introduced to him, and next evening he had a talk with him "in a small den, on the sunk floor of his father's house in George Square surrounded with dingy books." The friendship thus begun was maintained for forty years. No act of Jeffrey's parliamentary career gave him more pleasure than the moving of a bill providing for the appointment of an interim sheriff for Selkirkshire, thereby relieving Scott of the necessity of resigning owing to illness. It ought also to be remembered that when the stately Scott monument in Princes Street was planned, it was to Jeffrey that every one looked to write the inscription—a task which he admirably fulfilled.

An interesting friend of his later years was Joanna Baillie. Jeffrey criticised her plays somewhat severely in the *Edinburgh*, and for long she declined to be introduced to him. But there came a happy *dénouement* in the autumn of 1820 when they met in Edinburgh. For nearly thirty years they were good friends, Jeffrey seldom visiting London without calling on "nice Joanna Baillie . . . the prettiest, best-dressed, kindest, happiest, and most entire beauty, of fourscore that has been seen since the Flood." [1]

As a judge, Jeffrey did not win more than ordinary fame. He was conscientious, patient,

[1] *Life of Jeffrey*, i. 261.

urbane, learned; but he had two capital defects. He was loquacious, and he was long-winded. Circumlocutory himself, he rather encouraged than deprecated this failing in others. He never tired of argument. Cockburn says that though not exactly denying the necessity of rules for ending discussion, he scarcely liked them.

During the sitting of the Court of Session his duties usually took up nearly the whole day and most of the evening. But he always managed to get a little time for social intercourse, correspondence, walking, and reading. This last he indulged to the full, though it is amazing to think that so well-read a man should have had no library worthy of the name. He had a wretched collection of books, mostly unbound, and printed often in the vilest type. Volumes were frequently lost and others were misplaced on the shelves, but this did not seem to disturb him in the least. The Ciceronian adage that a house without books is like a body without a soul had less significance for Jeffrey than it would have had for most men occupying his literary position.

In his old age he formed a special friendship with Dickens, and was a warm admirer of his novels, frequently bursting into tears over the sentimental passages. Other favourite books of his declining years were the *Pilgrim's Progress*, Eldon's *Life and Correspondence*, also Burke's, "the greatest and most accomplished intellect which England has produced for centuries, and of a noble and loveable nature." [1]

Professor Gregory Smith has remarked upon

[1] *Life of Jeffrey*, i. 397.

the exceptionally limited nature of Jeffrey's literary output,[1] representing, as it does, a single type of composition almost entirely restricted to a single journal. Singular to relate, Jeffrey never wrote a book; he had not even the ambition to write one. Cockburn once exhorted him to try some original composition, and got for reply: "I have no sense of duty that way, and feel that the only sure or even probable result of the attempt would be hours and days of anxiety, and unwholesome toil, and a closing scene of mortification."[2] The modesty here displayed is most touching, but really Jeffrey had no cause to be nervous as to the result of any excursion into the domain of authorship.

In 1841 Jeffrey fainted while discharging his duties, and had to obtain leave of absence for the greater part of a year. He returned to the Court of Session in May of the following year, but his health was never quite restored, though he continued "to hobble along the broken arches" with as good a grace as most of his fellow-travellers. The vacations usually found him at "the paradise of Craigcrook," where he entertained on as lavish a scale as ever. In 1835 the beauty and comfort of his country home were augmented by a large addition to the mansion. During the building operations he spent several months at Skelmorlie, where he revelled in the magnificent scenery of the Clyde, lounged about the woods, and read snatches of Shakespeare, Keats, and Shelley.

[1] Article in *Chambers's Cyclopædia of English Literature.*

[2] *Life of Jeffrey*, i. 370.

The disruption of the Church of Scotland in 1843 moved Jeffrey profoundly. "I am proud of my country," he was heard to exclaim as he witnessed the procession, headed by Chalmers, on its way to Tanfield Hall to form the Free Church of Scotland. Though not much of a churchman, Jeffrey, by choice as well as by compulsion, took a deep interest in the events which led up to the Disruption. He was a warm friend of Chalmers, and had become convinced that the catastrophe was inevitable fully a year before it happened. In his judicial capacity he declared his sympathies to be with the non-intrusion party, and his hostility to what he held to be the novelty sanctioned by a majority of his brethren on the Bench, and confirmed in the House of Lords. "Did you ever see," he wrote on the eve of the Disruption, "a more tyrannical or short-sighted discussion than that on our poor Church in the House of Lords?"[1]

Jeffrey was also interested in the earliest efforts on behalf of social reform. Though too old to actively engage in the work he encouraged others. When Dr. Guthrie, the famous Scottish preacher, launched his scheme for the setting up of "ragged" schools, he had no more loyal and enthusiastic supporter than the judge.[2] Dr. Guthrie he envied "beyond all your contemporaries, though far less for your extraordinary genius and eloquence than for the noble use to which you have devoted these gifts." And he went on: "This last effort of yours is the most remarkable and important. . . . If I were young

[1] *Life of Jeffrey*, i. 389. [2] *Ibid.* i. 401.

enough to have the chance of tracing his passage to manhood, I believe I should have taken a boy on your recommendation; but, as it is, I can only desire you to take one for me, and to find him a better superintendent; and for this purpose I enclose a draft for £50, which I beg you to apply in the way you think best for the advancement of your great experiment."

The evening of Jeffrey's life was tranquil. He delighted much in the society of his grand-children, and was never tired of strolling through the grounds of Craigcrook. His intellect was as vigorous as ever, but his outward appearance was much changed. "The bright manly eye remained, and the expressive energy of the lips, and the clear sweet voice, and the erect rapid gait. But the dark complexion had become pale, the black hair gray, the throat told too often of its weakness, the small person had become still smaller, and the whole figure evinced the necessity of great care." [1] The last of the very few articles which he contributed to the *Edinburgh* after his resignation of the editorship, appeared in January 1848, and was an elaborate thesis on the claims of Watt and Cavendish as the discoverers of the composition of water.

On January 22, 1850, he attended the Court of Session for the last time. Though far from robust, he felt as well as he had done for some time, and was able to walk round the Calton Hill before returning to his house in Moray Place. That night, however, he had a bronchial attack from which he never rallied. He died on

[1] *Life of Jeffrey*, i. 394.

January 26, 1850, in the seventy-seventh year of his age, and was buried in the Dean Cemetery, Edinburgh, where he wished to sleep the long sleep.

Hazlitt says Jeffrey was neither a bigot nor an enthusiast.[1] The statement, unfortunately, is profoundly true. Had Jeffrey exhibited more enthusiasm, more sensibility, he would not have been so purblind a literary critic nor so impressive a failure as a political orator. He himself thought that his chief merit lay in "having constantly endeavoured to combine ethical precepts with literary criticism." It is indisputable that he raised the tone of periodical criticism, but his writing was cold, passionless, and mostly destructive, for he was without enthusiasm and without hope.

[1] *The Spirit of the Age*, 4th ed., p. 245.

XIII

LORD COCKBURN

(1779–1854)

CARLYLE on learning of Lord Cockburn's death, a few weeks after that of "Christopher North," wrote of him, with admirable point and picturesqueness, in his *Journal*, as "in all respects the converse or contrast of Wilson—rustic Scotch sense, sincerity, and humour, all of the practical Scotch type . . . Cockburn, small, solid, and genuine, was by much the wholesomer product; a bright, cheery-voiced, hazel-eyed man; a Scotch dialect with plenty of good logic in it, and of practical sagacity. Veracious, too. A gentleman, I should say, and perfectly in the Scotch type, perhaps the very last of that peculiar species."[1] Carlyle might have added that Cockburn was not only among the last gentlemen to flourish in a distinctly Scottish environment, but he was a link between the old school of Scots judges and the modern.

When Cockburn began his professional career, Monboddo and Braxfield were but newly dead. Eskgrove and Newton, however, were still to the fore, and were scrupulously maintaining the

[1] Carlyle's *Life in London*, ii. 158.

Photo, Swan Watson

LORD COCKBURN

From the Painting by Sir John Watson Gordon, P.R.S.A., in Scottish National Portrait Gallery, Edinburgh

standards of judicial decorum set up by their predecessors, the former by his drolleries, and the latter by his rakish accomplishments. On the other hand, the bacchanalian Hermand had just begun his judicial career, while Eldin had more than twenty years before him in which to display his coruscating talents as a pleader, before entering upon his brief and inglorious career as a judge. When Cockburn passed away the old type of Scots judge had long since vanished, and given place to the sedate and altogether irreproachable specimen of senatorial propriety that we know to-day. Whether the transition was accompanied by a substantial improvement in judicial ability is a point about which the wise man will prefer not to dogmatise; but there can be no question whatever that judicial morals were radically changed for the better.

Henry Cockburn was born in the year 1779. The place of his nativity was, curiously enough, a mystery to Cockburn himself, and a mystery it has remained. Two places the subject of this sketch suspected of the honour. One was an airy room in the tall " land " which formed the east side of the Parliament Close, Edinburgh. The other was the Mid-Lothian parish of Cockpen, where his father, who was sheriff of the county, subsequently Judge Admiral, and finally a Baron of Exchequer, had a small estate.

Cockburn, like Jeffrey, certainly did not become a Whig on the traditionary principle. He was nurtured in a hot-bed of Toryism. His father hated a Whig as he hated Satan, while his mother's sister was the wife of Henry Dundas, the most powerful representative of Scottish Toryism for a generation. The elder Cockburn was a sagacious man with a strain of austerity in his nature, which did not, however, prevent him from enjoying his joke. He was a good father, though a strict disciplinarian, his conception of the paternal office not permitting of easy familiarity with his children. Of his mother, Cockburn wrote: "If I were to survive her for a thousand years, I should still have a deep and grateful recollection of her kindness, her piety, her devotion to her family, and her earnest, gentle, and Christian anxiety for their happiness in this life and in the life to come." [1]

Cockburn's earliest memories were of an old-fashioned mansion standing within its own grounds on the south side of Edinburgh. To this house his father had removed from Cockpen. Adjoining it were the lands of Grange, Blackford, Braid, and Mortonhall, and as these were unenclosed, the boy roamed at pleasure as far as the Pentland Hills. In 1787 he was sent to the High School, a place famous for Latin, but so "notorious for its severity and riotousness" that he never could approach it without trembling.[2] And no wonder! During the four years he attended the school there were probably not ten days in which he was not flogged once. He never got a prize, once sat "boobie" at the annual public examination, and came to the conclusion that Latin was of no use except to torture boys. Be that as it may, he warmly admired Dr. Adam, the rector, whose industry

[1] Cockburn's *Memorials of his Time*, 1856, p. 2. [2] *Ibid.* p. 3.

was such that he would sit up all night trying to verify a quotation. But even this good man could not eradicate the hereditary evils of the school. The boys were coarse in their speech, uncouth in their manners, and spoke the broadest of dialects. To commemorate their final liberation from this hated school, Cockburn and some of his mates, among whom were Brougham and Francis Horner, erected a stone pillar in a hollow between the Braid and Blackford Hills.

What time Cockburn could spare from his school lessons was spent in rambles around Edinburgh, and in visiting relatives and friends. His Saturdays and Sundays were frequently passed at Niddrie House, the garden of which was to him "a thing of beauty and a joy for ever." "Eden was not more varied. And Eden is well worthy of its reputation, if it was the scene of greater happiness."[1]

Two of his father's near neighbours and friends were Principal Robertson, the historian, and Adam Ferguson. Robertson used to assist his grandson and young Cockburn in preventing the escape of their rabbits, and, when in a particularly amiable mood, the old man would permit them to have a pull at his favourite cherry tree. But Cockburn's most vivid impression of the historian was that he enjoyed a good dinner. Ferguson (who lived in Sciennes House, where Burns and Scott met for the first and only time), Cockburn thought looked "like a philosopher from Lapland," being always arrayed in a fur-lined greatcoat and fur-lined boots. In

[1] *Memorials of his Time*, 1856, p. 17.

the summer of 1793 Cockburn remembered shaking hands with the philosopher, who, aged seventy-two, was setting out for Italy in a strange sort of carriage, and with a single companion, his object being to prepare a new edition of his *History of the Roman Republic.*

On Sundays, between morning and afternoon sermons, Cockburn would go to the house of the mother of Sir David Dundas, Commander-in-Chief of the British Army, where he partook of Scotch broth and cakes. The lady, who was upwards of fourscore, was full of spirit, and keenly relished a joke. Cockburn having read to her once a newspaper paragraph which stated that a lady's reputation had suffered by some indiscreet talk of the Prince of Wales, she indignantly exclaimed: "The d—— villain! Does he kiss and tell?"[1] The house of Lady Arniston, the mother of the first Lord Melville, was another place of call. On one occasion she wished Cockburn and his companions to go an errand, and on it being represented to her that their lessons would be neglected if they complied, she answered: "Hoot! What o' that? As they used to say in my day—It's only het hips and awa' again."[2]

In 1793 Cockburn became a student at Edinburgh University, where he resumed grinding at "that weary Latin," but without much progress, the class being "a constant scene of unchecked idleness and disrespectful mirth." His prospects brightened, however, when he entered Dugald Stewart's class. The prelections

[1] *Memorials of his Time*, 1856, p. 59. [2] *Ibid.* p. 60.

of that eloquent metaphysician "were like the opening of the heavens,"[1] and changed his whole mental outlook. Then he joined the Academical Society, where he got his first notions of composition and debate, and "that delightful feeling of free doubting." A few years later he was admitted to the Speculative Society, became enamoured of its leaders, Jeffrey, Brougham, and Horner, and was soon completely emancipated from the high Toryism of his family and relatives.

Choosing the law as his profession, Cockburn was called to the Scottish Bar in 1800, and "with a feeling of nothingness" paced the Outer House. For some years he found time hanging rather heavily upon his hands. The reason was not far to seek. A Toryism, which had little affinity with the modern article, reigned supreme. For its monument one had only to view the Machiavellian statecraft of Henry Dundas, Scotland's uncrowned king. There were no public rights, no popular representation, no independent press, no free public meetings. The Whigs were conspicuous by their paucity, and both inside Parliament House and outside, they were "viewed somewhat as a Papist was in the days of Titus Oates."[2]

Cockburn had drunk deep draughts of the Whig poison, and could therefore expect no patronage. But the unexpected happened. In 1807, his all-powerful Tory uncle, Dundas, offered him an advocate-deputeship. Cockburn naturally demurred, but his uncle urged acceptance on the

[1] *Memorials of his Time*, 1856, p. 26. [2] *Ibid.* p. 90.

ground of family connection, and assured his nephew that there was no thought of his compromising his Whiggism. This being made clear, Cockburn yielded, though with considerable misgiving, for he did not see how he was to steer a safe course between the Scylla and Charybdis of party politics. For three years Cockburn made a bold effort, but in 1810 he had "the honour of being dismissed," it being represented to him that he was but an indifferent supporter of the Government, and had dared to vote against the Lord Advocate. He reminded his superior that he accepted the post on the understanding that he was to retain his Whig opinions. This was acknowledged, but those to whom he owed the appointment had buoyed themselves up with the hope that his Whiggism was a "mere youthful fervour," and would speedily vanish in the genial atmosphere of the political creed of his fathers.

But they were sadly disillusioned. Cockburn's Whiggism waxed stronger with the years. This, of course, meant scanty employment, and he took to volunteering, the "Napoleonic scare" being then at its height. Following in the footsteps of other Whigs (for whatever else those of this political persuasion lacked, they did not lack patriotism), he became captain of a company, which he systematically drilled for ten years.

In 1811 he married a niece of the famous Lord Hermand, and set up his "rural household gods at Bonally," at the foot of the Pentland Hills, and not far from Colinton. The property at that time consisted of a "scarcely habitable farm-house," but as he had vowed not to leave the place unless some avenging angel expelled him, he set about enlarging the house and improving the grounds. Soon he had reared himself a tower, and reached "the dignity of a twenty-acred laird."

At Bonally, Cockburn lived principally for the remainder of his days. Here his children were born, and here he enjoyed the acme of domestic felicity. It was his custom to spend as much of his life as possible in the open air. He revelled in the sights and sounds of outward Nature, and was never happier than when roaming over the Pentlands, not a summit of which he had not scaled a score of times. One summer he read every word of Tacitus in the sheltered crevice of a rock, called "My Seat," about 800 feet above sea-level, from which an enchanting view was obtained. The progress of his trees and flowers, most of them of his own planting, afforded him endless delight, and, on a summer day, he would sit for hours under the refreshing shade of the wooded slopes of Bonally, listening to the music of the two streams which ran through the estate. "Human nature is incapable of enjoying more happiness than has been my lot here," he wrote in his old age.

With the passing of the years political rancour abated, and Whiggism was seen not to be so diabolical after all. Cockburn was among the first of his professional brethren to benefit by this improved state of affairs, for whatever the world might think of his politics, it could not deny his abilities as a pleader. A striking presence, a highly expressive face, a flexible voice, a vigorous common sense, a lucid and persuasive speech, a fund of genial humour, and so perfect a knowledge of the emotions that "he could touch with a strong and certain hand any chord from uproarious merriment to the deepest pathos, or the most terrible invective"[1] —such gifts made him all but irresistible before a Scottish jury.

One of his most celebrated efforts was the speech in which he opened the defence of Stuart of Dunearn, who was tried in 1822 on a charge of having killed Sir Alexander Boswell in a duel. Sir James Mackintosh in the House of Commons characterised it as a speech which, "as a specimen of forensic eloquence, considered with reference to the peculiar difficulties with which the advocate had to contend, was unrivalled by any similar effort in ancient or modern times."[2] Hardly less memorable was his brilliant defence of Helen Macdougal, who was arraigned in connection with the notorious "Burke-and-Hare" murders. Cockburn, who was honestly convinced that there was not sufficient legal evidence to warrant a conviction of the woman, delivered a speech of tremendous power, which was rendered all the more impressive by the fact of its being delivered in the grey dawn of a winter morning.

It was in criminal cases that Cockburn shone. His attitude towards a jury had little of professionalism about it. He spoke as if he were an

[1] *Edinburgh Review*, January 1857.

[2] Cockburn's *Memorials*, 1856, pp. 397-398 (*n*.).

intimate friend of the accused, whose acquittal was a matter of the utmost importance to himself personally. His method was first to win the confidence of the jury, which the sincerity of his utterances and the appropriateness of his gestures rarely failed to do, and then to retain it by all the arts known to a consummate dialectician and a great orator. In civil cases, Cockburn was less successful. His technical knowledge of the law was distinctly inferior to that of John Clerk. But what he lacked in learning was more than counterbalanced by his nimble intelligence, his shrewd judgment, his clear and firm grasp of the points at issue, his cogent speech, and his knowledge of human nature.

Cockburn's reputation as an advocate was substantially enhanced by the part he played in the trials for sedition which took place in 1817–19. No person had been accused of political offences in Scotland since the days of Braxfield, and as political passion ran high, and the cry for reform was insistent, the trials created immense interest both in Parliament and in the country. Cockburn, as an ardent Whig and a thorough-going champion of political reform, regarded the trials as part and parcel of the general system of a despotic government; and the defence of its luckless victims called forth all his powers.

While dwelling upon his legal career, it ought to be mentioned that law reform was a subject which interested Cockburn deeply. By means of pamphlets, and articles in the *Edinburgh Review*, he strove incessantly to bring about improvements in the administration of justice in Scotland. In 1822 he published a pamphlet protesting against the now long-abolished practice which permitted the judge in a criminal case to select the jurymen. Cockburn also urged the anomaly of the Lord Advocate's combination of the functions of an English Home Secretary with those of an English Attorney-General, a view which Parliament adopted some sixty years later.

With aristocratic connections, social gifts of no mean order, and the instincts and breeding of a gentleman, Cockburn was well fitted to move in the highest circles of Edinburgh society. But the political views that hindered his progress at the Bar also hindered to some extent his social advancement. As a young man, his intimate associates were mostly Whigs. With Jeffrey and Brougham, whom he had known at the High School, he was on terms of special intimacy, and when the *Edinburgh Review* was started he, of course, was a leading member of the brilliant group which launched it. Popular Cockburn was, but the circle of his real friends was not large. In a gathering of persons with whom he was only partially acquainted, he was shy and reticent, and gave little evidence of that charm which, in congenial society, he invariably displayed.

In London society, which he rarely troubled with his presence, his Scottish traits, and more particularly his Scottish accent, circumscribed his powers of social conquest, and he was usually hopelessly dull. But at the supper parties of the Edinburgh Reviewers, or at the meetings of the Friday Club, where "the established taste was for quiet, talk, and good wine," he was in his element. Not that he was boisterous or obtrusive, or attempted to shine, but periodic and close contact with kindred spirits seemed to act like a charm, and to bring out all that was best in him. His conversational powers were considerable, and with a well-stored mind, a lively fancy, a quaint humour, and a talent for epigram, he could both entertain and instruct.

And he was what many good talkers are not—an excellent listener. Garrulous people he abhorred, and any one who attempted in his presence to usurp conversation which was the privilege of all, he timeously crushed with a withering sarcasm. He was also remorseless in the case of those who came merely to display their learning, or to give token of their intellectual prowess. Cockburn did not despise either the one or the other, but he rightly divined that the primary object of social intercourse is to afford enjoyment to all who engage in it.

Lockhart thought Cockburn the best teller of a plain story he ever heard.[1] "After Cockburn," he writes, "has been allowed to tell his story in his own way, for ten minutes, I would defy Diogenes himself to doubt it." It is, therefore, not difficult to conceive of Cockburn's success in the social circle, since the number of those who possess the art of telling a story is small compared with those who can pour out a stream of interesting talk.

He was also an effective platform speaker,

[1] *Peter's Letters to his Kinsfolk*, ii. 68.

though the opportunities for displaying the gift did not occur until he had almost reached middle life, there being no such thing as a public meeting in his young days. To an assembly of his countrymen, he never appealed in vain, his broad speech, homely style, and deft use of the images and allusions of common Scottish life at once catching the ear, and retaining the attention, of his audience.

Cockburn's interest in the *Edinburgh Review* was political rather than literary. He wrote many articles in its pages in which he discussed, with insight and knowledge, problems directly or indirectly connected with parliamentary and legal reform; but probably not one on a purely literary theme. While no worshipper of the ideas of 1789, and despising whole-heartedly those of his countrymen who affected republican airs and talked wildly of the superiority of things French, he yet viewed with disgust and indignation the political degradation to which Scotland had been reduced by an effete and tyrannical government, and early resolved to do what in him lay to bring about parliamentary and burgh reform on a drastic scale.

Identifying himself closely with Whig propaganda, he, along with Jeffrey, virtually led the forces of reform in Scotland. He addressed public meetings, he conducted a voluminous correspondence, and he became an indefatigable pamphleteer. Between 1822 and 1826 he wrote, and published anonymously, three pamphlets in which with much acumen and eloquence he pleaded for the extension of the parliamentary and municipal franchises of Edinburgh. The parliamentary representation of Scotland and the poor laws were scathingly condemned in articles in the *Edinburgh Review*. In short, Cockburn's political writings attracted wide attention, and soon it became evident to the most benighted Tory that the tide of reform in Scotland was rising, and could no longer be stemmed.

On the formation of the Grey Ministry in December 1830, Cockburn was appointed Solicitor-General for Scotland (Jeffrey becoming Lord Advocate), and for the next three years he was one of the hardest-worked of government officials. Immediately after his appointment he was summoned to London to confer with the Cabinet upon a measure of Scottish parliamentary reform, and in the following year he was mainly responsible for the drafting of the first Scottish Reform Bill, the passing of which marked an era in the political emancipation of the country.

In 1831 the monotony of his parliamentary career was to some extent relieved by his election to the Lord Rectorship of Glasgow University, an honour which had fallen to his friend, Jeffrey, some years previously. Joseph Hume, the economist, and Lockhart, the biographer of Scott, were also candidates, but, formidable as they were, Cockburn secured the highest number of votes. He delivered his address in January 1832, and became very popular with the students. When, in the following year, the next election came round, he was confronted with an extremely awkward situation, the votes of the electors being equally divided between himself and Sir David Sandford, the Professor of Greek in the University. Cockburn was much perplexed, and made a careful search for precedents, and for any information that might elucidate the position. Eventually, he decided that his opponent, being the occupant of a Chair in the University, was ineligible, and that he must needs give his casting vote in favour of his own re-election.

Cockburn's short but eminently fruitful parliamentary career came to an end in 1834, when he was elevated to the Bench. Three years later he was appointed a judge of the criminal court. His judicial career lasted exactly twenty years. As a judge he did not fulfil in all respects the highest expectations. The weak and the strong points which he had exhibited as a pleader were perpetuated on the Bench. His decisions in civil causes were frequently reversed by his colleagues, and as frequently confirmed on appeal to the House of Lords, a circumstance that has been attributed to the "utterly untechnical character of his mind, which made his exceptionally terse and lucid judgments read in the eyes of a foreign lawyer with a force not due to their intrinsic merits." [1] As a criminal judge, he was surpassed by none of his contemporaries, being not only a master of the criminal jurisprudence of Scotland, but a skilful reader of character.

Furthermore, the highest traditions of the Scottish judiciary were maintained by him.

[1] *North British Review*, November 1856.

Judges, he was wont to remark, "should never expose themselves unnecessarily—their dignity is on the Bench."[1] Cockburn never deviated from the spirit of this rule. He was decorous without being stiff and pompous; merciful as well as just. His industry was great, his impartiality unquestioned, his humanity the brightest trait in his judicial character.

Cockburn, it has been said, was one of the most popular Scotsmen of his time. But his popularity was not that of Scott, or of Jeffrey, or of "Christopher North," which was mainly literary, nor yet that of Chalmers, which was almost exclusively ecclesiastical. It was "good, honest, personal liking." The pervasive influence of his radiant nature made itself felt wherever he went. His magnetic personality drew to itself all sorts and conditions of men. The sedan-chairman who lounged about the streets of Edinburgh, the venerable lady spending the evening of her days in Trinity Hospital, the Moderator of the General Assembly, the smallest scholar at the High School, a peer of the realm—all were known to him, and all delighted to bask in the sunshine of his kindly presence, and to listen to his cheery and entertaining talk.

Nor was his popularity a mere local affair. When in 1837 he became a criminal judge, his duties took him periodically to every part of Scotland—from the wilds of Ross-shire to the highlands of Galloway. During the last seventeen years of his life he became known and respected throughout the length and breadth of

[1] *Circuit Journeys*, 2nd ed., p 17.

the land. Cockburn kept a journal, in which he jotted down anything which struck his fancy in the course of his judicial peregrinations. These notes, which were published in 1888 under the title of *Circuit Journeys*,[1] not only afford eloquent testimony of his own popularity, but are a highly instructive and frequently graphic record of men and manners in the smaller towns of Scotland during the second quarter of last century, as well as an interesting account of the writer's impressions of the scenery and historic buildings of his native land.

Cockburn, when he went on circuit, was usually accompanied by his wife and daughters, for it was his custom to combine pleasure with business. Immediately his duties at the court were over, he would go with his family to visit friends in the neighbourhood, or to view a noble landscape, or to inspect some picturesque ruin. Most of his journeys were made by coach, a mode of locomotion which enabled him to enjoy the delights of the country. For railways, he had no great liking, and where their construction was likely to spoil a beautiful landscape, he opposed them as uncompromisingly as did Wordsworth and Ruskin.

Deeply imbued with the æsthetic as well as the historic sense, Cockburn waged implacable war against all vandals. To mar a noble prospect, to destroy a hoary ruin, to injure a great work of architecture was, in his eyes, sacrilege of the worst kind. "Can there be any doubt," he remarks of a landowner who had made a howling

[1] A second edition appeared in 1889.

wilderness of his property, "that the rich brute who could allow five miles of wood, the ornament of a district, to be destroyed for £80, is now suffering for this in a hotter world? Spare him not, Devil! Give him his own faggots."[1] It was in the same spirit that he viewed an ancient building. Milton said, in an immortal passage: "As good almost kill a Man as kill a good Book." Cockburn would have added: "As good almost kill a good Book as destroy an ancient Building."

Nowhere, perhaps, could he have found a better field for the cultivation of his æsthetic tastes than Edinburgh—the fairest of all British cities, and venerable as well as fair. If Cockburn was not the first to discover the beauty of Edinburgh, he was, at all events, the first to rouse public attention to the fact that the preservation of its charms was of primary importance, even from a purely utilitarian standpoint. He would have heartily endorsed Ruskin's sentiment that "of all the cities in the British islands, Edinburgh is the one which presents most advantages for the display of a noble building; and which, on the other hand, sustains most injury in the erection of a commonplace or unworthy one."[2]

Cockburn saw clearly that being conspicuous neither as an industrial nor as a commercial city, the beauty of Edinburgh was a most important asset. Her face was her fortune. But the civic fathers of his day did not view the city in any such light, and were busy obliterating all

[1] *Circuit Journeys*, 2nd ed., p. 279.
[2] *Address to the Citizens of Edinburgh.*

that gave the Scottish capital its peculiar charm and distinction. Ancient landmarks were destroyed, historic houses were swept away, noble sites were bartered for ignoble uses, and the speculating builder was allowed to do his worst. Indeed, so strong a hold had the spirit of vandalism obtained, that had the voice of protestation not been lifted up the fair fame of Edinburgh would soon have been in the dust.

Marking how critical the situation had become, Cockburn dashed off his famous *Letter to the Lord Provost on the Best Ways of Spoiling the Beauty of Edinburgh*. This pamphlet did not arrest the hand of the despoiler, but it awakened him to the fact that in future his nefarious work would not only be severely circumscribed, but would be carried on in the teeth of a hostile public opinion. Cockburn proved that the beauty of Edinburgh was a fact, and, from every point of view, was a thing well worth being cared for.

Before Cockburn's day, nobody in Edinburgh talked of amenity; now it is the most honoured word in the vocabulary of every public-spirited denizen of the "grey Metropolis of the North." Not only is he proud of his city, but, as Ruskin put it, he feels it a duty to give himself a right to be proud of it. Edinburgh still harbours much architectural dissonance, is still liable to occasional bouts of vandalism; but with it all, Alexander Smith's words have not been falsified, nor are ever likely to be: "Residence in Edinburgh is an education in itself. Its beauty refines one like being in love. It is perennial, like a play of Shakespeare's. Nothing can stale its infinite variety."[1] That Edinburgh can still command glowing eulogies such as this, is mainly due to Cockburn and the association which worthily perpetuates his name and labours.

In the stirring ecclesiastical events of his time, Cockburn was an active participant. In May 1807, he pleaded his first case in the General Assembly of the Church of Scotland, and from that time onwards he was personally concerned in all its judicial proceedings. He could, therefore, hardly help being conversant with what was happening ecclesiastically in his midst. His attitude to religion and to the Kirk is, however, not easily defined. Lord Hermand, as we have seen, thought that every sensible man should be of the religion of his mother.[2] If Cockburn did not entertain this belief of his relative, he came very near doing so. In reviewing the state of religion in Scotland, he predicts an improvement if people "would only accept of that as religion, which was considered to be so by their devout fathers."[3]

But stray remarks scattered up and down his writings show that he accepted the traditional creed with substantial qualifications. Certainly, he was not an orthodox Presbyterian. A man who was a determined foe of fanaticism, who had a horror of long sermons, who frequently found his way into the fields instead of into the church on Sundays, and who was not averse to travelling and sight-seeing on the first day of the week, had

[1] *A Summer in Skye*, 1912, pp 14-15. [2] See p. 202.
[3] *Memorials of his Time*, 1856, p. 45.

assuredly wandered some way from the religious belief of his Presbyterian forebears.

Still Cockburn thought Chalmers a genius, recognised Guthrie as one of the greatest of preachers, and hailed the Disruption as "the most honourable fact for Scotland that its whole history supplies." As no reader of his *Journal* needs to be reminded, Cockburn was a close and shrewd observer of ecclesiastical events. He strongly supported the non-intrusion party, and when the matter came before the law courts, he took the same line as Jeffrey, and judicially declared in favour of the claims of the Scottish Church to spiritual independence. But the majority of his colleagues thought otherwise, as likewise Parliament, which caused Cockburn to remark: "We have now in Scotland a thing called a Church, the spiritual acts of which the law condemns and punishes."

Scant justice has been done Cockburn's merits as a writer. The historian of letters is inclined to say: "Jeffrey I know, and Sydney Smith I know, but who is Cockburn?" Without disparaging in the slightest Jeffrey's place in literary criticism, it is undeniable that not a line of what he wrote is read to-day, save by the student. Not so, Cockburn. The *Memorials of his Time*, which has been described, and not extravagantly, as "one of the pleasantest fireside-books of the (nineteenth) century," is not only "alive," but has recently entered upon a fresh lease of life. But more of this fascinating volume presently.

Meanwhile, we would remark that although Cockburn was not a bookman in the modern sense of the word, indeed had rather a contempt for bookish people, he was nevertheless a man who had read widely, and to some purpose. He was, despite the hard things he was wont to say about the ancients in his High School days, a reputable classical scholar, who enjoyed his Horace and his Tacitus. He had read, too, in many branches of modern literature, and had shown himself to be catholic in his taste, if not always sound in his judgments. It was his invariable practice to take a book with him on starting on his circuit journeys, and from stray jottings some idea of the breadth and depth of his literary understanding may be obtained.

He venerated his countryman and contemporary—Scott, both as a man and as a writer. "I can never forget," says Lockhart, "the pregnant expression of one of the ablest of the Whig school and party—Lord Cockburn, who, when some glib youth chanced to echo in his hearing the consolatory tenet of local mediocrity, answered quietly: 'I have the misfortune to think differently from you. In my humble opinion, Walter Scott's sense is a still more wonderful thing than his genius.' "[1] Cockburn greatly admired Scott's poetry, and revelled in the Waverley Novels. In 1828 he visited the author at Abbotsford, and in the *Memorials* draws a pleasing picture of the man. He was of opinion that a very good idea of Scott's conversation might be obtained by "supposing one of his Scotch novels to be cut into talk."[2] And

[1] *Life of Scott*, new pop ed., p 370.
[2] *Memorials of his Time*, p. 454.

Scott thought as worthily of Cockburn. "Jeffrey and Harry Cockburn are to be sure very extraordinary men,"[1] was his remark in trying once to determine why it was that he was often merrier when dining with a party of Opposition friends than with those of his own political persuasion.

Cockburn was also extremely fond of Dickens. Shakespeare and Scott excepted, he believed no man had "fancied and wrought out so many original characters."[2] Macaulay's style he did not like. He thought it more dangerous to youth than that of any other English writer with whom he was acquainted. Simplicity would, in his view, cure Macaulay of all his literary faults.[3] As for Burke, he was noble but dull. His letters told us nothing save the moves in the political game. "It is all Lord Rockingham against Lord Somebody else, or the King against them all. Did Burke never philander or go to the Literary Club?"[4] Among Scottish literary ladies, Cockburn favoured most Mrs. Elizabeth Hamilton, author of *The Cottagers of Glenburnie*, and Mrs. Grant of Laggan, whose *Letters from the Mountains* he considered "an interesting treasury of good solitary thoughts." Both "were excellent women, and not too blue. Their sense covered the colour."

Next to the pleasure of reading books, Cockburn placed the pleasure of collecting them. His library was not a large one, but it was much superior to Jeffrey's, which perhaps is not saying much. Plain, practical, unimaginative, he was

[1] *Life of Scott*, p. 652.
[2] *Circuit Journeys*, 2nd ed., p. 103.
[3] *Ibid.* p. 237.
[4] *Ibid.* p. 257.

interested most in what may be called "the human element in literature." He did not relish either the frivolous or the erudite book. Wholesome, instructive, and entertaining reading was what he craved for. If Cockburn had lived in our day, he would have devoured cheap reprints of the classics, with an occasional sevenpenny novel thrown in.

Five books came from Cockburn's pen, though only his *Life of Jeffrey* was published during his lifetime. His posthumous works were *Memorials of his Time* (1856); *Journal, 1831–44* (2 vols. 1874); *Circuit Journeys* (1888); and *Examination of the Trials for Sedition in Scotland* (2 vols. 1888). Let it be said at once that Cockburn never posed as a man of letters. He did not write for the sake of winning renown as an author, but simply because he had something interesting to say.

The *Life of Jeffrey* is the only work to which the literary test may be applied, because it was the only one that was written deliberately for public perusal, and had the benefit of his revision. Of this work we have already spoken, but a few additional comments may be set down. The *Life of Jeffrey* was undertaken at the request of the family and several intimate friends of the judge, and was published within two years of the death of the subject. It extends to two octavo volumes, the first containing the biography, and the second a selection of Jeffrey's letters.

In a modest preface Cockburn refers to the disadvantages under which he laboured. One was the difficulty of speaking frankly of persons still living or recently dead. He felt he was not in a position to abuse anybody. His position seems to have been that he would tell the truth, but not the whole truth—a principle as inadmissible in the writing of biography as it is in a law court. He writes agreeably, too agreeably, for at times he soars into the region of panegyric. Moreover, his narrative, for the most part, is dry, colourless, fragmentary, and very ill-proportioned. As for the letters, Cockburn's statement that they contain "scarcely three lines that might not be read with propriety to any sensitive lady, or to any fastidious clergyman,"[1] may be admitted. Presumably, however, the letters were selected not because they were morally unobjectionable—which would hardly be complimentary to Jeffrey—but with a view to disclosing the personality of the writer. But this is precisely what they fail to do. The career of Jeffrey still awaits a competent biographer. For the present we must look to Carlyle rather than to Cockburn if we would obtain glimpses of the personality of the "Delphic Oracle."

The *Examination of the Trials for Sedition in Scotland* was published more than thirty years after Cockburn died, and is, as its title suggests, an investigation of the factors that governed the trials of various prisoners charged with sedition in the days when Scotland was little more than the appanage of a Tory clique, of whom Henry Dundas was chief. The work can hardly lay claim to impartiality, since Cockburn, a staunch Whig,

[1] Preface to *Life of Jeffrey*.

and counsel for several of the prisoners whose trials are commented upon, sets himself to review the work of judges who made no secret of the fact that they were political partisans, and were using their powers to the utmost in putting down sedition, *i.e.* those who dared to impugn the Tory system of government. But when all allowance has been made for Cockburn's bias, it is indisputable that he makes out a very strong case.

The judgment he passes on Braxfield and his colleagues is severe, but not too severe. He is substantially correct when he says: "No quality which could disgrace a court of justice was absent from these proceedings; levity, insolence, and predetermined oppression on the Bench; a jury which had prejudged the case; evidence of the basest and most nefarious description; and a punishment which startled even that generation."[1] Even a Tory writer in *Blackwood's Magazine*[2] is compelled to admit that there was harsh and unconstitutional treatment, that Gerrald was tried under a superannuated law that had arisen under another state of things, and that a verdict was obtained against him which would not have been countenanced in any other part of the Empire. And the iniquity of the proceedings becomes singularly impressive when it is recalled that Muir and Palmer were transported in 1793 for doing what Grey and Brougham did in 1831. No wonder that Charles Fox should have exclaimed in the House of Commons, "God help the people who have such judges. . . . Were I a native of Scotland, I would instantly

[1] Vol. i. Introduction. [2] Vol. xxix. p. 908.

prepare to leave that land of tyranny and despotism." [1]

Pleasant it is to pass from this contentious work to *Memorials of his Time*, the book by which Cockburn is best known, and deservedly so. It was written between 1821 and the close of the year 1830, though it was not published until two years after his death. "It occurred to me," wrote the author in 1840, " . . . as a pity that no private account should be preserved of the distinguished men or important events that had marked the progress of Scotland, or at least of Edinburgh, during my day. I had never made a single note with a view to such a record. But about 1821 I began to recollect and to inquire." [2] Such was the origin of a book which gives the most brilliant, graphic, and entertaining account of the social and political condition of Scotland during the closing decades of the eighteenth, and the first thirty years of the nineteenth, century.

Primarily, the book tells the story of the political regeneration of Scotland. It may be described with just a suggestion of Whig hyperbolism, as "an illuminated catalogue of past abuses too preposterous to be believed if they had not been almost too inveterate to be conquered." [3] Cockburn, however, weaves into his narrative much extraneous matter illustrative of the men and manners of his time. His pictures of the Scotland of that day, and especially of the literary and social life of Edinburgh when Scott

[1] Speech on Sedition Trials, 1794. [2] Pref. to *Memorials of his Time*.
[3] *Edinburgh Review*, January 1857.

was the presiding genius, are full of charm and animation. The author had no eye for subtle shades of character, but he could deftly portray broad lineaments. And this he has done in the *Memorials*, where the men and women of his time, with all their virtues and foibles, stand out so prominently, that if they were to walk the streets of Edinburgh to-day, we should have little difficulty in recognising them.

In the *Memorials*, Cockburn does what he refrained from doing in his *Life of Jeffrey*—he writes with engaging frankness. The personages who play a part in his narrative are weighed in the balance, and the result is set forth straightforwardly. With his political adversaries he, of course, deals faithfully; but no malice lurks in his strictures. On the other hand, he is not unmindful of their good points, and can even be genial. Be that as it may, it was not to be expected that the Tories would be pleased with Cockburn's account. When the *Memorials* appeared in 1856, its veracity was seriously impugned. "Books like Lord Cockburn's," remarked the *Quarterly Review*, "are the bane of history." Indeed, the work gave rise to such an ebullition of Tory wrath that the *Edinburgh Review* had to come to the rescue, ably defending Cockburn in an article entitled "Scottish Lawyers and English Critics." [1]

Cockburn's *Journal*, published in two volumes in 1874, is practically a continuation of the *Memorials*, and brings the narrative down to the year 1844. But it is rather a disappointing

[1] *Edinburgh Review*, January 1857

book. Certainly, it is inferior in interest to the earlier work. Possibly this is due to the fact that whereas the dominant note of the *Memorials* was political and social, the theme of the *Journal* is mainly ecclesiastical. Cockburn, as has already been mentioned, was not a typical Presbyterian, though no doubt he thought himself one. Ecclesiastical affairs, however, did interest him, and he found the atmosphere of church courts tolerably congenial. Moreover, having lived through what was known as the "Ten Years' Conflict," and being compelled to pass judgment on its fruits from the Bench, it would hardly have been possible for him not to give the events which led to the disruption of the Church of Scotland a prominent place in his reminiscences. Nevertheless, his narrative of the contendings of Moderate and Evangelical is not attractive in anything like the same degree as his lively sketches of the quaint manners and quainter forms and speech of the people who dwelt in the tall "lands" of Edinburgh in the days when Scott and he were young.

Cockburn himself was the visible embodiment of many of the characteristics of an age he had long survived. He had a well-built, athletic figure, a thoughtful countenance, a lofty brow, an aquiline nose, and large bright eyes. High-spirited and chivalrous, he had a shrewd head, a sympathetic heart, and a tender conscience. Humour, too, he had in abundance—and wrath, which at times made him a most formidable adversary. But his normal mood was that of a well-bred and affable gentleman, though he would not suffer fools gladly under any conditions. He spoke with a Doric breadth of accent common among persons of his station at the beginning of the nineteenth century. His step was quick and light; and he was an excellent swimmer, an accomplished skater, and an ardent mountaineer. He was extremely fond of life in the open, and indulged his predilection to the utmost. Till within a short time of his death, it was his custom to sally forth at midnight to enjoy an hour's solitary communion with Nature, or a chatty stroll with any person who was also partial to nocturnal meanderings. He scoured the Pentland Hills in all weathers without either an overcoat or an umbrella, which said much for his constitution, if little for his common sense.

His clothes, like his figure, were antique. Scorning fashions, he dressed to please himself. The hat he wore was shapeless, while his shoes, constructed after a pattern of his own, are said to have been the ugliest in Edinburgh, which, no doubt, is saying a good deal. He adored young people, and when nights were long, and a "snell" wind was blowing across the Pentlands, he would gather them in the ingle-nook of his lonely tower, and tell them, in his own inimitable way, how their grandfathers lived, and struggled, and died.

Cockburn was gathered to his fathers like a stalk of ripe corn in due season. He had just returned from a circuit journey in the West when he was seized with a serious illness. A few days later, April 26, 1854, he breathed his last at

Bonally, and was laid to rest in the spot where he most wished to lie—by the side of Jeffrey in the Dean Cemetery.

So passed the last of the old school of Scots judges.

INDEX

THE END

Printed by R. & R. CLARK, LIMITED, *Edinburgh*

www.ingramcontent.com/pod-product-compliance
Ingram Content Group UK Ltd.
Pitfield, Milton Keynes, MK11 3LW, UK
UKHW021345300326
11569UKWH00043B/1037

9 781021 550231